D1598392

SELF-ANALYSIS
Critical Inquiries, Personal Visions

SELF-ANALYSIS
Critical Inquiries, Personal Visions

edited by

James W. Barron

With a Foreword by Stephen A. Mitchell

 THE ANALYTIC PRESS

1993   Hillsdale, NJ   London

RC
506
.S45
1993

The Analytic Press
365 Broadway
Hillsdale, NJ 07642

Set in Palacio by Lind Graphics, Upper Saddle River, NJ

Library of Congress Cataloging-in-Publication Data

Self-analysis / critical inquiries, personal visions / edited by James W. Barron.
    p.   cm.
    Includes bibliographical references and index.
    ISBN 0-88163-143-4
    1. Psychoanalysis. 2. Introspection. I. Barron, James W., 1944–
RC506.S45 1993
616.89′17 – dc20   93-15733
                                                                CIP

Printed in the United States of America
10 9 8 7 6 5 4 3 2 1

With Love and Gratitude to My Father
Ernest R. Barron, Ph.D.

Acknowledgments

My interest in and capacity for self-analysis are closely related to my experience as both psychoanalytic patient and practitioner. My motivation to engage in self-analysis, as well as my respect for its difficulties and limitations, increased in the years following termination of my personal analysis.

As several contributors to this volume ably demonstrate, self-analysis is not a solitary activity. It takes place in the presence of real and imagined others. Similarly my writing and editing are inseparable from my relationships with friends and colleagues within the analytic community, a number of whom deserve specific recognition.

At the beginning of my career, Earl Wedrow first stimulated my interest in psychoanalytic theory and technique. Bob Gardner has been an influential teacher and supervisor. In addition, he is a coparticipant, along with Al Margulies and Gary Goldsmith, in our ongoing study group on self-analysis and creativity.

Faculty members of The Psychoanalytic Institute of New England, East, and the Boston Psychoanalytic Institute, specifically Samuel Silverman, Axel Hoffer, Ana-Maria Rizzuto, Arthur Valenstein, Evelyne Schwaber, Howard Levine, and Anton Kris, have generously shared their ideas and helped shape my own. Barbara Pizer, Stuart Pizer, Jonathan Slavin, Malcolm Slavin, and other members of the Massachusetts Institute for Psychoanalysis have provided friendship, critical feedback, and an important intellectual context. I also wish to thank Pierre Johannet and Ciaran Ross for their skillful translations of the writings of Didier Anzieu and Martine Lussier.

The idea for this book gradually took shape in the course of conversations with Paul Stepansky, who helped me conceptualize the overall architecture and who provided invaluable assistance along the way. I am indebted to him, to Eleanor Starke Kobrin, and to their colleagues at The Analytic Press.

Most of all, I owe a debt to my wife, Marcy Bienen, my daughter, Mia, and my sons, Jesse and Alexander, for their sustaining and loving presence in my life throughout this creative process of exploring the self-analytic domain.

Contents

Contributors

Didier Anzieu, Ph.D. — Professor Emeritus, University of Paris-Nanterre; Vice President, French Psychoanalytical Association.

James W. Barron, Ph.D. (editor) — President, Division of Psychoanalysis, American Psychological Association, Massachusetts Institute for Psychoanalysis, and International Federation for Psychoanalytic Education; editor of *Psychologist Psychoanalyst*; Instructor in Psychology, Department of Psychiatry, Harvard Medical School.

Ricardo Bernardi, M.D. — Director and Professor, Institute of Psychological Medicine, National University of Uruguay Medical School; Training Analyst, Psychoanalytic Institute of Uruguay.

Beatriz de León de Bernardi — Training Analyst, Psychoanalytic Institute of Uruguay.

E. Virginia Demos, Ed.D. — Faculty Member, Massachusetts Institute for Psychoanalysis; Clinical Instructor, Beth Israel Hospital, Boston.

Rivka R. Eifermann, M.D. — Training and Supervising Analyst, Israel Psychoanalytic Institute; Faculty, Psychology Department, Hebrew University of Jerusalem.

Robert Gardner, M.D. — Training and Supervising Analyst, Psychoanalytic Institute of New England, East.

John E. Gedo, M.D. —Emeritus Training and Supervising Analyst, Chicago Institute for Psychoanalysis; author or editor of twelve books on psychoanalytic topics.

Adrienne Harris, Ph.D. —Clinical Associate Professor, New York University Postdoctoral Program in Psychotherapy and Psychoanalysis; Associate Editor of *Psychoanalytic Dialogues: A Journal of Relational Perspectives.*

Martine Lussier, M.A. —Director of the Library, Sorbonne, University of Paris.

Alfred Margulies, M.D. —Associate Professor, Harvard Medical School; Faculty Member, Psychoanalytic Institute of New England, East, Massachusetts Institute for Psychoanalysis, and Boston Psychoanalytic Institute.

James T. McLaughlin, M.D. —Training and Supervising Analyst, Pittsburgh Psychoanalytic Institute; Clinical Associate Professor Emeritus of Psychiatry, School of Medicine, University of Pittsburgh.

Stephen A. Mitchell, Ph.D. (Foreword) —Faculty and Supervisor, New York University Postdoctoral Program in Psychotherapy and Psychoanalysis; Editor of *Psychoanalytic Dialogues: A Journal of Relational Perspectives.*

Warren S. Poland, M.D. —Member, Editorial Boards *Psychoanalytic Quarterly, Psychoanalytic Inquiry,* and *Psychoanalytic Books;* private practice of psychoanalysis, Washington, DC.

Therese Ragen, Ph.D. —Candidate, New York University Postdoctoral Program in Psychotherapy and Psychoanalysis; private practice, Evanston, IL.

Henry F. Smith, M.D. —Faculty Member, Psychoanalytic Institute of New England, East; Assistant Clinical Professor of Psychiatry, Harvard Medical School.

Stephen M. Sonnenberg, M.D. —Clinical Professor of Psychiatry and Behavioral Sciences, George Washington University School of Medicine and Health Sciences, Washington, DC; Adjunct Clinical Professor of Psychiatry, Cornell University Medical College, New York City.

Ernest S. Wolf, M.D. —Assistant Professor of Psychiatry, Northwestern University Medical School; Training and Supervising Analyst, Institute for Psychoanalysis, Chicago.

Foreword

Stephen A. Mitchell

Perhaps the best kept secret in the life of a psychoanalyst is that his patient of longest duration, the patient he at times loves and hates the most, the patient who is often the most central and preoccupying, the patient who often provides both his most triumphant successes and his most disheartening and bitter failures—is himself. The necessity for keeping this secret can be traced back to the beginnings of Freud's development of the psychoanalytic method.

The first analytic patients were suspect in all respects. Hysterics were thought to be either malingerers or suffering from some unknown organic deficiency—either their nervous system or their moral fiber was weak. Breuer located the problem in a propensity to "hypnoid states," not a terribly admirable trait to possess. Many would date the beginning of psychoanalysis with Freud's claim that hysterics suffered from conflicts, but Freud also initially set hysterics and other neurotics apart from the rest of humanity; an unconscious was something out of the ordinary, acquired through trauma.

It was only with the abandonment of the theory of infantile seduction and the development of the theory of infantile sexuality and drive theory in the early years of the 20th century that the line between analytic patients and the rest of humanity began to become less sharp. Recent developments in the direction of the demedicalization of psychoanalysis have continued this trend, but there is still no clear consensus about whether analysands are best thought of as "patients," whether we are all best thought of as "sick," whether being an analysand undergoing an analysis presupposes that something is terribly wrong.

Yet, despite the bad reputation that inaugurated and has lingered around the role of the analysand, Freud was clearly, for many years, his own most important patient. Beginning in 1895, with his discovery of a method for finding meaning in dreams, Freud pursued his self-analysis with intense interest and deep passion. As his analysis of his own dreams and his feverish letters to Fliess suggest, this was no mere idle hobby. Freud suffered from disturbing neurotic symptoms; he was deeply preoccupied with the need to sort out and understand his relationships with his parents, to come to terms with his own childhood. Freud used his self-analysis and his discoveries about his own psychic functioning and inner world as the substratum for his clinical work with his analysands as well as his dazzling construction of theories.

Freud's presentation of his discoveries to the public never hinted at the centrality and importance of his self-analysis. It was not easy to establish psychoanalysis as a brand-new professional discipline, and considerable discretion about the role of self-analysis was crucial. The differences between doctor and patient needed to be emphasized. The analyst was portrayed as a wholly objective, detached professional. The deeply personal, disturbing, and provocative nature of analytic discourse was portrayed as evoking merely scientific interest and a purely therapeutic participation on the part of the analyst. (Ferenczi's [1932] *Clinical Diary* provides a striking exception to this portrait of psychoanalysis in its first several decades, but this account of "mutual analysis" was in fact, a private journal, not intended for publication.)

The place of self-analysis in the life of the analyst has remained a minor theme in the psychoanalytic literature throughout its history. Analysts are generally portrayed as professionals who, like other professionals, have mastered certain crafts and provide a particular expertise that enable them to analyze their patients.

Consider the enormously important and popular concept of the "working alliance," which has informed and influenced a great deal of clinical psychoanalysis and psychotherapy in the United States since the 1950s. The patient's experience is pervaded with irrationality and conflict. The analyst offers a "reality ego," a "work ego," with which the patient can increasingly form an alliance, to dispel gradually the illusory and fantastic in his own life. The analyst provides a model of rationality, objectivity, and nonconflictual productivity. To the extent that the analyst is functioning professionally, self-analysis is unnecessary.

It is only recently that alternative visions of the experience of the analyst, which grant a considerable importance to self-analysis, have emerged for public consideration. These alternatives have accompanied broad shifts in conceptualizing the analytic process in two-person rather than one-person terms, in the increasingly pervasive importance of object relations, and in the growing interest in countertransference in virtually all quarters of the analytic world. Ironically, these theoretical advances have made it possible for analysts to begin to write about what all analysts have known all along: people do not become analysts out of mere intellectual interest, but out of a deep need and passion for self-understanding; and the vitality of psychoanalysis with one's analysands is grounded in a continuing and perpetually evolving enthusiasm for self-reflection and self-healing.

This volume represents a major step forward in the new project of psychoanalysts writing openly and constructively about the self-analytic core of their profession. It contains a wealth of perspectives on the self-analytic process, from theoretical and developmental underpinnings, to instructional examples of self-analytic work, to innovative techniques through which self-analysis (both individually and with colleagues) might be explored.

One of the first and most interesting lessons of this volume, and a tribute to its diversity, is that self-analysis itself is theory bound. Like all other problems, how one understands the nature, the function, and the process of self-analysis is deeply embedded in one's larger theoretical perspective—in terms of both theory of mind and theory of the analytic process.

Many of these papers explore self-analysis by analysts in connection with their work as analysts. There are crucial differences with respect to how deeply personal the analyst's participation in the analytic process is thought to be. And those differences in where to place the analyst in the process greatly affect the way in which the analyst's self-analysis operates.

Analysts of earlier decades regarded countertransference—the intrusion of the analyst's personal dynamics and experience into a purely objective analytic understanding—as both avoidable and regrettable, requiring a return to their own personal analysis. Here the analyst is viewed as ideally listening to and understanding the patient with an ear that is untainted by the analyst's own subjectivity. Some contemporary authors (Abend, 1986; Silverman, 1985, 1991) have preserved this ideal but regard intrusions of the analyst's own dynamics and subjectivity as both unavoidable and not necessarily regrettable. For them, self-analysis is regarded as a perpetual tool of the analyst as she is inevitably pushed and pulled through the patient's transferences into departing from analytic neutrality. Rather than regarding self-analysis as remedial work for errant clinicians, self-analysis is now regarded as a necessary ingredient in analytic listening in the face of the buffetings of transference–countertransference interactions.

A second and closely related model of self-analysis in the analytic situation portrays the analytic process as rife with enactments of and resonances with the pasts of both the analysand and the analyst in the here-and-now interactions between them. Jacobs (1991), for example, applies the discipline and method of transference analysis to the analysis of the analyst's countertransference. Material from the analysand's past resonates with and evokes material from the analyst's past. The archaeological model Freud employed in unearthing the genetic roots of the analysand's transferences is now used to unearth the genetic roots of the analyst's reactions., Rather than contaminating, the analyst's experience provides useful clues to the patient's experience; the analysand's mind and the analyst's mind are parallel systems with isomorphic patterns.

A third model of self-analysis in the context of analytic interaction, drawing on the Klein/Bion notion of projective identification, considers analysts' awareness and analysis of their own experience as central. However, in analyzing themselves, analysts are uncovering pieces of their patients' psychic content, which have been displaced, projectively, into the experience of the analyst.

A fourth view of self-analysis is based on the assumption that the analyst inevitably has a great deal at stake, personally, in the here-and-now of the analytic encounter. Searles (1979) and Racker (1968) were ground-breaking pioneers in positing that all the deepest levels of the analyst's dynamics—his own infantile longings, his own primitive anxieties, his fears for his own sanity and value—all these become activated (perhaps provoked by the patient's projective identifications) in any live analytic process. Here self-analysis operates not as an occasional corrective or even as one among other important dimensions of the analyst's participation, but as the central focus of the work. It is only through the self-analytic process that one gains access to the patient's conflicts and struggles.

Searles and Racker tended to address what they regarded as universal, primitive dynamics: paranoid and depressive anxieties, longings for symbiotic fusion, fears of breakdown. Various contemporary authors (Donnel Stern, Greenberg, 1991; Hoffman, 1983, Tansey and Burke, 1989; Stolorow, Brandchaft, and Atwood, 1984; Ehrenberg, 1992) regard the analyst's participation not only as deep but as ideosyncratic, as mediated through the particularities of the analyst's own life history and own conscious and unconscious beliefs. Here the analyst's understanding of the patient inevitably and necessarily passes through the grid of the analyst's character, and a continual process of self-analysis becomes essential if the patient's self-discoveries are to be freed from the constraints of the analyst's habitual ways of listening and thinking.

All these models of self-analysis in the context of the analytic process are represented in the papers in this volume. We see analysts exploring their own experience on many different levels, with different degrees of urgency, and with a profound sense of responsibility for the welfare of their patients, above all else.

Self-analysis, as it turns out, is very hard to do and probably harder to write about.

On one hand, there is an omnipresent danger of self-absorption, self-indulgence, self-deception. One of the greatest privations of the job of being an analyst is having to keep quiet so much of the time, to resist so many of the impulses to say, "Something like that happened to me . . . " or "Let me tell you how I feel about that. . . . " Surely one of the reasons there is now so much interest in the analyst's self-disclosure, an interest that at times seems to approach the level of a fad, is that we have all had to remain so laconic and other centered for so long. So, practicing and writing about self-analysis is fraught with the dangers of a defiant reclaiming of the spotlight, the bursting forth of a thwarted exhibitionism.

On the other hand, it is very difficult for many analysts to care about themselves enough, and to take themselves seriously enough, to offer themselves their own resources as analysts. The chronic overwork most of us subject ourselves to, the masochistic elements of being drawn to the "helping professions," these factors make it difficult for us to be analysts to ourselves with the same dedication and discipline that we bring to our patients. I have not infrequently found myself noting, as I stumbled across some bit of neurotic distraction or familiar but unexplored psychic pain, that it would be a good idea for me to pursue it, in a sustained fashion, with the analytic skills I have honed over the years and regularly make available to my patients. But I rarely do.

According to legend, Erich Fromm, sitting in his garden at the end of the day, used to devote a daily hour to self-analysis. I have always found that image inspiring. The essays in this book may also serve as a source of inspiration. Notwithstanding the pitfalls surrounding the process of self-analysis, they provide us with provocative and constructive models for that essential project, in which we may learn better to avail ourselves of our own analytic resources.

REFERENCES

Abend, S. (1986), Countertransference, empathy and the analytic ideal: The impact of life stresses on analytic capability. *Psychoanal. Quart.*, 55:563–575.

Ehrenberg, D. (1992), *The Intimate Edge.* New York: Norton.

Ferenczi, S. (1932), *The Clinical Diary of Sandor Ferenczi*, ed. J. Dupont. Cambridge, MA: Harvard University Press, 1988.

Greenberg, J. (1991), *Oedipus and Beyond: A Clinical Theory.* Cambridge, MA: Harvard University Press.

Hoffman, I. Z. (1983), The patient as interpreter of the analyst's experience. *Contemp. Psychoanal.*, 19:389–422.

Jacobs, T. (1991), *The Use of the Self.* New York: IUP.

Racker, H. (1968), *Transference and Countertransference.* New York: IUP.

Searles, H. (1979), *Countertransference and Related Subjects.* New York: IUP.

Silverman, M. (1985), Countertransference and the myth of the perfectly analyzed analyst. *Psychoanal. Quart.*, 54:175–199.

Stern, D. B. (1991), A philosophy for the embedded analyst. *Contemp. Psychoanal.*, 27:51–80.

Stolorow, R., Brandchaft, B. & Atwood, G. (1987), *Psychoanalytic Treatment: An Intersubjective Approach.* Hillsdale, NJ: The Analytic Press.

Tansey M. & Burke, W. (1989), *Understanding Countertransference: From Projective Identification to Empathy.* Hillsdale, NJ: The Analytic Press.

Introduction

James W. Barron

We are witnessing a resurgence of interest in self-analysis. More articles specifically about self-analysis have sprouted in the literature during the past two decades than appeared altogether during the prior history of psychoanalysis. The historical underemphasis or neglect of this topic is paradoxical, since the origins of self-analysis and psychoanalysis are inseparable. In fact, psychoanalytic theory and practice are the intellectual children of Freud's self-analytic efforts (Anzieu, 1986; Gay, 1988). In his correspondence with Fliess, while engaged in writing *The Interpretation of Dreams*, Freud exclaimed, "My self-analysis is in fact the most essential thing I have at present and promises to become of the greatest value to me if it reaches its end" (letter to Fliess, 15 October 1897, in Masson, 1985).

Freud linked self-analysis to psychoanalytic technique in general and to the analyst's handling of countertransference in particular. The first time he referred specifically to countertransference in one of his essays (Freud, 1910), he emphasized:

> Other innovations in technique relate to the physician himself. We have become aware of the "counter-transference," which arises in him as a result of the patient's influence on his unconscious feelings, and we are almost inclined to insist that he shall recognize this counter-transference in himself and overcome it. Now that a considerable number of people are practising psycho-analysis and exchanging their

observations with one another, we have noticed that no psycho-analyst goes further than his own complexes and internal resistances permit; and we consequently require that he shall begin his activity with a self-analysis and continually carry it deeper while he is making his observations on his patients. Anyone who fails to produce results in a self-analysis of this kind may at once give up any idea of being able to treat patients by analysis [pp. 144–145].

Yet Freud's attitude toward self-analysis was profoundly ambivalent: "My self-analysis remains interrupted. I have realized why I can analyze myself only with the help of knowledge obtained objectively (like an outsider). True self-analysis is impossible; otherwise there would be no [neurotic] illness" (letter to Fliess, 24 November 1897, in Masson, 1985).

Citing its difficulties and limitations and contributing only a handful of articles on the topic until the 1960s, with the exception of Horney's (1942) explication of self-analysis for the lay reader, generations of analysts allied themselves with the negative side of Freud's ambivalence toward self-analysis. Kramer (1959) and Ticho (1967) investigated the development of self-analytic functions during the termination and posttermination phases of clinical analysis. Fleming (1971) wrote about self-analysis from the perspective of psychoanalytic training. Gray (1973), although not using the term self-analysis, spoke of the development of closely related self-observational capacities. Thomson (1980) also focused on the receptive functions of the analyst as they relate to self-observation.

A growing number of analysts have seriously explored their own pathways to self-analysis, as well as the relationship between their self-analytic efforts and their work with patients (Calder, 1980; Gardner, 1983; Beiser, 1984; Eifermann, 1987a, b; Silber, 1991; Sonnenberg, 1991). Others have focused more specifically on the utility of self-analysis in deepening our understanding of countertransference (Ross and Kapp, 1962; Jacobs, 1973, 1991; Kern, 1978).

We can no longer soothe ourselves with the belief that self-analysis was necessary for Freud and enabled him to make his fundamental discoveries, but that we ourselves do not need to make use of self-analysis as a basic discovery tool. We can no longer hide behind the myth of perfectly analyzed analysts (Silverman, 1985) who need to engage in self-analysis (or return to a dyadic analysis) only when we experience unexpected, unwanted countertransference reactions to our patients. Instead we have a growing appreciation of the ongoing necessity for self-analysis to illuminate the ways in which our inner worlds actively shape, and are shaped by, the inner worlds of our patients.

There is a quiet revolution taking place that fosters our renewed interest in self-analysis. Analysts have always been participant observers, but historically we have been more comfortable emphasizing our observer status. We were the blank mirrors reflecting our patients' transferences, maintaining our neutrality, and interpreting our patients' psychic realities from our privileged epistemological positions as the ones who knew.

Now we are redefining the psychoanalytic situation. Conceptually, we are moving slowly (and not without considerable anxiety and resistance) away from the periphery and toward the center of engagement with our patients in the analytic encounter. Our view of countertransference is undergoing corresponding changes. McLaughlin (1975, 1981, 1988) believes that the term countertransference is misleading; it suggests that the analyst's transference is solely or primarily counter to the patient's transference. Countertransference is not just an occasional aberration or perturbation of the analyst's neutrality; it is an ongoing part of his or her psychic reality. I agree with McLaughlin that we would more accurately dispense with the term countertransference and speak instead of the analyst's transference. As we attempt to appreciate more fully our patients' psychic realities (Schwaber, 1983, 1986), including our patients' perceptions of our inner worlds (Hoffman, 1983), we need to take greater responsibility for our own inward looking.

While the contributors to this volume represent diverse theoretical perspectives, they are united both by their recognition of the importance of self-analysis and by their commitment to its elaboration. They explore fundamental questions. What do we mean by self-analysis? To what extent and under what conditions is self-analysis possible? How is it different from ordinary self-reflection or introspection? What are the different modes of self-analytic inquiry? What are the developmental antecedents of the capacity for self-analysis? How do we make use of self-analysis in our work as analysts? Conversely, how do we make use of our analytic work as an impetus to our self-analytic efforts? What is the role of the "other" in self-analysis? What are the relationships among self-analysis, writing, and creativity?

The authors grapple with the formidable ambiguities of self-analysis without either idealizing or devaluing its potential. They paint a richly detailed picture of how the mind of the analyst works and how the psychoanalytic process really functions.

REFERENCES

Anzieu, D. (1986). *Freud's Self-Analysis*. Translated from the French by P. Graham. Madison, CT: International Universities Press.

Beiser, H. R. (1984), An example of self-analysis. *J. Amer. Psychoanal. Assn.*, 32:3–12.

Calder, K. T. (1980), An analyst's self-analysis. *J. Amer. Psychoanal. Assn.*, 28:5–20.

Eifermann, R. R. (1987a), "Germany" and "the Germans": Acting out fantasies and their discovery in self-analysis. *Internat. Rev. Psycho-Anal.*, 14:245–262.

_____ (1987b), Children's games, observed and experienced. *The Psychoanalytic Study of the Child*, 42:127–144. New Haven, CT: Yale University Press.

Fleming, J. (1971), Freud's concept of self-analysis: Its relevance for psychoanalytic training. In: *Currents in Psychoanalysis*, ed. I. Marcus. New York: International Universities Press, pp. 14–47.

Gardner, M. R. (1983), *Self Inquiry*. Hillsdale, NJ: The Analytic Press.

Gay, P. (1988), *Freud: A Life for Our Time*. New York: Norton.

Freud, S. (1910). The future prospects of psycho-analytic therapy. *Standard Edition*, 11:139–151, London: Hogarth Press, 1957.

Gray, P. (1973), Psychoanalytic technique and the ego's capacity for viewing intrapsychic activity. *J. Amer. Psychoanal. Assn.*, 21:474–494.

Hoffman, I. Z. (1983), The patient as interpreter of the analyst's experience. *Contemp. Psychoanal.* 19:389–422.

Horney, K. (1942), *Self-Analysis*. New York: Norton.

Jacobs, T. (1973), Posture, gesture and movement in the analyst: Cues to interpretation and countertransference. *J. Amer. Psychoanal. Assn.*, 21:77–92.

_____ (1991), *The Use of The Self*. Madison. CT: International Universities Press.

Kern, J. W. (1978), Countertransference and spontaneous screens: An analyst studies his own visual images. *J. Amer. Psychoanal. Assn.*, 26:21–47.

Kramer, M. (1959), On the continuation of the analytic process after psychoanalysis (a self observation). *Internat. J. Psycho-Anal.*, 40:17–25.

Masson, J. M., ed. (1985), *The Complete Letters of Sigmund Freud to Wilhelm Fliess 1887–1904*. Cambridge, MA: Harvard University Press.

McLaughlin, J. T. (1975), The sleepy analyst: Some observations on states of consciousness in the analyst at work. *J. Amer. Psychoanal. Assn.*, 23:363–382.

_____ (1981), Transference, psychic reality, and countertransference. *Psychoanal. Quart.*, 50:639–664.

_____ (1988), The analyst's insights. *Psychoanal. Quart.* 57:370–389.

Ross, D. W. & Kapp, F. T. (1962), A technique for self-analysis of the countertransference. *J. Amer. Psychoanal. Assn.*, 10:643–657.

Schwaber, E. (1983), Psychoanalytic listening and psychic reality. *Internat. Rev. Psycho-Anal.*, 10:379–392.

_____ (1986), Reconstruction and perceptual experience: Further thoughts on psychoanalytic listening. *J. Amer. Psychoanal. Assn.*, 34:911–932.

Silber, A. (1991), Analysis, re-analysis, and self-analysis. Presented at Symposium on Self-Analysis, meeting of American Psychoanalytic Association, New York, December.

Silverman, M. A. (1985), Countertransference and the myth of the perfectly analyzed analyst. *Psychoanal. Quart.*, 54:175–199.

Sonnenberg, S. M. (1991), The analysts's self-analysis and its impact on clinical work: A comment on the sources and importance of personal insights. *J. Amer. Psychoanal. Assn.*, 39:687–704.

Thomson, P. G. (1980), On the receptive function of the analyst. *Internat. Rev. Psycho-Anal.*, 7:183–205.

Ticho, G. R. (1967), On self-analysis. *Internat. J. Psycho-Anal.*, 48:308–318.

SELF-ANALYSIS
Critical Inquiries, Personal Visions

I

DEVELOPMENT OF THE CAPACITY FOR SELF-ANALYSIS

EXPLORATION OF OUR "PERSONAL EQUATIONS"

The self-analytic process is complex and multifaceted. No two persons engage in self-analysis in quite the same way. And each person's self-analytic capacity varies considerably over the life cycle. This variability has important development roots. Focusing on the infant research literature, Demos describes the "competent" infant with inborn potentialities which, when nurtured by a responsive caretaker, grow to form a network of interrelated skills (see Demos, 1992). These skills initially support rudimentary self-observation and eventually make more sophisticated self-analysis possible.

Demos conceptually divides early competencies into three realms: the construction and representation of experience, the modulation and regulation of affect, and the sense of personal agency. The elaboration and articulation of each of these competencies require a sufficiently empathic primary caretaker.

Although competence in each realm is necessary for the development of a self-analytic capacity, Demos draws heavily on the work of Silvan Tomkins and places special emphasis on the importance of affect. Along with Tomkins, she speaks of ideoaffect complexes, which function as primary psychic organizers and which play a central role in the self-analytic process.

As is well known, tolerance of negative affect is a sine qua non of psychoanalytic inquiry in either a dyadic or self-analytic mode. Less well appreciated is the role of positive affects (see also Gardner, chap. 8). Demos comments:

> The whole enterprise of attending to, elaborating on, valuing, and attempting to understand, change, or master one's inner experiences requires an affective and motivational investment. Certainly some of the motivation comes from a wish to escape from or master painful negative affective experiences. But that wish alone is not enough to produce a focus on internal psychic processes. Indeed, it often leads to strenuous efforts to control external conditions, that is, other people and events. The capacity for self-analysis requires the capacity to generate and sustain interest in one's own inner experiences and to experience excitement and enjoyment in the process of exploring and understanding oneself. This capacity for sustaining and elaborating positive affect about oneself does not just happen in the absence of intense or intrusive negative affects. It must be nurtured and fostered by the caregiver and by the analyst.

Demos explores the parallels between the infant–caretaker relationship and the analysand–analyst relationship. While not naively maintaining that they are isomorphic, she does note important similarities that influence the evolution of the capacity for self-analysis.

Consistent with Demos's description of the competent infant in a relational matrix, Ricardo Bernardi and Beatriz de León de Bernardi describe the conceptual shift from the mirror analyst to "the idea of an interaction in which the patient is also sensitive to that which the analyst contributes to their link."[1] They explore the influences of the self-analytic activities of the analyst on this interaction.

Of course self-analysis enhances our awareness of countertransference. Even more fundamentally, as Bernardi and de Leon point out, self-analysis leads to a more refined understanding of our own ongoing participation in the analytic process.

> The disposition toward self-analysis enables us to become aware of the assumptions that emanate from within our own psychic reality and shape our representations of the analytic process. As analysts, we each introduce our own "personal equation" between what we listen to and what we interpret.

---

[1]Other contributors to this volume (e.g., Gardner, Margulies, McLaughlin, Smith) explore facets of the patient's awareness of the analyst's inner experience. For further exploration of this theme, see Hoffman (1983) and Schwaber (1986).

Bernardi and de León examine the ways in which our assumptions generate our "personal equation." We are accustomed to considering as assumptions the content of our implicit and explicit theories, and perhaps even our attitudes toward those theories. Ordinarily, however, we do not think of our *Weltanschauung* and our personal ways of hearing, seeing, representing our experience, communicating, and relating as part of our assumptions. (There appear to be some similarities between Bernardi's and de León's extended definition of "assumptions" and Demos' description of "ideoaffect complexes.")

Bernardi and de León assert that the degree to which we carefully consider these factors as assumptions determines the scope and depth of our self-analytic efforts. They support their assertions with clinical vignettes illustrating the utility of their concepts.

In their clinical examples, they demonstrate that our work with patients may challenge our most cherished assumptions about ourselves and our identities as analysts, and may precipitate a sense of loss and mourning:

> In our interaction with patients, we must abandon well-known presentations (and inner representations) familiar to us and our patients. Such mourning and disidentification processes are necessary for us to be able to admit that our understanding is always only partial and possible within the parameters of our own psychic reality, which may not become a model for our patients or for our colleagues.

Loss and mourning are inevitable concomitants of the self-analytic process and simultaneously help to make it possible and contribute to its difficulty. Demos conceptualizes essential developmental antecedents of affect tolerance and related capacities necessary for self-analysis. Bernardi and de León focus on the widening scope of self-analysis, which includes our hidden assumptions and unexamined personal equations.

REFERENCES

Demos, E. V. (1992), The early organization of the psyche. In: *Interface of Psychoanalysis and Psychology*, ed. J. W. Barron, M. N. Eagle & D. L. Wolitzky. Washington, DC: American Psychoanalytic Association, pp. 200–232.

Hoffman, I. Z. (1983), The patient as interpreter of the analyst's experience. *Contemp. Psychoanal.*, 19:389–422.

Schwaber, E. A. (1986), Reconstruction and perceptual experience: Further thoughts on psychoanalytic listening. *J. Amer. Psychoanal. Assn.*, 34:911–932.

1

Developmental Foundations for the Capacity for Self-Analysis

Parallels in the Roles of Caregiver and Analyst

E. Virginia Demos

My task is to provide a developmental perspective for a discussion about the capacity for self-analysis in adulthood. What can such a perspective contribute? My goal is to present a view of the early beginnings of psychic life, focusing particularly on the developmental foundations for the emergence of the capacity for self-analysis. This will involve not only suggesting when psychic life begins, but also, and perhaps more importantly, describing the psychological processes going on in the young infant and the role of the caregiver in influencing these processes. It is assumed there are some continuities in the ways in which the infant organizes psychic experiences and the ways in which the adult does so, and therefore there are some parallels between the roles of the caregiver and the therapist. A developmental framework, then, may perhaps shed some light on the processes in the analytic situation that foster the analysand's capacity for self-observation, inquiry, and analysis.

I will argue that the capacity for self-analysis is multifaceted, drawing on a variety of basic human skills, that can themselves vary in their degree of development and in the extent to which they become coordinated with other essential skills and tendencies. Thus, it is a capacity that is not so much acquired, although it does involve learning, as it is one that emerges because it is inherent in the organization of innate human adaptive functioning. Through experience with the caregiver, this capacity can either be encouraged and elaborated on, or be interfered with, discouraged, and derailed. I would like to begin by briefly describing some basic psychological capacities of the infant that provide the essential ingredients for self-observation, and then illustrate some of the ways in which transactions with caregivers can shape and influence these capacities.

The radical increase in our knowledge about early infancy in the last three decades has prompted several efforts to integrate infancy research with psychoanalytic models (Lichtenberg, 1984; Stern, 1985; Sameroff and Emde, 1989). I have recently presented my own attempt at an integration (1992), which I will summarize briefly here. It differs from other available conceptualizations of early psychic experience in arguing more strongly for early competence and against stagelike models for understanding psychic organization, and in giving affect a central motivating role in psychic organization. I believe that the data we now have suggest that infants arrive in the world with preadapted capacities for feeling, for thinking, for perceiving, for remembering, for acting, and for coordinating these capacities in consciousness to produce voluntary acts. Thus, contrary to Winnicott's statement that "there is no such thing as a baby" (1965), I am arguing that there is indeed a baby with a functioning set of unique social, experiential, and organizational capabilities, and there is a mother with her unique history and capacities. The infant clearly needs a mother, but her role is now seen as enhancing, supporting, interfering with, discouraging, or ignoring her infant's ongoing processes and efforts. She has considerable influence, but this influence does not amount to creating de novo organization and basic capacities within the infant.

The unique characteristics of each participant are important in the relationship between the infant and the caregiver. Not all infants will be affected in the same way by a particular caregiver, and conversely, not all caregivers will be responsive in the same way to a particular infant. Each contributes something essential and unique to the transactions. Much of what goes on between an infant and a caregiver involves the complicated processes of getting to know each other and forming a relationship. Each must learn about the other's preferences, tolerances for intensity and pacing of stimuli, limitations, and distinctive modes of behaving. In other words they have to learn to live together, to understand each other's meanings, to find ways to manage clashing agendas, and to determine the balance between helping, hurting, and ignoring each other, and between enjoying, manipulating and dreading each other.

In this relationship, as in all relationships in which the participants are deeply engaged with each other, the potential for change for both participants can be great. Since much of the discussion to follow will focus on how the infant is influenced by the parent, I would like to emphasize briefly here, how the parent can be influenced and changed by the infant. Several researchers, most notably Bell (1977), have commented on how compelling and engrossing young infants are for adults, out of all proportion to their relative size and real world power. This is due in part to the nature of their stimulus qualities, for example, a large head, "cuteness," and preemptive affective expressions. It is also due in part to the meanings for the parents of their infant; for example, the embodiment of hope (a new beginning, a chance to "do it right this time") or a burden (someone who will drain all of one's resources), or a source of gratification (someone who needs me or loves me,) or someone to "take it out on" "to get back at." The infant, then, has the power to evoke within the caregiver a wide range of deeply felt meanings. These include a reexperiencing of unresolved issues and long forgotten transactional patterns of being with and feelings about one's own parents and oneself as a small child.

To the extent that the infant represents a hopeful new beginning, then the evocation in the parent of old patterns of experience and of unresolved issues will be felt as an opportunity for the parent to rework old solutions and to develop new responses, strategies, and solutions with this new transactional partner, namely, the infant and small child. Thus, while engaging in the complicated and difficult processes of empathizing with the infant or child, and becoming his or her ally and helper, the parent is also empathizing with, becoming an ally of, and helping her or himself. This process involves simultaneously experiencing oneself as a child and as a parent, and reparenting oneself. The success of these efforts, therefore, depends not only on one's capacity to empathize with the infant and small child in reality and in one's past, and not only on the qualities of the real infant, but also on the availability of good parenting models. Often the parent, in trying to avoid his or her own parents' mistakes, overcompensates and errs in the opposite direction. An overly strict upbringing can result, for example, in too much permissiveness in the next generation; a distant parent can lead to an overly involved parent in the next generation, thereby perpetuating the problematic nature of the same issue. Nevertheless, real change is possible and might well involve the caregiver seeking help in order to break out of a repetitive cycle that has now become quite conscious and intolerable. By contrast, to the extent that the infant is experienced as a burden or as a source of gratification to the parent, and evokes merely a wish to replay old solutions, then the opportunities for change and the reworking of unresolved issues are diminished.

Although in describing the characteristics of the infant–caregiver relationship, I have thus far emphasized how each contributes to the processes involved and how the infant possesses compelling qualities for the caregiver. Nevertheless, I must now acknowledge that this is not a relationship between equals. The caregiver has many advantages in strength, knowledge, experience, instrumental effectiveness, and emotional regulation. These are all advantages that the infant and growing child will gradually attain. But the infant is not totally helpless, and is far more competent than we have been ready to acknowledge. We have been slow to embrace one of the tenets of evolutionary theory, namely, the more capable a species is in adulthood, the more capable is the newborn of that species. This is not an argument for preformed ideas. Rather it argues that because of our long evolutionary history, all of the essential human functions and capacities are already present at birth. They exist in various phases of readiness and their elaboration requires interactive experience with the real world and with more experienced human beings, namely caregivers.

Before going on to describe the basic capacities of the human infant, I would like to suggest that already in our discussion there are parallels that can be drawn between this new view of the infant–caregiver relationship and the patient–therapist relationship. I would argue that our patients come for treatment with a multiplicity of possibilities and capacities, some nearly lost to them, and that our role as therapists is to help them reorganize their inner worlds, for example to help them to recognize, to have more access to, to use more effectively that which they have within themselves; or to help them to increase their capacities to bear negative affect; or to help them to learn to trust again. The analyst's or therapist's interventions can then be understood as encouraging, articulating, and lending support to certain organizational possibilities within the analysand or patient over others. From the analysand's or patient's point of view, the experience is one of recognizing in the clinician's responses a possibility that he or she already knows about from earlier experiences, such as a possible way of constructing reality that was not very well organized or coherent before; or that had been more available in the past, but has been overridden by other, more pressing forces in the present; or that was available but simply never received much confirmation from the outside world. Thus the clinician's interventions serve to shift the balance of organizational possibilities within the patient rather than introduce something totally new. Once a shift has occurred within the patient, he or she can then construct new possibilities. Indeed if the analysand's capacity for self-analysis is to be fostered, the analyst must believe that the analysand already possesses the essential ingredients.

There are also parallels in the importance of the unique characteristics of each participant in the theraputic relationship. Not all analysands will be affected in the same way by a particular analyst, and conversely, not all analysts will be responsive in the same way to a particular analysand. Each contributes something essential and unique to the transactions. There are parallels as well in the opportunities for change in the analyst. To the extent that the analysand evokes in the analyst a reexperiencing of unresolved issues, and the analyst can use that experience as an opportunity to reexamine his or her own patterns of responses, then to that extent, the therapeutic work with the analysand can enable the analyst to rework old solutions and to develop new responses and strategies in his or her own psychic organization. There are also parallels in the inequality of the relationship. The analysand has come for help in the particular areas in which the analyst possesses specialized training and knowledge. Yet it is also true that the analysand is not totally helpless, and that the analyst must depend upon and work with the analysand's strengths and capacities in order for the work to progress.

Let us return now to the infant and ask, what are these basic human capacities? I can only list them here, without supporting evidence, and must refer the interested reader to the authors cited earlier. There is a growing consensus among infant researchers that the infant has the capacity to experience the full range of basic emotions: enjoyment, interest, distress, anger, fear, startle, disgust, and shame. It is now agreed that the infant can recognize recurrent patterns of stimuli, can detect invariance in stimuli, and can detect contingencies between self-generated actions and effects on the environment. It is also agreed that the infant can make the distinction between internal and external events, and that the infant possesses perceptual biases inherent in possessing a human nervous system, brain, and body. Thus, the infant can hear sounds only within certain frequencies, can see colors only in certain wave lengths, can perceive motion only at certain rates, and visually prefers light–dark contrasts and contours.

Since many of these perceptual biases comprise stimulus characteristics that are routinely produced by other humans, it is inevitable, given an usual expectable environment, that the infant will be drawn to other humans. Thus, for example, while there is no evidence for a preformed idea or image of a human face, human faces contain many of the perceptual characteristics that the infant is most likely to pay attention to, therefore the infant will quickly construct a representation of the faces it sees most frequently. Finally, infants are capable of coordinating information emanating from affective, perceptual, cognitive, memory, and motor functions in order to try to bring about desired events and to limit or escape from undesired events. In a remarkable experiment reported by DeCasper and Carstens (1981), newborn infants quickly learned to lengthen the pauses between their bursts of sucking in order to turn on a recording of a female voice singing. These same infants became upset 24 hours later when they discovered that the singing voice was no longer contingent on the length of their pauses, and that they no longer had control over this stimulus.

This experiment reveals an amazing amount of organization within the newborn, for in order to succeed in this task the newborn had to coordinate perception (detecting the contingency); emotion (interest in the stimulus); cognition (generating a plan to repeat this interesting event); motor patterns (voluntarily lengthening the pause between sucks); and memory (remembering the plan and comparing the outcome to the goal). This experiment also highlights another important potentiality in the newborn, namely the newborn's capacity and preference for being an active agent in influencing events. Infants quickly begin to exert voluntary control over built-in reflexes; nonnutritive sucking is perhaps the best known example of this phenomenon.

Each year will bring more research data increasing our knowledge about the infant's competence. This knowledge will also help us to describe more accurately the infant's limitations, and by extension, to describe with more precision the caregiver's role in the infant's development. Or to put the matter somewhat differently. If we now have such a competent infant, what is developing over time, and how does the caregiver influence that development? Since our knowledge of the competent infant is relatively new, so too are our attempts to reformulate development and the caregiver's role. I would like to present my current thinking on these issues, focusing primarily on the development of capacities that support the development of the capacity for self-analysis, and on the caregiver's role in this development. The parallels to the analyst's role will also be discussed. I will describe three capacities, distinct yet interrelated. The first is the capacity to construct representations of events and/or objects that are encountered in the inanimate world, in the social world, and in the inner, psychic world. The second is the capacity to modulate and regulate emotional experience. And the third is the capacity to maintain one's sense of active agency in relation to the inanimate world, the social world, and the inner world.

The infant begins life with the perceptual, cognitive, memory, and affective capacities to construct representations of the world as it is experienced. What the newborn lacks initially is knowledge of and experience with the world. To use a computer analogy, the hardware is built in, but there is no software; human beings have to construct their own software, gradually, over time. Thus the newborn rapidly becomes engaged in two complementary yet opposing processes that will occupy him throughout his life. One involves moving from being a generalist to becoming a specialist, and the other involves disembedding knowledge from specific contexts and applying it to broader contexts.

The newborn is a generalist because at the outset of life a condition of omnipotentiality exists; any newborn can become a speaker of any language, or a member of any human family or culture. For example, newborns will brighten and smile at any human face, and can discriminate phonemes from any language. But several months later, after living in a particular family, these same infants will smile only at familiar faces and can only discriminate phonemes from the specific language spoken in their environment. Thus this omnipotentiality is lost as the infant accumulates experience with particular objects, with particular people, and with particular intensities and qualities of inner states. It is in this sense that the infant becomes a specialist, as a member of a particular family or group, in a particular place, at a particular historical moment.

This process of becoming a specialist involves constructing representations of the particularities of experience. Since the infant already possesses the capacity to detect invariance, to recognize recurring patterns, to detect contingencies, or, in other words, already possesses the basic tools needed to construct representations of particular experiences, what is the role of the caregiver? There is still the need to regulate the infant's exposure to stimuli or to experiences, which involves regulating variables such as pacing, intensity, clarity, and the optimal mix of redundancy and novelty. Infants possess only modest capacities in this realm. They can shut their eyes or turn their heads away from intense visual stimuli; they can spit out or regurgitate bad-tasting food; but they cannot turn off their ears (neither can we), except by falling asleep; and they cannot rid themselves of excessive or painful tactile stimulation; nor have they yet learned complicated cognitive maneuvers for dealing with information overload. Thus infants are dependent on caregivers to maintain their stimulus worlds within optimal ranges for making sense of their experiences.

The caregiver also plays a role in presenting the conceptual frameworks available in the family and culture, as well as the caregiver's own idiosyncratic concepts for organizing experience, and thus helps to shape the representations the infant is constructing. Perhaps the best example of both the regulating of stimuli function and the conceptual shaping function is contained in "motherese"— the universal language mothers speak to infants. It is slow, redundant, exaggerates important features, and is affectively modulated. It also builds on redundancies by introducing variations on a theme. All of these characteristics make it easy for young infants to construct representations of these exchanges, and to learn about the world the mother personifies. Infants will differ in their preferred rates, intensities, and patterns of stimuli; each mother must discover what works best for her infant. Motherese, of course, represents only one context in which the infant encounters the world. There are a multiplicity of others, which will vary on all of these parameters.

The issues at stake for the infant are the style or stance he or she will develop toward new information, new people, and new experiences, as well as the adequacy of the representations the infant will be able to construct. If the infant's world or parts of that world are too noisy, lack clarity, are too labile, too intense, or too invariant, if the conceptual frameworks are too idiosyncratic, or too confining, or too global, or too inflexible, the infant's task of accumulating experience and knowledge about the world will be compromised. The capacity for self-analysis is dependent to some degree on the skills the infant, child, and adult have been able to develop in this realm.

The parallel here for the analytic situation underscores the importance of perceiving the analysand's style of organizing information, and of being alert to difficulties the analysand may have in this area. The analyst must then regulate the pace, the intensity, the mix of redundancy and novelty, and the clarity of communications accordingly in order to enhance the analysand's ability to process and integrate the material. It also underscores the need for the analyst to understand the analysand's conceptual framework, its strengths and liabilities, and, at least initially, to work within that framework.

The second process, which involves disembedding knowledge from specific contexts and applying it to broader contexts, is the counterpoint to constructing particular representations. I have used the term "decontextualization" to describe this process (Demos, 1992). Early learning is tied to specific contexts and is characterized by gestalts—the inclusion of the whole scene. The infant has to develop skills in abstracting the essence from the whole and in recognizing that essence in a different context. This is to some extent a figure and ground problem. Infants already possess the capacities to perceive invariances and to recognize recurring patterns, but they lack experience in applying these capacities. Passive motion and locomotion aid the infant in being able to perceive objects, people, and events from different perspectives, and thus to focus on which aspects remain invariant and which change and are less essential. Language also provides another enormous gain in this area, since it offers nouns and verbs that represent classes of objects, actions, and experience. It allows an expansion of time into the past, present, and future, as well as an expansion of space. Reading and schooling represent further extensions of this skill as knowledge becomes increasingly abstract and removed from the immediate context.

The caregiver's contribution to this process involves communicating whether or not such endeavors are valued, and in influencing how and which content areas can be explored, talked about, and elaborated. Thus the degrees of freedom allowed and the amount of support given to the infant and child to physically, verbally, and mentally explore aspects of the inanimate world, social interactions, and inner experiences, and the degree to which the caregiver becomes involved in and sanctions such activities, are central variables in developing this skill. There are a great variety of possible outcomes; for example, this skill can be highly developed in some content areas and relatively undeveloped in others, or unevenly developed within a content area. The content areas most closely related to the capacity for self-analysis involve inner experiences and interpersonal relationships. The capacity for self-analysis, then, will depend to some extent on the degree to which and the ways in which the valuing of and the exploring, verbalizing, and elaborating of inner experiences of the self and others (e.g., feeling states, impulses, memories, wishes, intentions) have occurred in the person's life.

The parallel to the analytic situation is direct, since it is the situation par excellence where valuing and fostering the exploration, verbalization, and elaboration of inner experiences and relationships occur. There will, nevertheless, be tremendous variability in analysands' valuing of these content areas and in their level of knowledge in these areas. Thus, the analyst's role is not merely to communicate the value of exploring one's inner experiences and one's relationships, but also to become familiar with the particular ways in which these content areas were devalued, overvalued, or ignored for each analysand, in order to help them to unlearn a maladaptive value system and to learn a more therapeutic one. The analyst must also pay attention to the particularities of the analysand's conceptual organization in these areas. To the extent that the analysand's difficulties can be attributed to a lack of knowledge, or to inaccurate knowledge, the analyst's role can be described as that of a teacher. In this, the role parallels that of the caregiver in providing a safe, stimulating environment, useful information, and facilitating involvement.

This completes our discussion of the first of the capacities related to the capacity for self-analysis, namely, the capacity to construct representations of experiences encountered in the inner, psychic world. This has been described as involving several processes, each with a range of variable outcomes. Because of the focus on representations, this capacity deals primarily with the cognitive aspects of the capacity for self-analysis. Clearly it does not operate in a vacuum. I would like to turn now to a discussion of the second capacity, which interacts with the capacity to construct representations and which also underlies the capacity for self-analysis; namely, the capacity to modulate and regulate emotional experience.

To review briefly, we stated earlier that the human infant is capable of experiencing the full range of basic emotions, which are enjoyment, interest, distress, anger, fear, startle, disgust, and shame. Much of the work on infant affect has been based on the work of Silvan Tomkins (1962,1963), which I will briefly summarize here. He argues that we have inherited affect programs which are correlated sets of responses that include facial expressions, vocalizations, respiratory patterns, autonomic responses (heart rate, skin temperature, visceral) and skeletal responses. These affect programs function as general and abstract amplifiers of stimuli impinging on the organism and create, through facial, vocal, and autonomic responses, an analogue which is experienced as inherently rewarding or inherently punishing. Tomkins postulates that there are both innate and learned activators of affect, and that each discrete affect is activated by a particular pattern of stimulation, such as increases and decreases in rates of stimulation densities, and differing levels of nonoptimal stimulation. When internal or external sources of neural firing suddenly increase, the organism will startle, become afraid, or become interested, depending on the suddenness of the rate of the increase. When sources of neural firing reach and maintain a high, nonoptimal level of stimulation, the organism will experience anger or distress, depending on the level of stimulation. When the sources of neural firing suddenly decrease, the organism will laugh or smile with enjoyment depending on the suddenness of the decrease. Shame is activated when positive affect (e.g., interest) is interrupted and attenuated without being completely reduced.

Tomkins (1962,1963) distinguishes between the affect program per se, and affect-related information, such as the perceived trigger of an affect, and the response to an affect, including memories, plans, fantasies, perceptions, and motor responses that may or may not be coassembled with an affect at any given moment. He refers to these coassemblies as affect complexes or as ideoaffect organizations. Ideoaffect is an abbreviation for ideo-perceptual-memorial-action-affect, which refers to the involvement of all of the critical subsystems that together constitute a human being. Ideoaffect complexes, then, are organizations in which affect is seen as the core element in flexible and changing assemblies. Ideoaffect complexes are constructed over time as the infant experiences emotions and gradually connects these experiences to a variety of causes and to a variety of outcomes or consequences.

The newborn infant then, has the capacity to experience affect, but does not yet have past experience to draw on. Thus the crying neonate neither knows why she is crying, nor that there is anything that can be done about it. The cry in this initial experience represents an innate affective response to a continuous level of nonoptimal stimulation, such as hunger or fatigue, which, in conjunction with a correlated set of facial-muscle, blood-flow, visceral, respiratory, and skeletal responses, will amplify the original stimulus and produce an inherently punishing experience of distress for the infant. This initial experience of distress is as close to pure affect as is possible. As Tomkins (1978) has said: "affect either makes good things better or bad things worse" (p. 203). In contrast to Freud's idea that crying (affect) represented a discharge of drive tension (Freud, 1895), Tomkins argues that crying (distress) amplifies the tension and makes it feel worse. The evolutionary function of such a mechanism is to make the organism care about what is happening and to provide the motivation to organize a response. For Tomkins affects are the primary motivators, amplifying drives, cognition and memory etc.

We return to our crying neonate, who, because she is crying, now cares about what is happening, is now motivated to pay attention to what happens next, to remember what these punishing sensations felt like, and to begin to connect them to antecedents and conse-quences. For example, if a caregiver has consistently responded in a helpful way to the infant's crying, within 3 or 4 weeks, the infant will stop crying at the sight or sound of the caregiver's approach. This phenomenon occurs because the infant has already connected the experience of distress with the approach and comfort of the caregiver, and thus anticipates that the sight of the caregiver means that comfort will soon follow. This expectation represents the construction of an ideo-affect complex, and allows the infant to stop crying and wait.

The construction of ideoaffect complexes is the primary process by which the infant gradually learns how and if affective experiences can be modulated. I would like first to explore the factors that influence the infant's capacity to modulate negative affects, and then discuss the modulation of positive affects, relating both to the capacity for self-analysis.

Under ordinary circumstances, distress and anger are the most frequent experiences of negative affect for the young infant. (In more pathological families, fear, startle, and disgust may be more prominent. See Gaensbauer, 1982, as an illustration of fear in early infancy.) Thus, my examples will focus on distress and anger. Initially, infants have only a very limited repertoire of responses for managing an experience of distress or anger, and these work best at relatively low levels of intensity. Fussy infants can be seen to try to get their hands, fists, or fingers into their mouths and to suck vigorously if successful, or to move their heads and limbs around, as if searching for something. The sucking, with its rhythmical pattern of stimulation, will override the constant or arrhythmical pattern of stimulation that is causing the low-level distress. Many of the universal techniques for soothing infants, such as singing, rocking, or offering the breast or a pacifier, rely on a rhythmical pattern of stimulation. The moving around of the head sometimes allows the infant to succeed in finding an object to gaze at. This activity evokes the affect interest, which will feel more organized and focused than the pattern of stimulation evoking the low-level distress. Caregivers also use this technique with fussy infants by offering their faces or a novel object for the infant to gaze at. They are in effect using one affect to override another affect.

Beyond this low-level of distress, however, infants do not possess the instrumental capacities, the experience, or the knowledge to help themselves. They need a responsive caregiver to help them modulate and manage more intense negative affect. Since negative affects are an inescapable part of living and are inherently punishing, and since they can escalate, in a positive feedback loop, to higher and higher densities if no one intervenes, the potential for traumatic experiences of negative affect exists for the young infant. If such experiences occur, they are likely to set in motion massive defensive efforts. Infants left to cry will cycle up into higher and higher densities of distress and anger, and will eventually fall asleep from exhaustion. But this is an extremely punishing sequence, and on future occasions the infant will try to prevent it from happening again. For example, several decades ago, a number of observers (e.g., Provence and Lipton, 1962) noted that infants cared for in institutions did not cry. At that time, institutions operated by the clock; infants were fed and changed every four hours, and otherwise were not responded to. It is my hypothesis that these infants, left to cry for hours at a time in their sterile cribs, experienced such punishing doses of distress and anger that they learned to shut down at the first sign of any distress or discomfort. The caregiver's role in helping the infant to modulate negative affects is therefore crucial.

What is the right amount of crying or of negative affect? If affects have evolved in order to amplify experience and to motivate us by making us care about what is happening, then we must learn to be able to tolerate and endure our affects in order to use the information contained in them and to organize an adaptive response. I am suggesting that there is an optimal density of negative affect that is neither too low, thereby preventing the infant from exercising and developing his or her regulating capacities, nor too high, thereby overwhelming the infant and evoking defensive responses, but that ranges from moderate to moderately high. This optimal level will vary from infant to infant, from moment to moment, from context to context, and is therefore difficult to specify. But it is nevertheless recognizable, because it is a level that will allow the infant to remain in the situation, to continue to organize these experiences, and to try to do something about the situation. (I will say more about the infant's role in this process in the next section.)

The caregiver's role in helping the infant to modulate the intensity and density of negative affects is essential in two ways. First of all, the caregiver can protect the infant from traumatic experiences of negative affect that threaten to disrupt the infant's efforts to persist and that set in motion a defensive retreat. And second, the caregiver can help the infant to endure and manage more moderate densities of negative affect and thereby enhance the infant's capacity to remain in the situation and to persist in solving the difficulty. Both of these caregiver functions lead to a sense of trust within the infant—a trust in the reliability and manageability of one's inner experience. For if the caregiver succeeds in maintaining the infant's experience of negative affects within optimal densities, then the infant will have learned that the onset of negative affect does not signal the end of a task, or a dreaded escalation, but rather that the experience can be borne, that finding a resolution is possible, and that the punishing quality of the experience will come to an end.

The infant will learn many other things as well from these experiences; for example, that the caregiver is reliable and that the world is trustworthy. But since the activity of self-analysis generally occurs when one is alone with oneself, the learning about the reliability and manageability of one's inner world is most relevant to our focus on the capacity for self-analysis. The capacity to explore one's inner experiences will be enhanced to the extent that one is not surprised by, disorganized by, or defended against intense negative affects. In other words, the more one has developed the capacity to tolerate and endure moderately intense negative affective experiences, the more one will be able to probe and explore one's inner experiences.

In the analytic situation, the analyst must quickly assess the analysand's capacities in this realm; for example, what tolerance does the analysand have for experiencing distress, anger, fear, shame, and disgust; what are the characteristic defenses used for each affect. In many respects, the analyst's role is parallel to the caregiver's role in both of the functions mentioned above. The analyst protects the analysand from traumatic doses of negative affect and helps the analysand to endure and manage more moderate densities of negative affect so as to be able to remain in the situation and resolve difficulties — although the methods used in the two settings are quite different. Both the caregiver and the analyst must be skillful in their timing and pacing, and in the amount and kind of help offered, and both will use vocal modulation to some extent, but the caregiver will rely primarily on physical holding and soothing, and the analyst will rely primarily on words and meanings. Their point of entry into the situation is also quite different. Generally the caregiver is operating in a time period before the infant has developed extensive defenses, and is responding to negative affective states already underway in the infant or is acting to prevent the occurrence of such states. By contrast, the analyst is dealing with failed defenses or strong defenses and is often working to uncover or to bring into awareness the experience of negative affect. Despite these differences, both are trying to help the infant or analysand maintain their experiences of negative affect within an optimal range of density.

The ease or difficulty that an infant–mother pair or an analyst–analysand pair experiences in trying to achieve this goal is influenced by the characteristics of both participants in relation to affect. For if the affect mechanism is designed to amplify experience, then expressions of affect will evoke more of the same affect in a positive feedback loop, both within the person expressing the affect and in the observer. Infant affect, because it has not yet been socialized, tends to be more full-voiced, full-faced, and full-bodied than adult affect, and thus it is very likely that a caregiver who is engaged with a distressed or angry infant will experience a variant of the affects expressed by the infant. In the analytic situation, as the intensity of the affects expressed by the analysand increases, so too does the likelihood that the analyst will experience a variant of the same affects. When affects are evoked in the caregiver or the analyst, then their ability to respond in a helpful or therapeutic way will depend on their response to their own affective experience at that particular moment. This phenomenon of affective resonance, which is an important aspect of empathy, will activate the caregiver's or analyst's unique personal history of learning relevant to the evoked affect, and will both inform and complicate their task of perceiving and understanding the infant's or analysand's experience and of providing a helpful intervention. To the extent that the caregiver or the analyst is unable to bear the density of negative affect evoked within him-or herself by the infant or the analysand, then to that extent they will be unable to foster the development of the tolerance for negative affect in the other, and thus will be unable to foster the capacity for self-analysis. Here, the analyst's own therapeutic history is relevant. For if the analyst's own analysis has enhanced his or her capacity to bear negative affect, and thus has increased the analyst's capacity to continue his or her own self-analysis, then the analyst will be more able to foster this capacity in the analysand.

The regulation of positive affect does not involve the same kind of traumatic risks just described for the negative affects, but it is nonetheless an important aspect of the capacity for self-analysis. Earlier we described the various cognitive aspects of the capacity to construct representations of inner experience. Here we will focus on the affective and motivational aspects of that process. The whole enterprise of attending to, elaborating on, valuing, attempting to understand or change or master one's inner experiences requires an affective and motivational investment. Certainly some of the motivation comes from a wish to escape from or master painful negative affective experiences. But that wish alone is not enough to produce a focus on internal psychic processes. Indeed it often leads to strenuous efforts to control external conditions, such as other people and events. The capacity for self-analysis requires the capacity to generate and sustain interest in one's own inner experiences and to experience excitement and enjoyment in the process of exploring and understanding oneself. This capacity for sustaining and elaborating positive affect about oneself does not just happen in the absence of intense or intrusive negative affects. It must be nurtured and fostered by the caregiver and by the analyst.

In early infancy the experience of interest is manifested in a variety of ways—by gazing intently, by reaching toward an object, by vocalizing, and by other persistent, organized motor patterns. These behaviors become more elaborate as the infant becomes more mobile and active. The caregiver's response to these manifestations of interest is important in determining to some extent how well and in what areas the infant will be able to invest and sustain his or her interests. For example, the early face-to-face interactions between infant and caregiver provide complex information about what it is like to be with another person. Several infant researchers have described the synchronized patterns of behaviors that occur and the infant's capacity for early learning of these patterns (Stern, 1977; Beebe and Lachmann, 1988). I would like to emphasize here, the affective component of these experiences, and the consequences for the infant's experience of positive affects. If the caregiver is responsive and attuned to her infant, the infant will gradually come to experience that he or she is a source of interesting events and of delight for others, that interests can be sustained and shared with others, and that one's own experiences are important and matter to others. But there are many other possible scenarios. If the caregiver cannot become engaged with, or cannot sustain interaction with her infant, or becomes too intrusive or too controlling, the infant will learn that internal states, including interest, are not very important, or that one is not a source of interest for the other, or that one needs to concentrate on avoiding intrusions rather than on pursuing interests.

As the infant becomes more active, the messages from the caregiver may become more explicit. The caregiver may verbalize and continue to act in ways that communicate an investment in and support of the child's interests, curiosity, plans, and initiatives. Or caregivers can verbalize and convey in actions the message that the child's wishes, concerns, and activities are insignificant compared to those of the adult, and that the most important thing is for the child to comply with the adult's wishes. Or the adult can be too preoccupied or too self-absorbed or too depressed to pay much attention to the child, and conveys the message "don't bother me." The more the infant and child receive support in expanding, sustaining, and communicating affective states of interest and their related ideoaffect organizations, involving, for example, fantasies and plans, the more they will be able to experience themselves as the source of interesting ideas and events, to sustain their interests when alone, to invest their interest readily and easily, and to experience excitement and enjoyment in the process. There must be this investment of interest, excitement, and enjoyment in inner experiences in order for self-analysis to prosper.

In the analytic situation, the analyst's hovering attention and focus on the analysand's thoughts, fantasies, and wishes provides the necessary support for self-analytic activity. But the analyst's stance alone may not be sufficient to overcome the analysand's lack of interest and enjoyment in his or her own internal processes, or the analysand's learned conviction that his or her internal processes do not matter or are shameful, or that such a focus represents selfishness. Each of these issues will be a hindrance in developing the capacity for self-analysis, and therefore must be addressed and worked through in the analysis.

The third and final capacity related to the capacity for self-analysis is the capacity to maintain one's sense of active agency in relation to the world, to others, and to one's inner processes. By a sense of active agency, I mean the knowledge that one's own efforts are effective in causing something to happen, or in recreating and prolonging a positive state, or in limiting, ending, or avoiding a negative state. The DeCasper and Carstens (1981) experiment described earlier, in which neonates became upset when they could no longer turn on the singing voice by lengthening the pauses between their sucking bursts, suggests that the issue of agency is pertinent from the beginning of life, and that the fate of the infant's initiatives is being determined from birth on. Sander (1982) has suggested that if a family can facilitate the infant's own efforts at goal realization and provide opportunities for the infant to initiate goal-organized behaviors, then it will provide "the conditions which establish not only the capacity for self-awareness, but conditions which insure the use of such inner awareness by the infant as a frame of reference in organizing his own adaptive behavior" (p. 17). Sander goes on to say that "the valence of this inner experience under these conditions of self-initiated goal realization will be felt as the infant's own" (p. 17). By contrast, when self-initiated goals are not realized or facilitated by the family, then the valence of this inner experience will not be felt as the infant's own, but rather as external to the self, and the use of inner awareness by the infant as a frame of reference for organizing behavior will not be enhanced or supported. It follows then, that the perception that the locus of control of events is within oneself, and that therefore inner awareness is a relevant frame of reference for organizing one's behavior, is an essential foundation for engaging in self-analysis.

Infants and caregivers must negotiate this issue of the infant's agency and initiatives and the inevitable clash of agendas between the infant's goals and the goals of other family members. This can happen in a variety of ways (Demos, 1986, 1988, 1989a, 1989b), and both the timing and the content of the caregiver's responses will be important in determining the fate of the infant's sense of agency. I will present brief examples of each of these variables.

Earlier, when discussing negative affect, I stressed the need for the caregiver to help the infant to modulate these experiences. Here I will

focus on the timing of the caregiver's interventions and their consequences for the infant's sense of agency. Let us assume, for the
moment, that the infant begins with a low level of distress, manifested by whimpering and motor restlessness, and gradually works
up to a rhythmical cry and more vigorous motor restlessness. If the
caregiver responds by providing comfort too early in this sequence of
events, for example, at the very first sign of restlessness or of vocal
whimpering, the infant will receive a remedy before he or she has had
the opportunity to become aware of a problem. The comfort will calm
the infant, but it will in this instance bypass the psychological process
within the infant of becoming aware of a distressed state (A); of
experiencing an intention to end it (I); and of mobilizing behaviors to
achieve that goal (M). I will refer to this entire process as AIM. Here
again we see the importance of the concept of an optimal zone of
affective experience, that will vary from infant to infant, and that is
neither too brief and weak for AIM to occur, nor too prolonged and
intense, which might overwhelm or disrupt AIM. If the infant is
allowed sufficient psychological time for AIM to develop, then the
infant will be able to relate subsequent events, such as receiving
comfort, to all of the components of AIM—affect, intention, and
mobilization, and will feel actively involved in the outcome.

The caregiver's ability to determine and allow for the optimal
psychological interval that would permit AIM to emerge within the
infant involves a variety of factors. First of all, the caregiver must be
able to perceive the infant as a separate, autonomous little person
with the capacity for experiencing affect and intentions, and for
mobilizing a response. A perception of the infant as "totally helpless"
or as not capable of any of these experiences will clearly work against
supporting the infant's self-initiated goals. Second, the caregiver
must believe in the importance of fostering the infant's sense of
agency and value the infant's initiatives, while at the same time
recognizing the infant's limitations and need for support. In some
circumstances the experience of personal agency for the infant will
become compromised by conflicts and difficulties. For example, the
caregiver may experience the infant's initiatives as a battle over who
will be the boss in the family and try to override the infant: Or the
caregiver may experience so much gratification in anticipating the
infant's every need and in being indispensable to the infant that he or
she fosters the infant's dependency: Or the caregiver may overesti-
mate the infant's capacities and fail to offer sufficient support.

Third, the caregiver must be able to tolerate the level of distress or
negative affect in the infant sufficient to mobilize the infant, which
raises many of the issues already discussed earlier in the section on

the modulation of negative affects. Fourth, the caregiver must be able to tolerate the somewhat bumbling and awkward efforts the infant will make to try to help him or herself. All initial learning of skills at any age is characterized by ineptness. Thus caregivers are frequently in the situation of watching their infants and young children struggling to try to master a task, for example, to get their thumb in their mouth, or to feed themselves, to take their first step, or to tie their shoes. The capacity to gauge just the right amount of struggle that will be experienced by the infant or child as a challenge and will foster growth in their capacities and in their sense of themselves as agents involves judgment, skill, and empathy on the part of the caregiver. It also involves the capacity to tolerate the child's initial ineptness without becoming overly ashamed or afraid of potential failure, or contemptuous of and impatient with ineptness.

The parallels in the analytic situation are direct. The discovery that the timing of interventions is crucial is not news. But the infancy data underline the importance of timing for fostering the analysand's sense of agency in order to promote the capacity for self-analysis. It may be useful to articulate the separate components of AIM as a psychological process that must emerge within the analysand before an intervention can be experienced as one's own. It may be helpful to describe the components of the caregiver's ability to determine and allow for an optimal psychological interval that permits AIM to emerge. This description might evoke some echoes when one thinks about the analyst's ability to allow for a similar kind of psychological interval within the analysand.

This brings us to a discussion of the contents of the caregiver's and analyst's interventions and how they will help determine the sense of agency in the infant or analysand. As an illustration, let us begin with the infant–caregiver situation and examine the following sequence. A young infant is gazing intently at a nearby object and reaching toward it (manifestations of AIM—the affect of interest, the intention to explore the object further, and the mobilization of a reaching action). The infant is unable to fully execute this plan, however, and begins to express fussy sounds of frustration and mild anger. If a caregiver does not understand or believe that infants are capable of the psychological processes involved in AIM, then he or she will be highly unlikely to respond in a way that will facilitate and enhance the infant's efforts. The infant's fussiness might then be perceived as fatigue or hunger, or as inconsequential, or as irritating, and will be responded to accordingly. However, if the caregiver perceives the young infant as capable of the processes involved in AIM, then he or she will be far more likely to offer some kind of assistance, such as changing the infant's posture or moving the object closer to facilitate the infant's reaching efforts. This assistance will enable the infant to remain interested, to persist with the intention to explore the object, and, possibly to attain some success in executing this plan.

I am suggesting that the infant experiences these events as affective sequences, such as positive-negative-negative sequences, or positive-negative-positive sequences. Thus, the specific kind of caregiver response helps to determine the motivational meaning of the whole sequence for the infant. Returning to our illustration, a positive affective state of interest with its related intention and mobilization of behavior, leads to a negative affective state of mild anger, which can then lead to any of the following affective states, depending on what the caregiver does and how it is perceived by the infant: (1) an angry protest if the infant is put to bed for a nap; (2) a decline in interest if the infant is fed or merely comforted; (3) an increase in frustration and anger if the infant is ignored and left to his or her own limited resources, or to a giving up of the interest out of failure; (4) an increase in distress and/or anger if the infant is punished for being fussy; or (5) an increase in interest and enjoyment if the infant receives help in achieving a self-initiated goal.

Many varieties of affective sequences occur in the ongoing experiences of young infants, each providing meaningful information to infants about what to expect when they experience a particular affective state and try to carry out the intentions and actions mobilized by such a state. In the above example, in which the infant had experienced interest and then mild anger, clearly only the last possibility (5), which produces an affective sequence of positive-negative-positive affect will facilitate the infant's own efforts at goal realization. But all of the sequences described above will contribute to the determination of the degree to which an infant will feel in control of internal and external events, and the degree to which an infant will therefore continue to use inner awareness as a relevant frame of reference for organizing behavior. I have described in other contexts (Demos, 1989a, b) how the frequent occurrence of positive-negative-negative affective sequences can lead to experiences of ineffectiveness and helplessness in the infant, which then heightens the infant's need for the caregiver. As the infant puts more and more effort into obtaining and sustaining the caregiver's involvement, and becomes skilled at reading parental states and availability, he or she relies less and less on using an awareness of inner states as a useful frame of reference for guiding behavior.

Another way in which the content of the caregiver's intervention is important in influencing the infant's sense of agency has to do with the amount or degree of help the caregiver provides for the infant. Once again we are dealing with an optimal range of support. Both too much and too little support will undermine the infant's efforts to achieve some success in self-initiated goals, and thus to be able to experience him- or herself as effective. The old maxim "don't do anything for an infant and child that they can do for themselves" is relevant here. But the maxim speaks only to the error of being too controlling or too intrusive or too impatient with the child's efforts, or too enamored of one's own competence to allow the infant and child to do for themselves. The other side of this issue is equally problematic. Providing too little support, abandoning, ignoring, or sadistically putting or leaving the infant and child in difficult situations, and letting them fend for themselves, will create the positive-negative-negative affective sequences described above and undermine the child's sense of agency.

The relevance for the analytic situation is once again direct. The analyst's failure to perceive the analysand's need for support in particularly painful moments of the therapeutic work can lead to feelings of increasing helplessness in the analysand, which may result in a greater dependence on the analyst, or even in a premature termination of the work. On the other hand, if the analyst provides too much interpretation and does too much of the therapeutic work, the analysand will have difficulty experiencing a sense of agency and will not feel encouraged to pursue the hard work of self-analysis. If good ideas can come only from the analyst, then the analysand will begin to wonder why he or she should even try to figure things out. Both of these failures are endemic in the analytic situation. The emphasis on remaining neutral can cause an analyst to feel uncomfortable with the need to provide support for an analysand at particular moments in the therapeutic work. There may also be a lack of training or models for how to provide support without violating a therapeutic stance. On the other side, the long training and the prestige of the profession may inflate the analyst's notion of his or her own expertise, wisdom, or authority and lead him or her into errors of doing for the analysand what the analysand can do for him- or herself. The infancy data can help to reinforce the analyst's vigilance to avoid these errors. For if the goal is to promote the capacity for self-analysis, then the analyst must be very attuned to the analysand's own efforts to understand his or her experience, and work to support such efforts.

This concludes my discussion of the developmental foundations for the emergence of the capacity for self-analysis and of the parallels in the roles of the caregiver and analyst. I have maintained throughout this discussion that the capacity for self-analysis is multifaceted, in that it combines a variety of basic human skills, each of which can vary in the degree to which and in the ways in which they are developed and influenced by the caregiver and by the analyst. By describing the early manifestations of these capacities in infancy, and by detailing the diversity of transactions that can occur, I have endeavorred to articulate the complexity and subtlety of the processes involved and to point out the many parallels in the role of the caregiver and the role of the analyst/therapist. It follows from this approach that as these various skills become coordinated and focused on the task of self-analysis, the capacity to pursue and sustain this activity will be as variable from person to person as the variability of each of the component skills. In other words, no two people will engage in self-analysis in quite the same way, or bring to the task exactly the same combination of strengths and weaknesses. As with any multifaceted capacity, there will be a myriad of ways in which it can be exercised. It also follows that given the multiplicity of factors involved in the process of self-analysis, it is highly probable first, that every component of the process will not be developed to its utmost potential, and second, that new experiences will continue to challenge and change individual components. Thus, there will always be room for growth and new discoveries as we engage in the life-long task of understanding ourselves.

REFERENCES

Beebe, B. & Lachmann, F.M. (1988), The contribution of mother–infant mutual influence to the origins of self-and object representations. *Psychoanal. Psychol.,* 5:305–337.

Bell, R. (1977), Socialization findings re-examined. In: *Child Effects on Adults,* ed. R. Bell & L. Harper. Lincoln: University of Nebraska Press, pp. 53–84.

DeCasper, A.J. & Carstens, A.A. (1981), Contingencies of stimulation: Effects on learning and emotion in neonates. *Infant Behav. & Develop.,* 4:19–35.

Demos, E.V. (1986), Crying in early infancy: An illustration of the motivational function of affect. In: *Affective Development in Early Infancy,* ed. T.B. Brazelton & M. Yogman. Norwood, NJ: Ablex, pp. 39–73.

_____ (1988), Affect and the development of the self: A new frontier. In: *Frontiers in Self Psychology: Progress in Self Psychology, Vol. 3,* ed. A. Goldberg. Hillsdale, NJ: The Analytic Press, pp. 27–53.

_____ (1989a), Resiliency in infancy. In: *The Child in Our Time: Studies in the Development of Resiliency,* ed. T.F. Dugan & R. Coles. New York: Brunner/Mazel, pp. 3–22.

_____ (1989b), A prospective constructionist view of development. *The Annual of Psychoanalysis,* 17:287–308. Hillsdale, NJ: The Analytic Press.

_____ (1992), The early organization of the psyche. In: *Interface of Psychoanalysis and*

Psychology, ed. J.W. Barron, M.N. Eagle & D.L. Wolitzky. Washington DC: American Psychological Association, pp. 200–232.

Freud, S. (1895), Project for a scientific psychology. *Standard Edition*, 1:283–387. London: Hogarth Press, 1966.

Gaensbauer, T. (1982), The differentiation of discrete affects: A case study. *The Psychoanalytic Study of the Child*, 37:29–65. New York: IUP.

Lichtenberg, J. (1984), *Psychoanalysis and Infant Research*. Hillsdale, NJ: The Analytic Press.

Provence, S. & Lipton, R. (1962), *Infants in Institutions*. New York: IUP.

Sameroff, A.J. & Emde, R.N., (1989), *Relationship Disturbances in Early Childhood: A Developmental Approach*. New York: Basic Books.

Sander, L. (1982), Toward a logic of organization in psychobiologic development. Presented at the 13th Margaret S. Mahler Symposium in Philadelphia.

Stern, D. (1977), *The First Relationship*. Cambridge, MA: Harvard University Press.

_____ (1985), *The Interpersonal World of the Infant*. New York: Basic Books.

Tomkins, S.S. (1962), *Affect Imagery, Consciousness: Vol. 1*. New York: Springer.

_____ (1963), *Affect Imagery Consciousness: Vol. 2*. New York: Springer.

_____ (1978), Script theory: Differential magnification of affects. In: *Nebraska Symposium on Motivation*, ed. H.E. Howe, Jr. & R.A. Dunstbier. Lincoln: University of Nebraska Press, pp. 201–236.

Winnicott, D.W. (1965), *The Maturational Processes and the Facilitating Environment*. New York: IUP.

2

Does Our Self-Analysis Take Into Consideration Our Assumptions?

Ricardo Bernardi
Beatriz de León de Bernardi

Our analytic activity always begins with certain assumptions. At the most obvious level, these assumptions influence our theoretical predisposition. From our theories, in turn we derive our ideas of psychic structure, pathogenesis, the rules governing the treatment process, the elements contributing to psychic change, and other matters that vary from one theory to another. Rather than being associated solely with the contents of theories, our assumptions are also linked to our attitudes toward the theories themselves. In a less obvious manner, our assumptions find their way into our *Weltanschauung*. Finally, and even less noticed, are our highly personal ways of communicating and relating, of perceiving and representing our experience. As analysts we generally do not think of these factors as assumptions; we may not experience them as such. Nevertheless, those who try to communicate with us know they must take these aspects into account if they wish to achieve real contact with us. All our patients get to know us in the analytic situation: how, when, and to what we reply; how, when, and to what we react (or do not react).

We incorporate these assumptions into our analytic identities and into our theoretical and technical tools. Each of us often gets the impression that these assumptions are self-evident truths that need not be psychoanalytically investigated. Sometimes they are preconscious, and we simply fail to notice them. Yet—and this is of the utmost importance—we frequently consider that our idiosyncratic ways of seeing, feeling, and responding are the only possible ones, and thus we ourselves unwittingly hinder our ability to notice the distinct features of our patients, of our colleagues, and even of unknown and potentially creative parts of ourselves.

These assumptions belong uniquely to us and predate our relationships with our patients; in this sense, they differ from our countertransference reactions to our patients. These assumptions have a twofold relationship with self-analysis. On one hand, they may narrow its scope by causing us to ignore a portion of our psychic activity. On the other hand, our achieving greater awareness of these assumptions may open new areas of understanding of how our minds function in interaction with our patients' minds. Yet this is not an easy self-analysis: only the intellectual aspects of these assumptions tend to become conscious, while their unconscious roots remain concealed. As shown later in this chapter, it is difficult to reach those roots in the course of our analytic training or even in our personal analysis. And, if indeed we succeed in learning more about them, our assumptions nevertheless evolve during our lifetimes and therefore need to be accessible to our ongoing self-analytic activities. We argue that these assumptions should become the object of our self-observation, supported by a disposition toward self-analysis. Let us explain the meaning we assign to this expression.

DISPOSITION TOWARD SELF-ANALYSIS

We may assume general agreement with certain notions of self-analysis: that Freud's self-analysis had a deep impact on the very origin of psychoanalysis; that all successful analytic treatments must result in an increase in the self-analytic ability of the patient; and that, in our work as analysts, we must use our self-analytic skills to deepen our understanding of transference–countertransference relationships.

Yet many issues seem to be open to discussion. Do we actually engage in self-analysis in the systematic sense that Freud himself did? If we adopt a more spontaneous and fluctuating attitude toward self-analysis, what is the scope of the insight we achieve? Is that scope adequate to preserve the therapeutic achievements of analytic treatment or to recover them when threatened? What kind of self-analysis does our analytic work require? What are the regions in our minds that should be open to suspended attention focusing on ourselves?

We belong to the psychoanalytic tradition of Uruguay and of the River Plate at large, where analysts are expected to be able to develop and maintain self-analytic activity that will help them in their work and in their personal lives, with no infringement on their freedom to go back to the couch when they deem it advisable. Some authors (Grinberg and Lichtmann, 1981) state that any access to the unconscious through self-analysis is bound to be incomplete and vulnerable to compromise solutions. Yet others insist on the need to develop a "psychoanalytic function" in the patient that allows for separation from the analyst and the culmination of the analysis (Berenstein and Fondevila, 1989).

We have suggested that we analysts need to put the assumptions on which we base our interactions with patients at the disposal of our self-analytic activity. This activity might be characterized by some of the features described by Ticho (1967, 1971): to allow thoughts to drift in free association without too much anxiety, to notice the signs of unconscious conflicts, to be able to take the necessary time to understand those conflicts, and to be able to make use of the insight achieved.

Baranger et al. (1969) referred to a "disposition to be analyzed" that should exist in future analysts and that involves curiosity about inner world, a drive to investigate the unknown, and the ability to tolerate doubt.

We define disposition toward self-analysis as an orientation to the inner world. There is a suspension of judgment and a possibility of exposing our own ways of thinking and feeling to a questioning spirit that stimulates free associations while allowing them to be noticed. This is only a first step toward self-analysis; yet it is an important one, since it determines the size of the internal areas to which we gain access. These new areas will give us not only a deeper understanding of the signs of internal conflicts involved in countertransference, but also a more refined understanding of our own participation in the analytic process. Thus several aspects of our personal ways of listening and interpreting, which usually go unnoticed, become part of the observational field. This self-analytic activity may develop during the session, but its continuation and enhancement are necessary once the session is over.

SELF-ANALYSIS DURING THE SESSION

The disposition toward self-analysis of our assumptions is particularly clarifying when our interaction with patients becomes most intense, when there is a transformative process based on strong transference–countertransference elements. These particular moments in analysis have different degrees of significance and have been considered from different viewpoints. Thus, for instance the Kleinian tradition insisted that what occurs in the mind of the analyst must be considered to be an effect of the projective identifications of the patient. Others have demonstrated that this viewpoint may blur the participation of the analyst in this process (Jiménez, 1989). Baranger and Baranger (1983) suggested the idea of a "common field" between analyst and patient that would permit a more sophisticated understanding of the exchange taking place between them.

The moments of intense analytic interaction are, in fact, nodal points where it becomes necessary for us to make approaching and discriminating movements in relation to our patients. This is what we want to examine in further detail. Here again, different schools have tried to explain the phenomena involved (e.g., separation processes, individuation, integration of split and projected parts of the ego, desymbiotization, disidentification, and symbolic castration). Although from different theoretical contexts, they all acknowledge that the issue at stake is the psychic pain of the patient when faced with the need to be differentiated. But as analysts we must also face feelings of renunciation and loss. In our interaction with patients, we must abandon well-known presentations (and inner representations) familiar to ourselves and our patients. Such mourning and disidentification processes are necessary for us to be able to admit that our understanding is always only partial and possible within the parameters of our own psychic reality, which may not become a model for our patients or for our colleagues.

Schwaber (1986) has clearly shown the theoretical and clinical implications of the concept of psychic reality introduced by Freud:

> It is very difficult to enter another's inner world and to recognize that the only truth that we can seek is the patient's psychic truth—of the past or of the present—and that what we so firmly believed about ourselves may be perceived quite differently, given meanings quite unlike our own and with as much validity . . . [p. 930].

The disposition toward self-analysis enables us to become aware of the assumptions that emanate from within our own psychic reality and shape our representations of the analytic process. As analysts, we each introduce our own "personal equation" between what we listen to and what we interpret.

For purposes of considering the scope of self-analytic activity during the session and of developing and illustrating several of the preceding issues, we shall describe a sequence of three instances in a clinical case previously referred to by one of us in a recent paper (de León, 1991a). To capture the personal nature of the self-analytic experience, the case will be narrated in the first person.

CLINICAL EXAMPLE

First Instance

During a session the patient narrates three dreams, but my attention is caught by the second one. Although it was very short, it showed in a concise and deep manner the patient's feelings regarding the effect of my words.

> I dreamed that . . . somebody guessed that I had a fracture in my ear bone. "It's fractured," they said . . . No wonder the little bone hurt me . . . it was my right ear . . . There are so many, so many things I wouldn't want to hear.

Let us now turn to my reaction. The words "fracture" and "hurt" immediately trigger an association with blurred presentations of falling and suffering, not only visual or kinesthetic images, but also an emotion. Simultaneously I feel an undefined motoric impulse and experience the image of holding[1] the patient in my arms. I then recall previous sessions, when the patient referred to two falls in her childhood, once when she suffered a fracture. I say nothing; the session continues; and the patient and I work on her associations to all three dreams.

Let us now go back and rethink this clinical situation. Actions are suspended, and it seems there is a formal regression (Freud, 1900) in the session. The patient relates a dream, and her words create in my mind a deep expressive sense. Yet, some aspect of my interpretations or my voice is likely to have operated as day residues in the elaboration of such a dream. The dream refers both to painful corporal experiences, falls and fractures, and to emotional experiences of psychic pain revived in the analysis.

My internal response is immediate and appears in a form that is syntonic to the patient. The image of "holding the patient in my

---

[1]The Spanish word used in this case (and elsewhere in this chapter), "sostener," is the same word that later in the text was translated into "support." The words "sostén" and "sostener" refer to both holding and supporting and require different translations depending on the context in which they are used.

arms" assumes an intensive representational quality, including the wish to actualize the gesture.

In this case, the image in my mind is a sensorimotor presentation depicting the gesture that has been arrested in the analytic situation. This presentation evokes previous related instances in the analysis. My imagined gesture implies an emotional identification that is empathic with the corporal and psychic pain of the patient and with her wish to avoid the repetition of a traumatic fall.

Racker (1960) made a distinction between concordant and complementary identifications inside the countertransference. In this case, concordant countertransferential feelings prevail; yet, the resulting image has the nature of a complementary action—to hold the patient.

A week later, I am surprised to hear the patient say, "And here I struggle to defend my last layer of strength as otherwise I'll fall. I'll really fall." And she adds that away from the session, while she lay in an armchair that looked like a couch, she felt that she was falling, and she became quite anxious. The patient associates this situation with her analysis, but I am struck by the excessive care with which the patient tries not to express any complaint against me. I feel her hostility toward me and my words, which cause "fracture" feelings. I then interpret the patient's fears regarding the changes the analysis might entail and her uneasiness about whether I will be able to hold her, including her most aggressive feelings.

In this instance, the patient verbalizes and fully expresses the fear of falling and being fractured, which I had intuitively felt in the previous session. The patient then associates her anxiety to past situations in her life, those I had previously evoked. And I recall and feel once again the images and drives I had experienced while the patient was telling me her dream.

Second Instance

One month later, while I am greeting the patient as she is entering my office, she slips and falls. I am forced to help her up[2] and let her take support in my hand.

I experience several different responses to her action. The necessary physical contact produces in me a certain discomfort, but I still think that I cannot let her fall. I wonder whether I have seduced the patient into or induced her action. Maybe I experience pleasure in the mutually homosexual aspect of the relationship, which prevents the analysis from moving toward painful fracture points we both wish to

---

[2]Once again, the Spanish word is "sostener."

avoid. Or is this route our only approach to such affects? Was this action a warning by the patient that only a fracture between us would make room for further growth?

In both the first and second instances, my patient and I engage in gradually increasing, concordant movements. The dream narrative stimulates my reveries to a level evocative of oneiric hallucination. There is considerable permeability between our psyches. My words and her listening (voice and ear in the dream) are harmoniously adjusted, suggesting the evolution of the psychic process. I start from the assumption that I am supplying the patient with what she lacked in her previous traumatic situations and that the analysis is now in a position to provide.

Yet the patient's stumbling, the disruptive nature of her action, generates questions. I wonder how much my own conflicts, experiences, personal patterns, or theoretical formulations affected the clinical situation and shaped the analytic process. I also wonder about the role of the patient's personal contributions that we have not yet understood. The image of holding the patient in my arms that appears in my mind, was it an anticipation of the future needs of the patient? Was it a coincidence of patient and analyst? Did I induce anything into the patient? I feel a certain uneasiness. I must be alert.

Third Instance

The following sessions turn toward the homosexual aspects of the transference, associated to memories of certain features of the patient's link with her mother. The patient is deeply affected by any separation from me. During an interruption in our work she dreams:

> I was lying ("tirada") on a public square . . . there were some drug addicts and prostitutes . . . I was naked. I was not a part of the group but anything might happen. I was just lying there. I had fallen low. I was a whore.

Once again a fall. I feel I am often in the position of "throwing" (*tirar*) the patient, of not making enough room for her. (Usually the patient leaves some of the things she is carrying on the floor although there are other places where she might put her things.) At this stage of the analysis, the patient evidences deep suffering. The sadomasochistic aspect of her link with her mother is presented: "This weekend has been like an ink stain. Like death. I felt sick, like the image of my most awful feelings." My countertransference often includes discomfort and impotence regarding my patient's self-destructive aspects.

Another dream shows the intensity of my patient's demands on me and her request for my personal involvement in the link: "I dreamt that I came here and that an elderly lady would be the analyst, your mother. . . ."

I feel I must now face countertransferential feelings involving certain areas that are usually outside the analytic work. Some time later, the patient dreams about my husband, who appears as an insane and homosexual man who may drive her mad. I feel my patient's demand is that she and I form an exclusive mother–daughter link. (These aspects were, later on, the object of further consideration.)

I have already commented on the hyperintensity of some of my images in relation to my patient, images that focused my suspended attention toward them. Until my patient actually stumbled, my impression was that the analytic process was following a regular pattern. Her action and my reaction lead me to question both my own participation in the process and the defensive nature of my own experiences.

I sense the activation of aspects of my own infantile oedipal constellation and of my own family history, along with memories of some analytic experiences when I too was a patient. This process did not lead me to new insights or to the discovery of repressed personal aspects. My disposition toward self-analysis did, however, enable me to be alert to this activation and reelaboration of my own conflicts. But there is still something else.

It is worth noting that over this period, even while evoking my own personal history, I was able to notice clearly the differences between my patient's experiences and my own, between the ways chosen by my patient in her analysis and those I would have taken or at least would have anticipated my patient's taking. This period was marked by my awareness of similarities and differences and a deeper uncertainty, as well as by a feeling of disappointment and loss, related, I believe, to the pain of differentiation.

The disposition toward self-analysis helps us as analysts to tolerate the diversity of vital solutions and to overcome a tendency to blur the differences between us and our patients. It also contributes to a greater degree of freedom to face anything new. As analysts, we must be aware that our own ways of analyzing are not the only possible ones and that the analysis of the same patient with another analyst might follow different paths and arrive at different solutions.

According to the Barangers (1983),

> either expressly or implicitly, each of us makes use of a sort of
> *countertransferential dictionary* of his own (corporal experiences, move-

ment phantasies, images, etc.) which mark the moments when the suspended attention attitude is abandoned and the analyst turns to a second-glance attitude, questioning that which is occurring in the field [p. 529; italics added].

In my work with my patient, I had at my disposal the different ways of holding, being held–or not holding or being held–from my childhood and in my own analysis. And even my own ways to express these experiences through my body, including Stern's (1985) "vitality affects"–affective tones marked by the rhythm of acts rather than by their emotional content.

My uneasy, alert attitude appeared when my patient introduced words that did not belong in my "dictionary," or at least that I had not anticipated hearing at the time. Following my patient's action, I experienced a kind of mourning. To be able to progress in the analysis, I had to set aside the way I had concordantly linked my experiences to my patient's communications. I had to set aside something of my own, something valuable for me, in order to leave room for the onset of new, unanticipated aspects.

DISPOSITION TO SELF-ANALYSIS AND ITS RELATIONSHIP TO THEORIES

In the foregoing account, we shifted from the idea of the mirror analyst to that of an interaction in which the patient is also sensitive to what the analyst contributes to their link. Patients perceive and react to our contributions and are also undoubtedly responsive to aspects of our *Weltanschauung*–our attitudes toward life, death, aggression, self-love, and love of others.

Our explicit theories are only the tip of the iceberg of our *Weltanschauung*. Even more important than the contents of those theories is the way in which we relate to them, including the way we express those theories in our practice and incorporate them in our analytic identities.

The analysis, and consequently our self-analysis, of the unconscious aspects of our relationship with theories is a subject on which research is scarce. The obviously rational components in our field tend to obscure emotional aspects, even if they are highly visible in our psychoanalytic institutional life. These unconscious aspects must be open to analysis, a life-long task. We must learn from our experiences, enrich and transform our ideas through our work. Yet it is worth taking into consideration that the attitude adopted toward theories, both individually and collectively, may influence our disposition toward, and the scope of, our self-analysis, either favoring or hindering awareness of problems requiring investigation. In this chapter we focus our attention not on a description of the connection between these problems and the unconscious problems of the analyst, but on the initial step that allows a problem to be within the reach of self-analytic investigation.

A disposition toward self-analysis helps place our theoretical convictions in a position favorable to processes of change and revision. It allows us to perceive overvalued ideas that we might otherwise consider to be unquestionable truths, and to examine recurrent or unsolvable doubts or hesitations which are due to inhibitions or blind spots. These challenges require both self-analytic efforts and a new, conscious reflection supported by a greater degree of emotional freedom. To contact the raw material within them, we must treat our theories indeed like infantile sexual theories (Lijtenstein, 1976).

Let us return to our clinical example. The patient and the analyst, through the formal regression that took place, lived, in their interaction, the vicissitudes and transformations of a fantasy expressed through different sensory modalities. Stern (1985) has emphasized the importance of the transmodal elaboration of information for the evolution of the child's self, that is, the integration of different sensory channels, both at the level of the child's own self and at the level of "affect attunement" with the mother. Maybe an aspect of the patient's psychic growth, related to the expression of affects, requires support by nonverbal interaction showing the degree of adjustment between patient and analyst.

From a different theoretical standpoint, although reaching similar conclusions, Marty (1985) and the psychosomatic school of Paris have emphasized the mentalization processes that lead from the "primary mosaic" of body functions to the development of the preconscious as a highly individual and specialized organ, uniquely featured by its degree of richness, fluidity, and stability.

The foregoing conceptualization allows us to conclude that when the interactive processes of the analysis must be interpreted, understanding the form and content of the verbal interpretation is possible only through the unique features of the preconscious organization of the analyst. We can talk only with our own words. In summary, a clinical record shows us the analytic process only as it is presented in the mind of the analyst (or of any third party reinterpreting the material). In Freud's (1915) early terminology, the union of thing presentation and word presentation is always unique and idiosyncratic. This is why the analyst's formulating interpretations in his or her own words will be a step toward the patient's finding his or her own words.

Now we come to a particular problem, namely, that the *formulation* depends on the theoretical viewpoint of the analyst. Hence, we must be alert to the variations generated between analysts who have different orientations. These variations should be open to self-analysis, particularly when we try to apprehend the other's viewpoint, to think and say things as he or she would. This application of self-analysis allows us to achieve a deeper understanding of the features and limitations of our own way of thinking.

It seems useful now to go back to the clinical example and try to analyze which verbal presentations would be shared by analyst and patient and how they would vary, depending on our ways of listening. We may refer to several hypothetical possibilities. The first of these shared verbal presentations may be assumed to be expressed by the patient as, "I want my analyst to hold me because I am falling." In response to this request by the patient, the analyst experiences the drive-wish to avoid a traumatic fall, later enacted when the analyst holds the patient to prevent her from falling when she stumbles. Yet, as Freud (1911, 1919) showed, this kind of statement is subject to several transformations.

A second statement might be: "I want to fall because you do not hold me tight." This statement might include subtle variations of fantasies enlivened by the current analytic process: "I need to repeat my falls in order to show how badly I need support; I've fallen; I've been thrown; it is your fault; you have not been able to hold me"; and so on. The second statement, in its various forms, implies both the return of self-aggression (masochism) and an accusation directed at the analyst. The statement also contains an additional element: "You can hold me if you are very close to me," implying the patient's homosexual wish-demand.

Finally, we might "hear" a third statement: "I want you to feel that you cannot hold me, that your support is useless." This third version places the emphasis on hating the object and attacking the link.

The analytic process shows us these transformations and fluctuations. Yet, for the sake of intelligibility, when we move to the theoretical level, we must necessarily set an order. In fact, what the various theories suggest, despite their differences, is the understanding of something equivalent to Freud's (1937) "underlying bedrock" (p. 252)—that is, a basic hypothesis capable of determining others because of its higher explanatory and predictive power.

Since each analysis is a unique process, it is impossible for us to know how analysts belonging to different schools would interpret this material. But we do know the different opinions analysts express in their discussions of clinical material and control cases. Kleinian analysts would emphasize the investigation of the destructive aspects of the patient's fantasies as evidenced by her open demand for support. They might consider the analyst's drive truly to hold the patient as a lack of confidence in her own analytic resources, a lack stemming from the patient's attacks on her analytic ability. These attacks cause the analyst to counteract in an effort to soothe the patient and avoid activation of the negative transference. In this conceptual schema, the patient's aggression would be targeted at the analyst/"good breast" precisely because of the analyst's kindness and her ability to offer support, which becomes intolerable to the envious part of the patient. From this point of view, the third version of the fantasy ("I want you to feel that you cannot hold me, that your support is useless") represents the deepest and truest because it approaches the bedrock—envy as the primary expression of the death instinct.

From other viewpoints, the different fantasies of the patient would be considered to be the effect of early deficiencies, which might be interpreted in different ways. Kohutians might emphasize the patient's need for a self-sustaining selfobject fit to hold her self. Winnicottians might stress the search for the experience of having a "good-enough mother." Lacanians might say that "hold" is a signifier knotting together multiple meanings that trap both patient and analyst in an imaginary net out of which they may neither "fall" nor release themselves in order to gain access to the signifier of castration.

It would also be possible to discuss in depth whether the patient's central conflict should be placed at the oedipal or the preoedipal level, and whether the sexual, aggressive, or narcissistic aspects should be privileged. Although we may argue that clinical events favor some of these possibilities over others, our arguments would be far from conclusive and would certainly be the subject of debate.

We are not emphasizing the content of these various theoretical formulations; rather we are questioning how these different conceptual frameworks influence the analytic process. Fortunately, most analysts do not use these frameworks in such schematic form in their actual clinical work (at least we hope they do not). But this very fact causes the presence of these schemata to be more subtle and perhaps go unnoticed. We suggest guiding our self-observation in this direction, so as to open the way to self-analysis and to a more precise, critical reflection on the theories as they exist in clinical practice.

In this self-observation, we discriminate (1) What belongs in our theories and not in our patients—the role of theories during the session; (2) What belongs in us and not in the rest of the psychoanalytic community—pluralism as a problem; (3) What belongs in us but does not yet belong in our theories—potential for changes.

Theories During the Session

How do our theories affect our listening and interpreting? Since Freud, we have known when listening to our patients that we must set aside our theoretical assumptions. Different schools have emphasized this important point. Lacan (1973) referred to the analyst as the "sujet supposé savoir" from whom the patient expects an imaginary support; yet this expectation only moves the patient away from the truth of his or her own desire, which may be heard only from the patient's unconscious.

Based on different theoretical assumptions, Bion (1967) suggested that analysts listen without memory or desire. He referred to the reverie ability of the analyst, who, like a mother with her child, must contain the projected elements, metabolize them, and then return them to the patient to facilitate the patient's mental and emotional growth (1962, p. 309).

But the wish to reach a theoryless listening is idealistic rather than descriptive. The analyst's theories preexist the patient and set the frame that organizes the space where the analysis is to develop. Yet what should we do with our theoretical convictions during the session? Suspended attention implies a similar paradox. How is it possible to maintain alert attention if we do not fix it on a particular issue? How can we fail to look for what we have already found?

During her pregnancy, through changing presentations that include different kinds of anticipations, the future mother prepares for the new and unexpected in her child. Those presentations and anticipations, which are relatively free of conflict, are often not subject to analysis and remain in the preconscious. They may be briefly apprehended by the conscious, but they are easily forgotten (Bernardi, 1991). Similarly, we analysts have different anticipating presentations through which we prepare for our patients but that we often must abandon for the purpose of allowing the unknown to flow. We here have tried to demonstrate this phenomenon in our clinical example, but the problem remains for all of us as analysts, according to the degree of fixation of our convictions.

In our opinion, during the session, theories should be treated as fantasies are treated, since they operate as working models in a part of the mind of the analyst that is subject to a formal regression process, thus becoming more pervious to primary process. In that form, theories enrich the perceptive capacity of the analyst (de León, 1991b). This regression is also a necessary condition for theories to be alive and susceptible to modification through the analyst's experience. It creates a fruitful, even if difficult-to-manage, tension between our deepest theoretical convictions, incorporated into our analytic identity, and the concrete, particular, affectively charged presentations gathered from our experiences as we interact with our patient. Developing and maintaining this tension is what we mean by being "in a disposition toward self-analysis of our assumptions." Further, we believe that the pathology of theorizing is linked to distortions of this process.

Grinberg (1983) noted the treacherous and subtle role of resistances when there is a concordance in the theories and beliefs of patient and analyst. When such situations lead to the overlapping of the patient's resistance and the analyst's counterresistance, they give rise to what the Barangers (1961–1962) referred to as "bastions": areas that are excluded from analysis, although their contents are within easy reach of the conscious. When these bastions become a "complex of beliefs" (Rosolato, 1979), theories begin to assume the features and potency of a religious system. Grinberg analyzed the case of Guntrip, who, in his narrative account of his analyses with Fairbairn and Winnicott, explained that he had chosen analysts with whom he shared the "same wave length." Concurring with Pontalis (1967), Grinberg (1983) wrote:

> The demand of undergoing analysis again is many times due not so much to the fact that the first analyst has not been able to meet the demand, but above all because he was a prisoner of his own theory, that is to say, because he himself was involved in a personal process of elaboration and belief, in which he would drag his patient [p. 31].

Theories are for the analyst, as for any scientist, strongly idealized objects that are incorporated into his or her professional identity. Groups are formed when an ideal is shared (Freud, 1921).

Given their partially incompatible double purpose as personal analysis and professional training, didactic analyses are particularly vulnerable to the kinds of identification and disidentification processes operating between candidate and training analyst. As we have pointed out, because these processes continue in different ways once the analysis is over, it is essential that they be open to continuing self-analysis. Blind spots involving theories develop, in our opinion, precisely in those areas where the analyst may not expose his or her convictions to suspended attention because defensive processes exclude them from regressive, free-associative questioning.

Pluralism as a Problem

It is not easy to determine accurately in what ways and to what extent our theoretical opinions differ from those of other analysts; it is even more difficult to determine how and to what extent our analytic work differs from that of another analyst operating with a different theoretical conviction. Wallerstein (1988) suggests that psychoanalysis at present comprises "multiple (and divergent) theories of mental functioning, of development, of pathogenesis, of treatment and of cure" (p. 11) and is characterized by an increasing diversity of theoretical standpoints, linguistic conventions, and regional emphasis.

The present pluralism seems to be an undoubted fact. Comparing the records of the Wolf Man with subsequent readings by Klein and Lacan, one of us (Bernardi, 1989) has shown that each of these paradigms: (1) conditions the way in which we listen to the material (e.g., focusing our attention on different aspects of the same dream); (2) formulates different questions and discovers different answers to the same "facts," and each has its own ideal of what it means to understand those facts; and (3) begins the process of understanding from its own metapsychological assumptions.

It is quite difficult to determine the extent to which these different paradigms are coincident, contradictory, or supplementary, or whether their relationship to one another would be rather incommensurable, that is, whether they behave as logically and semantically different languages which can only be partially translated one into the other (Bernardi, 1991).

We wonder, for instance, if the Spanish term "sostener" has the same theoretical connotations as the English terms "hold" and "support." In Spanish, "sostener" does not evoke Winnicott, since in our psychoanalytic community the English term "holding" is used when making any reference to Winnicott. Translation difficulties show clearly the subtle problems embedded in implicit theoretical contexts.

Such increasing diversity causes Wallerstein (1988) to ask what it is that "holds us together as common adherents of a shared psychoanalytic science and profession" (p. 19). This question is particularly relevant to our subject. Any reply to it will open or close a path to analytic exploration.

Let us return to Freud's idea that groups share a common ideal.

What is the ideal that holds us together as analysts? If such an ideal is a set of replies or techniques, we shall experience diversity as a threat of fragmentation and shall insist on reinforcing the shared areas and safeguarding their existence, as Freud himself entrusted the Committee to do. This approach turns the task of homogenization into an essential need, beyond any question, and consequently beyond the necessity or possibility of analysis. If, on the contrary, we place our common ideal in the field of the problems we share rather than in the replies we offer, we stumble onto a new difficulty. How can two minds communicate precisely about those issues that differentiate them in their unique ways of envisioning the world?

This task implies acknowledging the untranslatable remainder of individual standpoints and the full scope of the scientific and ethical challenge inherent in problems of pluralism: to facilitate contact between different visions, when each considers itself as the only valid one (Bernardi, 1992).

We are not advocating tolerance, which might also derive from an eclectic or skeptical position or from an empathic (emotional rather than intellectual) attitude. Instead we are suggesting the goal of being able to operate within (Bion's) multiple vertices. This goal implies not only a more flexible splitting of ego functions and identifications, but also an ability to expose oneself to disidentification processes and a willingness to start all over again. Such splitting and disidentification are undoubtedly essential. How can we listen to that which is different in our patients if we fail to listen to our colleagues?

Potential for Change

Present epistemological trends force us to face the challenge of achieving a deeper understanding of the processes of theory election and change and, consequently, of our own changes. In this sense, such a challenge also involves our self-analytic activity. Kuhn (1972), operating within the field of epistemology, described this challenge quite accurately:

> The election of a new theory is the decision to adopt a different native language and to display it in an equally different world. This is not a transition where the terms "election" and "decision" are well used, but the motivations to use them once the transition is over are evident. When exploring into another theory . . . we may find that we are already using it. . . . We were never aware that we had already made such a decision, such election. This kind of change is, however, a conversion and the techniques which lead to it may well be described

as therapeutical, at least insofar as they are only successful when we know that we have previously been wrong. It is not surprising that resistances should arise towards such techniques and that in subsequent descriptions the nature of change will be disguised [p. 448].

These aspects need to be open to analytic research. Perhaps a first step toward understanding these transformations is to determine more precisely the areas in our own creativity that may enrich our theories or give rise to changes. Sandler (1983) focuses on the "implicit theories" of each analyst, those generally preconscious (only rarely conscious) structures that operate as models or schemata that organize the experience of the analyst with his or her patients. In spite of their potentially creative role, these implicit theories are often isolated from "official" theories that gain access to our consciousness. Why do we find it so difficult to develop our most personal ideas? Perhaps because we are afraid to be disloyal, to differentiate ourselves, and eventually to be alone and helpless. Maybe these fears lead us to ask theories (and those who represent them at an unconscious level) to hold us in the most difficult part of our work. Yet Freud taught us to link self-analysis and discovery. This link is still a challenge for each of us, even if it takes us along unique pathways. Maybe ahead of us we as colleagues have a task similar to the one we must face with each patient—how to achieve differentiation and still be together.

REFERENCES

Baranger, M. & Baranger, W. (1961–1962), La situación analítica como campo dinámico. In: Baranger, W. & Baranger M., *Problemas del Campo Psicoanalítico*, Buenos Aires: Kargieman, pp. 129-164, 1969.
_____ & _____ (1983), Proceso y no proceso en el trabajo analítico. *Rev. de Psicoanálisis*, 68:527–549.
_____ Besouchet, I. Nieto, M. & Ribeiro, I. (1969), Sobre la enseñanza del psicoanálisis. *Revista Uruguaya de Psicoanálisis*. 11:243-247.
Berenstein, S. P. de & Fondevila, D. S. de (1989), Termination of analysis in the light of evolution of a link. *Internat. Rev. Psycho-Anal.*, 16:385-389.
Bernardi, R. (1989), The role of paradigmatic determinants in psychoanalytic understanding. *Internat. J. Psycho-Anal.*, 70:341-359.
_____ (1991), Plurality of theories in psychoanalysis: Bases for a comparative study. Presented at 37th IPA Congress, Buenos Aires.
_____ (1992), On pluralism in psychoanalysis. *Psychoanal. Inq* ., 12:506-525.
Bion, W. R. (1962), The psychoanalytic study of thinking. *Internat. J. Psycho-Anal.*, 43:306-310.
_____ (1967), Notes on memory and desire. *The Psychoanalytic Forum*, II, 3. [Notas sobre la memoria y el deseo. *Rev. Psicoanál.*, XXVI, 3, 1969.]

de León, B. (1991a), Images and words in psychoanalytical work. Presented at FEPAL Symposium, Punta del Este, Uruguay.

―――― (1991b), Changing views on the dynamics of the analytic process and its relationship with theories in psychoanalysis. Presented at 37th IPA Congress, Buenos Aires.

Freud, S. (1900), The interpretation of dreams. Standard Edition, 4 & 5. London: Hogarth Press, 1953.

―――― (1911), Psychoanalytic notes on an autobiographical account of a case of paranoia (dementia paranoides). Standard Edition, 12:1–79. London: Hogarth Press, 1958.

―――― (1915), The unconscious Standard Edition, 9:159–215. London: Hogarth Press, 1957.

―――― (1919), A child is being beaten. Standard Edition, 12:175–204. London: Hogarth Press, 1955.

―――― (1921), Group psychology and the analysis of the ego. Standard Edition, 18:65–144. London: Hogarth Press, 1955.

―――― (1937), Analysis terminable and interminable. Standard Edition, 23:209–254. London: Hogarth Press, 1964.

Grinberg, J. (1983), Theory, belief and resistance. In: Investigación psicoanalítica [Psychoanalytic Research], ed. L. A. Allegro. Buenos Aires: Ediciones Psicoanalíticas, pp. 25–32.

―――― & Lichtmann, A. (1981), El verdadero autoanálisis es imposible. Presented at 32nd IPA Congress, Helsinki.

Jiménez, J. P. (1989), La contribución del analista en los procesos de identificación proyectiva. Presented at 36th IPA Congress, Rome.

Kuhn, T. S., del Popper, K. R. and others. (1972), Consideración en torno a mis críticos. In: Criticism and the Growth of Knowledge, ed. I. Lakatos & A. Musgrave. Cambridge, U.K: Cambridge University Press, pp. 391–455.

Lacan, J. (1973), Les Quatre Concepts Fondamentaux de la Psychanalyse. Paris: Seuil, pp. 209–220.

Lijtenstein, M. (1976), Sobre la noción de teoría en psicoanálisis. Revista Uruguava de Psicoanálisis, 55:381–388.

Marty, P. (1985), L'Ordre Psychosomatique. Paris: Payot.

Pontalis, J. B. (1967), A propos du text de Guntrip. Nouv. Rev. de Psych., 15:29–31.

Racker, H. (1960), Estudios sobre Técnica Psicoanalítica. Buenos Aires: Paidós.

Rosolato, G. (1979), La scission que porte l'incroyable. Nouv. Rev. Psych., 18:15–27.

Sandler, J. (1983), Reflections on some relations between psychoanalytic concepts and psychoanalytic practice. Internat. J. Psycho-Anal., 64:35–45.

Schwaber, E. A. (1986), Reconstruction and perceptual experience: Further thoughts on psychoanalytic listening. J. Amer. Psychoanal. Assn., 34:911–932.

Stern, D. N. (1985), The Interpersonal World of the Infant. New York: Basic Books.

Ticho, G. (1967), On self-analysis. Internat. J. Psycho-Anal. 48:308–317.

―――― (1971), Selbstanalyse als Ziel der psychoanalytischen Therapie, Psyche, 25:44–56.

Wallerstein, R. S. (1988), One psychoanalysis or many? Internat. J. Psycho-Anal. 69:5–21.

II

ANALYTIC WORK AND SELF-ANALYSIS

Locating both his patient and himself within an intersubjective space, Margulies explores the complex interplay, the mutual shaping and influencing, of patient's and analyst's inner experiences. His clinical vignettes link the self-analytic process to the reciprocal nature of the transference–countertransference dialogue.

In an effort to understand the multiple sources of the striking parallels between his patient's dreams/associations and his own, Margulies wonders about the ways in which patient and analyst communicate at the edges of each other's awareness. These communications may then function as day residues influencing the manifest content of each other's dreams. "In parallel dreams my patient and I search for missing fathers, and we enact this search in the uncanny concordance of our mutual dream experience. . . . In the multiplicity of roles and reciprocal roles, transference and countertransference, inner world and outer life, my patient and I are both father and child."

Although initially repressing his dream-memory, after reviewing his clinical notes[1] detailing his patient's dream, Margulies then recaptures his own. "I had in effect regained entrance to my own repressed dreamscape by first entering my patient's similar

---

[1] See Sonnenberg (chap. 12) for a fuller description of the function of clinical/theoretical writing on the analyst's ongoing self-analysis.

dream. . . . In the circularity of empathy and in the resonance of our unconscious overlap, *I empathize with another—and am startled to find myself.*"

Linking his experiences with his patients to the phenomenon of finding oneself in the gaze of the other, Margulies recalls the opposite views of Kohut (1977) and Lacan (1977). Kohut believed that a cohesive self comes into being largely through empathic mirroring by the other. Lacan believed that the initial alienation of the self occurs at precisely those moments of reflected mirroring—"a return with a difference." Margulies argues that both the empathic sense of sameness and the empathic sense of difference are necessary. Like Bernardi and de Leon (chapt. 2), he calls our attention to the pain associated with fuller awareness of difference and aloneness.

Margulies suggests the inter-dependence of the analysis of the patient and the analyst's ongoing self-analysis: "Each of us had our own rhythms and singularities, our own ways of working through. Because our griefs were similar enough, we could make contact; because we were each different, we could deepen the particularities of understanding."

McLaughlin also focuses on the reciprocal relationship between our self-analytic efforts and our work as analysts. Our encounters with patients, particularly those who confound our expectations, stimulate our self-analytic activity. "Seeking open resonance to each patient made it inevitable that new facets or aspects of old concerns could come alive in me, and impel further self-searching." Our self-analysis, as it leads to a clearer definition of our own inner experience, in turn enables us to explore more fully the particulars of our patient's psychic reality.

In a clinical vignette, McLaughlin explores the intersection of patient's and analyst's transferences. As was the case with Margulies' example, McLaughlin was also struggling with incomplete mourning following the death of a parent. His incorrect attribution of a dream fragment to his patient provides the impetus for his self-inquiry into the "fluid shifting of transference-laden mother/son identifications. . . ."

A second clinical example illustrates an impasse in the treatment of a patient who relentlessly attacked the meaning and value of the analyst's interpretations. McLaughlin's self-analysis of his transference to his patient gradually led to a way out of that impasse. His self-analysis could not be encompassed entirely within the treatment sessions themselves, but required continued working through outside of those sessions in private transitional spaces which McLaughlin refers to as "transference sanctuaries."

His work with these and other difficult-to-treat patients, who aroused strong transferences in the analyst, provided an impetus to McLaughlin's ongoing self-analytic efforts and led to a significant shift in perspective:

> Work with these patients drove home the recognition of the relativistic nature of the analytic enterprise when perceived from the different reality views of the two participants. I had no choice but to consider the extent to which my stance of superior knowing invalidated the psychic reality of the patient, and kept us both from understanding how that unique reality view had necessarily come to be.

These changes in understanding led to a more collaborative way of working with his patients.

Smith explores the nature of engagement of both analyst and patient in the analytic work. He focuses on the uses of that engagement in the analyst's ongoing self-analysis, although he cautions:

> I am not suggesting that the work exists primarily for the benefit of the analyst, nor am I speaking of modifications in technique that would alter our intrapsychic focus on the patient. I *am* suggesting that the two individuals are involved in an interactive process that lends itself to "reciprocal inquires," in Gardner's (1983) term, that these inquiries are at times simultaneous, parallel and symmetrical; and that whatever the analyst's self-inquiry *may* tell us about the patient, it *will* tell him something about himself if he chooses to listen.

In his clinical vignettes, Smith demonstrates the ways in which he advances his self-inquiry through an exploration of the symmetries and asymmetries of his own and his patient's experiences within the analytic hour. His analysis and self-analysis proceed simultaneously, at times parallel, at times intersecting, part of an ongoing process of finding, losing, and refinding in new ways both himself and the patient. For example, Smith describes his dream during the termination phase with one patient:

> My dream was a compromise formation that had borrowed some of the narrative style of her dreams to express my conflicting wishes and fears and, strangely, hers. My dream seemed to contain elements of her intrapsychic life and mine, simultaneously intertwined and yet discrete.

Smith relates the concept of engagements in the psychoanalytic work to that of enactments which he sees as both necessary and inevitable. He argues for a "taxonomy" of enactments that includes an examination of their multiple functions, and distinguishes between enactments that are analyzable (dependent to a significant degree on the analyst's capacity for self-analysis) and those which are not. In the midst of those enactments, Smith suggests that the greatest stimulus of the analyst's self-analytic efforts are the patient's perceptions of the analyst's actions and motivations, particularly when those perceptions are at considerable variance with the analyst's self-perceptions.

REFERENCES

Kohut, H. (1977), *The Restoration of the Self*. NY: IUP.
Lacan, J. (1977), *Ecrits: A Selection*, (trans. A. Sheridan). NY: Norton.

3

Contemplating the Mirror of the Other
Empathy and Self-Analysis

Alfred Margulies

"Each contemplating the other in both mirrors of
the reciprocal flesh of theirhisnothis fellowfaces."
—James Joyce, *Ulysses*

Several years ago my father was very sick over a year's time, and I knew that he was dying. I did not intentionally share this information with my patients. Clinically though, I heard it everywhere, and I wondered how much my preoccupation colored my empathic listening.

I usually take an extended vacation around Christmas and this was anticipated with my patients. During this vacation period my father died, and so by happenstance I was not away unexpectedly from my practice. I wanted my grieving to be separate from my work; none of my patients consciously knew of these recent events. On my return to my practice after the Christmas break, I looked forward to settling into the reassurance of my workaday routine.

My first patient had been in psychoanalysis for several years, and so our face-to-face interaction was brief and, to me, unremarkable. We greeted each other and got quickly down to business. After lying on the couch my patient's associations went to a Christmas card he had sent to his previous therapist. In his note he described himself as being at a crossroads. He reflected to me that for many years it

seemed as if he needed to have some crisis going on. Now he felt
preoccupied with death, "as if death is more important to me than a
woman is." This was about five minutes into the session and, other
than our initial greeting, I had said nothing. I was curious about this
almost immediate reference to death. "Why," I asked, "do you think
this concern has come up now?"

It was nothing new, he explained, and he went on to talk about
trips and his fears of plane and car crashes, sudden death, and life
being snuffed out. He then moved to a recent television program. It
was about elderly people, and it had upset him. In one segment an
older woman was trying to nurse her sick husband who could no
longer care for himself, which was crushing her emotionally and
physically. What must it be like to be in that circumstance, too
enfeebled to care for yourself? How can one live that way?

I had not seen the program, but my patient described many of my
own concerns during my father's illness. His devoted wife (my father
had remarried after the death of my mother) was becoming overwhelmed in her attempts to nurse him around the clock. In her
desperation and grief she was not caring for herself. Having lost the
ability to attend to his own bodily needs, my father felt a deep
humiliation about being a helpless old man—it was no way to live.

While listening to my patient, my head swam with meanings and
layers of meaning. How did my patient's ruminations reflect the
developing and ever-changing transference–countertransference matrix? He filled his analysis with bitterness toward his father, and for
me he reserved a relentless deprecatory quality. Fate made it impossible to continue treatment with his prior therapist who was the kind
of real man his father had never even approximated. While I had been
away, he had written this beloved therapist: Things, he noted, had
been going well. Though in his estimation I had never matched up to
his previous therapist, I, too, seemed to be improving. Did my going
away (and coming back) reawaken his deep paternal grief and
resentment, echoed in the loss of his prior therapist, and now, as I
returned from vacation, expressed in his fantasies of planes crashing?

Before analysis this man often longed for death, but, ironically, as
his life became more worthwhile to him, he dreaded the passage of
time. Time seemed omnipresent, breathing down his back (Yet
another Christmas card to his old therapist? How can it all go so fast?).
Crises had marked the path of my patient's life: He lurched from one
to another as if, looking back, they gave him a sense of direction.
Now he was at a crossroads, and the realness of death punctuated the
still unlived quality of his life.

In attempting to empathize with this man's bitterness about what did not happen in his life, I must draw on the resonant affective stores of personal experience, echoes of my own bitterness with life and its disappointments—empathy demands it. And so, while turning over in my mind the shapes of his life, I reflect on my own. My vicarious introspection, mirrorlike, flashes back into my own eyes.

Though I was behind the couch and out of sight, this man had always been extraordinarily attentive to my bodily reactions (sneezes, shifts in position that seemed subtle to me, my occasional quiet daydreaming—he had an animal-like vigilance). Had he been unconsciously aware of my anticipatory grief about my father before my being away? Were our unconscious minds in powerful, nonverbal dialogue? Did he somehow know about my grief? Did I *need* him to know? Was I transmitting my own distress in my choice of words or through my body? Was I, to paraphrase Freud, chattering with my fingertips?

I did not know. This was my first patient upon returning from my father's funeral, and all of this had taken place ten minutes into the session. I said nothing. My patient soon moved on to other concerns seemingly far afield from death.

My second patient of the day was in psychotherapy. Yet again the first ten minutes of the session confronted me. My patient had dreamt that he and his father were hugging, and he thought, *"Oh. You're back."* (His father had died five years before.) Moreover, a phone call in the night awoke my patient from his dream—his wife's uncle had passed away. This anecdote was both fascinating and disturbing to me, for this patient almost never reported dreams. Of course, one *reads* it as a transference dream upon my return from a scheduled vacation.

Nevertheless, I was unnerved. My second patient was so different from my first—and yet we, too, were rapidly into grieving. This man was open and loving, gregarious and proud. His transference had been positive and idealizing, and reflected his deep love for his father. Moreover, though fate had snatched away a young wife through cancer, he was not bitter, but heartbroken. He was almost by constitution celebratory of life and libido—it was in his marrow. With this man, my affective resonance drew on a different reservoir within my psyche. Listening to him, I recalled with love my own life and those who mattered.

A week later the second patient returned to his dream of hugging his father. He carefully explained a feature of the dream whose nagging significance he did not understand. In the dream his father was hugging him, but oddly, with his arms beneath the patient's. (He demonstrated on himself, putting his arms crosswise and with his hands beneath his armpits.) I was astonished—in the interim I had experienced a remarkably similar dream. My own dream had been very powerful to me and with a primitive force, one of childlike love and grief. In my dream my father had hugged me, too, and with his arms beneath mine, just in the confusing manner reported by my patient about his dream. The uncanny similarity of our dreams defied and haunted me. I was baffled on many levels. It was only later, though, that I realized the bodily significance of the hugs in both my patient's dream and my own.

One afternoon, waking from a nap, my daughter was crying for attention. Delighted to see her, I leaned over her crib to pick her up — putting my arms beneath hers to both lift and hold her, a spontaneous gesture embraced hundreds of times in my life as a parent. The position of my arms and hands was precisely that of my father's in my dream, and, to be sure, of my patient's father in his dream. In both dream instances the odd hugging posture did not make overt sense — only with the realization that *this is how an adult picks up a child* did the significance fall into place. Whatever the mechanism of our resonant concerns, I gained a precise sense of the unusual hug of my patient's dream — and my own — a hug of a young child being picked up by a loving adult. This, I'm convinced, was an early preverbal memory — or wish — of my own, a memory caught in the net of my own childhood body-ego and refracted through my adult experience as a father. The body, as it were, remembers in love and grief.

The origin of this particular empathic precision remains a puzzle to me. Did my patient pick up my grief? (His dream, though, occurred before my return — but, then, I had been preoccupied before I left.) What nonverbal cues did he transmit at the first telling of the dream? Had he subtly and out of consciousness indicated to me a kind of hug only more fully elaborated in the next session? Did I respond in kind, registering in my body his bodily reaction, and then drawing on his manifest dream content of the hug to serve as a day residue for my own dream? Were we fueling each other's unconscious processes in circular fashion, or was I more attuned to his preexisting grief for his father now that I was grieving for my own? Regardless, our pain was in surprising synchrony. Moreover, even without this insight *during the first telling of his dream*, I later resonated deep within the regression of my own dream body.[1] No doubt, the dreams reflect an intense

---

[1]The role of nonverbal cues in empathy is a still barely explored area. I am reminded of the "let-down" experience of nursing mothers. The very cry of the baby creates a resonance in the mother that affects her in a hormonal/physical fashion. I wonder, does let-down occur in sleeping mothers? Such complementary affective/physical states seem the prototype of interpersonal communication and, of course, empathy.

state of transference and countertransference—in our parallel dream lives we were hugging one other.

Later I was relating to a colleague that a patient and I had experienced remarkably similar dreams. In the midst of this discussion I forgot my own dream and could not remember my patient's and, perplexed, moved on to talking about other things. Only when I returned to my clinical notes did I recall my patient's dream—and only then did I retrieve my own. I had in effect regained entrance to my own repressed dreamscape by first entering my patient's similar dream. This is to say, his inscape (Margulies, 1989) was more bearable than my own. In the circularity of empathy and in the resonance of our unconscious overlap, *I empathize with another—and am startled to find myself.*

REFLECTIONS ON/IN/THROUGH THE MIRROR

Kohut (1977) stressed the parental mirroring function as critical to one's sense of inner coherence, a function that finds its way into the myriad selfobjects of adulthood. Mirroring and empathic resonance create a sense of wholeness; the failure of parental empathy is the fall from grace. Rage, then, is a breakdown product, an unnatural state of being, a consequence rather than a first mover. In Kohut's formulation, the reflected and vicarious joy of the empathic parent obviates the potential disaster of the Oedipus of everychild.

With a different web of meaning the Lacanian notion of "desire" captures the reciprocal quality underlying interaction—the baby desires-to-be-desired (1977). Lacan, in contrast to Kohut, saw a metaphorical mirroring stage of development as the beginning and inevitable moment of one's creation of self-image and simultaneous self-alienation. One sees oneself in reflection as more coherent than one is or experiences oneself to be. This is to say, one becomes an illusion to oneself: One identifies with one's ideal of coherence, which then becomes as elusive as the Holy Grail.[2]

Kohut and Lacan are in fundamental opposition. And because they are opposed, they sharply illuminate one another, revealing in the radical nature of their positions an essential paradox: We are both healed and torn by our reflections within the gaze of the other. The other reflects ourselves back to ourselves, but always in a "return

---

[2]Sartre (1956), by way of further contrast, saw the gaze of the other as the moment of existential annihilation: This is the other as Medusa. One's essential freedom is destroyed as one becomes an object within the other's script.

with a difference." Lacan speaks of "reconciliation" with the unknowable of the unconscious: We can hope for little more in the search for
that which will always remain beyond our grasp.

The empathic sense of sameness in the other gives us certainty—
this is someone adrift in the same boat that I am; I recognize myself
in him, and this gives our experience a sense of shared authenticity.
The empathic sense of difference gives us nuance, the clarity of
specificity, of existential contingency and uniqueness. I am just like
him—but with a difference that is me, can only be me, given my
unrepeatable existence.

It is the return with sameness but also the return with a difference
that is implicit in my metaphor of the self-spiral. That is, the self
comes into being in the spiral of self-reflection itself, and is doomed,
like Sisyphus, to a task that never ends. That this is more than an
empty metaphor seems apparent to me in witnessing those who can
no longer spiral recursively (e.g., secondary to organic deficits in
memory), and who lose themselves without even knowing it (Margulies, 1989).

THE RESURRECTION OF POSSIBILITIES: MEMORIES OF
THE FUTURE

In the midst of many simultaneous dialogues, I am constantly
working through pieces of myself, each dialogue shaping me and
being shaped by me. Because this is a paper on self-analysis I
emphasize my own half of the clinical dialogues that I have presented: It is my countertransference obligation. Both of my patients
amplified different aspects of grieving, and, not surprisingly, both
needed to get to the unfamiliar side, the resisted side, of the
ambivalence inherent in their griefs. I did, too. Each of us had our
own rhythms and singularities, our own ways of working through.
Because our griefs were similar enough, we could make contact;
because each of us was different, we could deepen the particularities
of understanding.[3]

My surprise of self-recognition helped me understand my patients

---

[3]Given the vicissitudes of my scheduled absence simultaneous with my father's
death and funeral, I did not share my life's events with my patients. This is a complex
and debatable decision (see, for example, the sensitive discussion in Givelber and
Simon, 1981). Perhaps I was avoiding more difficult feelings, toughing it out as if
everything was okay. Clinical practice (indeed, life) is always a first take, and without
the opportunity for editing, much less parallel control experiments.

in a deeper way, and—with and through me—both of my patients came to a fuller reconciliation with their own fathers. My first patient on my return from my father's funeral held a visceral hatred of his father (and, often, of me). The next patient's feelings for his father were bright and affirming. As I resonated with each in turn, I awakened parallel memories of my own father. Other patients, each reflecting back to me my own partial experience, confront me with aspects of myself. With each turn of my spiral of self-reflection, I reshape my memories, remaking my history of myself to myself.

To say that we are being empathic with someone is always a crude simplification of a fluctuating process that cannot easily be captured. Attempting to find the other, we are always in motion, now closer, then further away, now shallow, rarely deep. Empathy occurs in pieces, and only sometimes is it immediate and compelling. There are those moments, though, when the experience of empathy is of touching something profound. It is not merely that we share a similar experience with the other, but that something ordinarily inaccessible—deep and hidden—emerges.

By connecting profoundly to another, one transcends the essential aloneness of experience. No doubt this is one of the attractions to doing psychotherapy for a living and is a hazard for a therapist who is mourning—the patient is needed. In my mournful questing am I more vulnerable to using my patients? As a colleague put it, this is the moment of the earthquake before one has the words to know it. Even in my sleep I am searching. Now I am too heartsick about life: Death, the Real, has flooded in. Is what is real to me, real to my patients?

Any dream is a limit of subjectivity, a pure "inscape" reflecting the dreamer's singularity of worldview (Margulies, 1989). Because my dream is distinctly my own, it discloses my unrepeatable uniqueness, and because it is unique, it ensures my aloneness. O'Flaherty (1984) wrote: "Why do people write stories about people who share the same dream? The answer to all of these questions begins, I think, in our recognition of the human terror of solipsism" (p. 73). This terror comes home to me in my mourning—a deep connection has been severed, and I am groping, needing.

And yet the deep connection of intimate, shared understanding and empathy need not be only regressive. Though the pseudoempathy of need can breed a keen awareness of the other's mind, it remains partial and sectored, a piece of empathy that seldom rises above its frightened urgency and subtle manipulation. The deeper ongoing process of empathy, in contrast to urgent merger states, carries a sense of epiphany for the empathizer; one's relationship to oneself and humanity is illuminated. Moreover, in the finding of deep mutual concordance, one encounters separateness. Time itself underscores this separateness: Deep empathy is fleeting, leaving a residue of wonder.

Freud (1919) explored the uncanny in relation to obsessionality, but mourning, like obsessionality, always carries seeds of the uncanny. The grieving process attaches to obsessional mechanisms in the context of cultural prescriptions of repetitive rituals and in the obsessional defenses of mourning and depression itself. Moreover, one confronts in its very uncanniness the metaphysical inconceivableness of death: Though we know rationally about the annihilation of existence, the grieved other is too much a part of us. In letting go of the other, we must, as Freud (1917) so sharply observed in "Mourning and Melancholia," let go of a piece of ourselves: The death of the other divides us internally. And we are divided on many levels—cathexis/decathexis, rational/irrational, internal/external, conscious/unconscious, wish/reality, self/object—we are unable to relinquish our hold on the internal other so evenly; relinquishing itself is always partial and sectored. It is this very unevenness of letting go, of decathecting, that keeps the internal object (and so ourselves) in a mixed state of live-and-dead, and this amalgam itself manifests in the experience of uncanniness.

Parallel dreams underscored the uncanniness of the clinical moment with my second patient: Time turns upside down; the dead have come back to life. My unconscious exerts itself, magically and paradoxically, demanding to be heard. The dream taps into the timelessness of the unconscious, but the collapse of dreamtime remains only partial and uneven. We construct possibilities that are no longer present—and perhaps never were present, but only subjunctive, "as if." I see my father in the dream present, but my body ego folds on itself with me simultaneously an adult and a small child. Manchild, I resurrect a body memory, but a memory that is also a fantasy that is now dream-actualized. And now I own it, I possess it as part of who I am, and I come to experience my father, real and fantasized, as possessing it too, even though it was only a dream possibility. My wish, my desire, my grief crystallize into a lived symbol: The dream seems given as a gift from my unconscious, a legacy from my father—and it is healing.

Grievers often experience dream visitations as gifts. I recall Freud's notes on the case of the Rat Man (1909), in which his patient describes "a pale lady who comes to meet him" (we the readers remember his beloved, dead sister, pale on her sick bed): "He cherished this . . .

dream as though it was his most precious treasure."[4] Clare Winnicott's (1989) memorial description of her husband ends with a
precious dream. In that dream, she and her husband spend a
wonderful day together, filled with vitality and love. At the end of the
day, she looks her husband in the eyes and says, "There's something
we have to say to each other, some truth that we have to say, what is
it?" Looking unflinchingly into her eyes, he says, "That this is a
dream . . . I died a year ago." In both dreams the grieved-for other
comes alive as a vision; the dream itself is a keepsake. (And how
fitting it is that his wife's dream should become a Winnicottian
transitional phenomenon, a tribute to Winnicott's own warm brilliance.) The keepsake is the resurrection of the broken, groping
conversation, of the good-bye that cannot yet let go.

In resurrecting the other in a dream, one's own inner deadness-
in-loss comes to life, but through the medium of becoming identified
with the other. And so the uncanny dream connection with my
patient is a desire for that connection to my father that happened too
seldom, a promise sustained by the unconscious childhood illusion of
infinite future and possibility, a promise now death-frozen and lost
forever except within the illusion of my dream life. In parallel dreams
my patient and I search for missing fathers, and we enact this search
in the uncanny concordance of our mutual dream experience—all left
unverbalized, and so, I now realize, unanalyzed. In the multiplicity of
roles and reciprocal roles, transference and countertransference,
inner world and outer life, my patient and I are both father and child.

In working through, one works through that which never happened because it couldn't happen the way that one wanted. The
dream enacts the wish to be a boy, a baby, to start once again in *that*
relationship, to have time stand still within the promise of a future.
That there were and are fearful hatreds and longings is certain; this is
after all Freud's leveling humanity. And though apparent to me in my
own analyses (I must hesitate here: Is this disingenuous? Can one
ever acknowledge the full force of one's feelings? We touch them—
and move away), the work remains incomplete.

---

[4]Consider Keats's dream image of Moneta in *The Fall of Hyperion*, written shortly
before his death: "Then saw I a wan face,/ Not pin'd by human sorrows, but bright
blanch'd/ By an immortal sickness which kills not . . ."
Aileen Ward (1963) wrote that this was the Goddess of Memory and the Goddess of
Melancholy, and: "In the end it is the face of death itself, in the most beautiful and
terrifying aspect in which Keats had met it—the face of his dead mother, shrouded for
her coffin. . . . It is the very foundation of Keats's poetic structure, the metamorphoses
recurrent throughout his poetry of the 'Beauty that must die' and the dead miracu-
lously brought to life again . . ." (p. 340).

And the work of self-knowledge must remain incomplete. With each new life stage, we work through once again, but from the vantage point of new consolidations (I understand more and differently); new life's challenges (facing my children's life stages, each child and each stage with a unique passion); new empathic understandings (I know better what it is like to be a father); new anxieties (I, too, am facing the mortality only understood by one in the midst of generational shifts); and new mysteries (I understand better the limits of my present understanding). Self-recursion, *Nachträglichkeit*, "deferred action," *après-coup*, memories of memories, empathy with oneself in the empathic spiral. My internal father, my internal-and-so-constructed father, evolves with me: I create and find him yet again in an internal discourse that is endless.

The timelessness of the unconscious—that there will be a time someday to go back and work things through with those you love—encounters the finality of death. The unconscious wins, but just for a while. Grief is staved off, and then confronted and (literally) embraced: One cannot go back and replay life, make it go differently; one is caught in mortality. Moreover, in accepting my father's death, I must accept my own.

EDITING ONESELF: POSTSCRIPT TO A DRAFT REVISION

Lived life, as Milan Kundera (1984) observed, is always a first sketch. The act of writing gives the illusion of perfection, of having transcended one's limitations in space and time. I can revise my work, as if to revise myself, and, as with the repetition compulsion itself, perhaps this time I can get it right. This is, after all, in the tradition of *The Interpretation of Dreams* (Freud, 1900), which is in its essence a self-analysis conducted not only through the examination of dreams, but, more importantly, through the self-recursive act of writing about the process itself. In my dialogue with my imaginary audience, with the text itself, I end up talking to myself, my most patient, critical, and capricious audience.

In the context of writing this chapter, my spiral of grieving reawakens now years later. The writing itself serves as a day residue for the larger process of self-analysis. In my musings over this text, I again remembered Clare Winnicott's dream. To my surprise, I then incorporated her dream into one of my own, molding it to my own inner purpose. My unconscious enters into a dialogue with Clare Winnicott's dream, and I spiral in the contemplation of the mirror of her-my grief.

October 29, 1991

Last night I had another dream about my father. And once again we were hugging (the only other hugging dream that I can recall is the one related previously). This time, though, my father was sick, thin, and haggard. My daughter was present and I was alarmed for her to see him so near to death, I wanted to shield her from this knowledge. (Of course, it is myself I wish to protect. Moreover, by implication I anticipate a parallel, unbearable future in which I am in my father's role to her.)

My father's second wife was going away in a train, and I was saying good-bye. (She is his living symbol, and my father had some wonderful years with her. My own mother had left on that train many years before.)

The scene shifted. I was then with some high-school/college friends at a reunion (I had, in fact, recently been to such an event), and having a wonderful, raucous time. Suddenly I became aware that the reunion events were over, that we had to say good-bye, and I announced sadly to my friends that though the events felt everyday, as if they could go on forever, they had come to an end. Would we ever be able to come back together this way again? I knew that we wouldn't, though I hadn't the heart to tell them in the dream. We had all moved along, pushed by time and chance itself.

In my dream I still flinch from the truth interpersonally—I cannot yet summon myself to say that we will not see each other again. Perhaps, in my dream awareness, I await another reunion. But when I awoke, I felt a deep sadness, relief, and a sense of finality. My self is running ahead, with me ever one step behind . . .

REFERENCES

Freud, S. (1900), The interpretation of dreams. Standard Edition, 4 & 5. London: Hogarth Press, 1953.

_____ (1909), Notes upon a case of obsessional neurosis. Standard Edition, 10:151–318. London: Hogarth Press, 1955.

_____ (1917), Mourning and melancholia. Standard Edition, 14:237–258. London: Hogarth Press, 1957.

_____ (1919), The "uncanny." Standard Edition, 17:217–252. London: Hogarth Press, 1955.

Givelber, F. & Simon, B. (1981), A death in the life of a therapist and its impact on the therapy. Psychiat., 44:141–149.

Kohut, H. (1977), The Restoration of the Self. New York: IUP.

Kundera, M. (1984), The Unbearable Lightness of Being (trans. M. Heim). New York: Harper & Row.

Lacan, J. (1977), Ecrits (trans. A. Sheridan). New York: Norton.

Margulies, A. (1989), The Empathic Imagination. New York: Norton.

O'Flaherty, W. (1984), *Dreams, Illusion, and Other Realities*. Chicago: University of Chicago Press.
Sartre, J. P. (1956), *Being and Nothingness* (trans. H. E. Barnes). New York: Philosophical Library.
Ward, A. (1963), *John Keats: The Making of a Poet*. New York: Viking Press.
Winnicott, C. (1989), D. W. W.: A reflection. In: *D. W. Winnicott: Psycho-Analytic Explorations*, ed. C. Winnicott, R. Shepherd & M. Davis. Cambridge, MA: Harvard University Press.

4

Work with Patients and the Experience of Self-Analysis

James T. McLaughlin

An ongoing capacity for self-analysis is what working analysts commonly expect of themselves, and hope their patients will acquire. Many of us carry some conviction about having attained fresh and mutative understanding of ourselves through reflective self-scrutiny. Yet we are chronically uneasy about the authenticity of self-analytic discoveries, are wary of openly claiming them as analytic, and write sparingly about them.

For some analysts self-analytic work is an inescapable, expectable, and desirable part of their living, whether experienced as deliberately sought (Calder, 1979; Sonnenberg, 1991) or as fortuitous (Gardner, 1983; Beiser, 1984; McLaughlin, 1988, 1991; Jacobs, 1991).

From this second position I shall address some questions central to the matter of self-analysis. What pressures in and around analysts urge them to introspective inquiry? What is the nature of the self-analytic experience and of the circumstances in which the work takes place? How can we weigh the significance of self-analytic endeavors for analysts in their work and in the other important relationships in their lives and distinguish the effects of self-analysis from the profusion of changes inherent in the vicissitudes of the life cycle?

MOTIVATIONS FOR SELF-ANALYSIS

My response to such questions can only be partial. I have picked for my focus just one sector: the ongoing impact on the analyst of clinical work with patients.

It is my premise that work with patients, especially work with those patients who stretch and burden us, is a potent pressure impelling analysts to introspection in their reach for adaptive changes in their theoretical view and technical approach. In other words, I see our clinical work as the compelling motive, especially for those analysts whose need to do therapeutic work with others derives from adaptive and reparative urgencies learned in mastering troubled relations with primary others of their childhood. Such a therapeutic investment fosters the deep involvement necessary for significant analytic work. At the same time, it may well lead to a revival of conflict in the face of fresh provocation.

In saying this I suppose I could be wide of the mark for those whose reasons for being analysts, therapists, lie elsewhere—perhaps, like Freud, more in the direction of exploration and discovery. Yet, there is much that our strange calling demands of each of us, in our cave dweller mode of restricted range and mobility, that points to an altruism of dynamic significance. How else are we to account for our willing acceptance of a working lifetime of muted affective and motoric outlet, so that those few others we bring close to us might attain just those freedoms we have put aside? How else may we account for the inner turbulence and struggles that can take place in us as we live out the hours and years as working analysts whose accomplishments are dependent upon achievements not our own?

In my years of analyst-watching, my respect has grown for the integrity and tenacity of the need, in each of us, to wrestle with those liabilities in ourselves that impede us from doing our best work on behalf of our patients. Though the pain of lapse and shortfall may have its narcissistic base in prompting us to do better, our dogged return to the engagement with our patients reveals the strength of our need to relate intimately to and help other people. It is our rueful readiness to look to our own part in shaping the complications in the analytic venture that points to the deeply personal roots of responsibility felt and taken.

Here, I think, we tap the lifesap of what moves us to a continuing self-search that seems, for some analysts, a natural resource and replenishment. It is a way of seeing and sorting, akin to dreaming, that eases the way between the patients and our selves.

I am inclined to place the power of analytic work with patients to impel self-inquiry above even the poignancies of marriage and children. In familial relationships we are less aim-inhibited and, rightly or otherwise, allow our personal needs a far greater legitimacy of claim to fulfillment, and a more forceful voice in the compromises of intimate relating than we do with our patients.

My hesitance in speaking of these self-searchings as self-analysis is a carryover from the Grail-seeking times of my training, when insights fell short if they did not with certainty identify the primitive stuff of the infantile neurosis, or were suspected of harboring an inexact interpretation as rationalization masking a deeper truth.

The climate of psychoanalysis has moderated, however, and our lush hopes of recapturing veridical truths for and with our patients have since withered. Little of the immense territory claimed by Freud for his psychoanalysis is left, nearly a century later, that has not been fought over and new ownership variously asserted. Yet there remains evident among us a group reluctance to lay full claim to digging rights for exploring that one portion of the analytic field, self-analysis, which remains the unique property of Freud.

We may have here a wry insight into our group dynamics in noting how much of the residual ambivalence we retain toward the astonishing reach of Freud's vision lies in just this point. As we have gradually deidealized analysis as a body of theory and technique, we collectively seem to have grown able to see and acknowledge that the analytic work done with patients by others whose viewpoint differs from our own can be authentically analytic. In the province of self-analysis, however, we are still apt to be skeptical toward the claim of others for the validity of their self-analytic sorties, and defensive of our own.

I see these constraints as a reflection of our reluctance to share our ignorance and to join in the necessary deidealization of this essential part of our professional identity that eventually we must claim.

I am comfortable thinking of the work entailed in attaining these insights as self-analysis, particularly when some subsequent enhancement of self-understanding is discernible. I feel that there are more meaningful, experience-near indicators that we can discover and apply in judging the cogency of self-analytic moments than the application of a theoretical construct such as the infantile neurosis, or similarly idealizing expectations. I will dwell upon these clinical criteria a little later.

Insight is a concept central to most definitions of self-analysis. In its broadest sense, I regard insight as any fresh perception of oneself (Webster, 1952). In particular, the type essential to our work is mutative insight, that fresh perception of self, conscious or otherwise, which accompanies a developmental increment in the patient's psychic organization as a consequence of analytic work (Moore and Fine, 1990, p. 99). Such mutative work is necessarily done in the course of struggles to replace or alter old perceptions of self and other, when they are replayed in new variations in the very different context of the analytic relationship. In these intensities patients can come to experience more of themselves and others than they have been able to see while constrained by their transferences. Without such an intense need to bring their intrapsychic conflicts to light, patients are likely to experience little psychic change, and few felt insights. In my experience, this affectively driven process holds equally for the analyst.

THE ANALYST'S UNFOLDING PERCEPTION OF PATIENT AND SELF

As a frame for exploring self-analytic sorties, let me first sketch what I have noticed to be a familiar sequence in the unfolding of an analyst's perception of self and patient, spurred by the challenge of ongoing clinical work. Oversimplified, this march carries from the comfort, when at a loss, of first behaving like one's own analyst; to the confusion of finding likenesses to oneself in each patient; then the sobering acknowledgment of the ambiguities and opacities inherent in those differences between self and patient that cannot be merged (Mclaughlin, in press). That each step in this journey of discovery of patient and self makes its particular demands upon us for self-scrutiny is what I shall try to convey. The data that I shall draw upon will be from my own experience, unless otherwise acknowledged.

SHAPING OF A VINTAGE FIFTIES ANALYST

The training of the late 1940s required that we work from a position of cool detachment, confident in the fidelity of our unconscious attunement to our patients that would yield the accurate decoding of the patients' manifest concerns. We were to trust our intuition, buttressed by the theoretical formulations provided us, to lead us to the exact interventions that would guide the patients through the morass of their infantile misconceptions. One result of these serene expectations was that, when faced with clinical situations outside the span of my supervised experience, as was too often the case, I would come up short. In such moments I was most likely to steady myself by drawing automatically upon the experiences of my own analysis for a remembered stance of my analyst that might meet the crisis. For me this meant much well-intended silence broken by throat-clearing, as a sign of life still extant behind the couch, then a gently intended "yes?" as signal/plea to the patient for more data; for such had been the major modes of my first analyst. This could be helpful, but too often led to impasses which left me with accretions of what was then pejoratively designated as countertransference. For this disorder the sole prescription of the time was more analysis.

I was moved to seek a second analysis in my early years as an analyst because of the large number of physicians in my analytic caseload. All males, they comprised a mixture of psychiatrists and other medical brothers with backgrounds often similar to mine. The trial identifications that Robert Fliess (1942) would have us make came easily, but did not so easily go. Being receptively close to my physician patients was at times to be in a hall of mirrors. What we came gradually to recognize, in the terms of the times, were conflicted nurturing maternal identifications anchoring a renunciation of direct satisfaction of one's own needs, except as attainable through service to others. Notably these defenses against phallic-aggressive wishes tended to include an inhibition, sometimes massive, of intellectual strivings and other self-effacements consonant with the image of the "Old Family Doctor," and with the particulars of the Hippocratic oath as well (McLaughlin, 1961).

Work with each physician-patient stirred resonances in me of personal matters that I had thought comfortably resolved through my own analyses. At times I was unable to sort out which dynamic shadings belonged to the patient and which belonged to me. I was concerned over the validity of the dynamics I was discovering in my patients. Was I really understanding what lay in them; or was I reading my own organizings into them? Incidents would occur during analytic hours that startled or bewildered me and, often, the patient, too.

THE IMPACT OF LIKENESSES: A CONFUSION OF VOICES

One instance in particular from these early times stands out. I was working with two analysands, both psychiatrists, one of them in training analysis. Each was struggling to express and deal with yearnings for the beloved woman lost to him in his past. One had lost his mother through her protracted dementing illness and death when he was a latency child; the other his wife through her sudden death from a cerebral vascular catastrophe during the early years of their marriage. Neither, for quite different reasons, had been able to mourn, to make peace with his loss and hurt over having been left, or to resolve his remorse over his part in shaping the loss. Both were caught up in these tensions, and both reproached me for not doing more to comfort and resolve their distress.

I felt burdened and at a loss. About a year earlier, I had been with my own mother in her dying hours at her summer place.

During an hour with my training analysand I made an incredible gaffe. I was caught up in noting new tones of distress in his otherwise familiar recounting of having been a 10-year-old immersed in his boy's world, only peripherally mindful of his mother's deterioration. He was wondering now why his father had not reached out across the distance between them to help him see what was happening. I felt he was ready for a formulation that I had been holding back for quite awhile. I spoke to him of his need to defend himself against his anxiety and anger about his mother's slow desertion of him, leading him to squelch his distress and direct his anger upon his drunkard father. As support for my interpretation I spoke of a dream from a recent hour depicting an empty Eskimo kyack bobbing helplessly in turbulent rapids, surviving only because its decking held out the whitewater.

The trouble was that this dream belonged to my other patient. I realized this as I finished speaking, and sat in a silence of shared shock. Our working through of the consequences of my mistake was arduous and complex. Three points stand out: I acknowledged my gaffe. I meant it when I apologized, saying that my confusion of the two surely involved something in me that I would work to identify and resolve. Second, I had a vague inner perception that there was some sense in my involving the candidate analysand in my misadventure rather than his counterpart. I had been put off and dissatisfied for some time with the obduracy of his distancing idealization of me, which I conceptualized then as a defense against his competitive aggression. Yet I had seen him as not yet capable of being confronted with this disavowed aspect of himself, and I had felt bogged down. Third, the qualities of my immediate distress during our charged silence were familiar: chagrin and anxious vigilance, the flush of foot-in-mouth shame, and misery over having done some irreparable harm. I had long known that this flood of affects was central to my most painful experiences of misdeeds and blunders in childhood and adolescence. Through much prior analytic work this affective state had largely attenuated to a signal-cluster that I could recognize as a call for more self-inquiry. On this occasion, however, the impact was full and I was shaken by it.

In my own analytic hours I had been obliquely reproaching my second analyst for helping me so little to get in touch with the grieving for my mother that we agreed was surely there and must be tapped. I came now to sense how necessary it was that I avoid full awareness of my mixture of need and vengeful distancing toward her, now my analyst and then my mother, feeding into my habitual resort to solitary coping. An important referent to the depths of my own problem came in my realization that I had become caught up in strong resonances of likeness to both these patients, especially to the one who suffered my slip. In the work with my patient I had brought us into the replaying of unresolved son-to-mother entanglements, snarled and made static by uncompleted mourning. Who had shamefully and hurtfully neglected, rejected, deserted, or abandoned whom, and who ought to feel shame and remorse toward whom, were shifting uncertainties alive in each of us. These transference configurations had become animated in and between us in the intensities of the analytic relationship. In each of us these conflicts were further magnified by paternal absence, and a consequent lack of the presence and support of one parent by which the vicissitudes of ambivalence in relationship to the other can be mitigated. This lack of the father I saw as contributing to the strong sense of responsibility for the well-being of others that could be identified in the patients and myself, as a way of countering guilt and concern over aggression in self and other.

It was in this fluid shifting of transference-laden mother–son identifications that I merged my patients and me in my enactment. Prompted to come to grips in my own analysis with my own delayed mourning, I could see my gaffe as an aggressive act against my patient whose candidacy furthered my sense of the likeness between us. This confusion of likenesses struck me as a kind of self-inflicted wounding and expiation, a compromise expression of my wishes to punish and to help, to reproach and to seek the forgiving rapprochement of shared understanding.

In the years following the ending of my second analysis I became accustomed to dwell outside the analytic hours upon events with patients that had left me uneasy and unsettled. Such gropings were not deliberate, but took place when I puttered in the garden or in my workshop, immersed in the serenity of familiar tasks. I learned to welcome these reflections and the dreams that drifted in upon their heels, for together they somehow illuminated an aspect of me that now meshed with or matched my patient in the ways in which we were alike and different. Only gradually did I grow aware of how much I counted on shop and garden as places of entry to paths toward insight; how invariably I would seek them out when beset with an unsettled problem with family and patients, or when getting an analytic paper underway.

Seeking open resonance to each patient made it inevitable that new facets or aspects of old concerns could come alive in me, and impel further self-searching. Working on the impediments that befell me, signaled by sleepiness, boredom, excessive intervening or steering, brought me to recognize disturbing similarities between us, and added fresh perspectives on my old history. This resulted in a restored stance in the work and a modest harvest of clinical papers for my colleagues to endure (McLaughlin, 1975, 1981, 1987).

THE IMPACT OF DIFFERENCES

What flushed me out of my refuge in the illusion of detached objectivity were my daily encounters with some patients who seemed very different from me and beyond my expectancy range. Here were individuals who just could not tolerate being dealt with from a distance and through minimal communicative contact. They monitored with anxious vigilance my ways of trying to relate to them. All were liable to rapid decompensation in the analytic setting and disruptive behaviors outside, taking refuge in regressive withdrawal and somatic and emotional distress in response to behaviors of mine that they experienced as slighting, preemptive, intrusive, or abandoning.

I was dismayed and puzzled by these reactions to interventions I considered on target and tactful, and to my silences, which struck me as humanely intended. It took me longer than I would wish, and more iatrogenic pain inflicted than I care to recall, before I could hear more in those negative responses than defensive avoidance and transference-driven resistances against a truth.

Work with these patients drove home the recognition of the relativistic nature of the analytic enterprise when perceived from the different reality views of the two participants. I had no choice but to consider the extent to which my stance of superior knowing invalidated the psychic reality of the patient, and kept us both from understanding how that unique reality view had necessarily come to be. I was impelled to address the complications that my limitations imposed upon the work in consequence of my acquired biases of theory and technical preferences, influenced at times by regressive transferences of my own. I have written elsewhere in some detail about the enactments shaped between the patient and myself under the impact of our shared regressive transferences, and the nature of the spontaneous self-analytic inquiry prompted by these experiences (McLaughlin, 1988, 1991).

Triggering these self-explorations have been varied cues and signals, in addition to the cluster I described above. I am in agreement with Poland (1992) about heightened psychic tension as the immediate driving force impelling us, or many of us, to the task. Unlike some who have the self-discipline and capabilities to engage regularly in self-analysis (Sonnenberg, 1991), I have not been able to get very far in habitual self-analysis. What usually has moved me has been some degree of anxiety, an uneasiness while at work with a patient, building up gradually and often out of my full awareness. Eventually, I catch myself in some form of withdrawal or therapeutically intended steering, or get caught up in a more obviously regressive enactment. The distress signals that follow press me to off-hours reflection.

CLINICAL VIGNETTE: THROUGH A GLASS DARKLY

Here is a thumbnail sketch from one of the many cases that have put their weight behind my ongoing need for self-appraisal and change (McLaughlin, 1991). Mrs. P had come into analysis in the 1970s for help with her long-standing isolation, bouts of depression, and chronic inability to find satisfaction and fulfillment in any aspect of her life. Her suffering was evident and her pleas for help insistent. I had grown weary in my year-long effort to reach her through her incessant and ambiguous circumstantiality as she detailed her hopeless failures as wife and mother. When I intervened (more accurately, had to interrupt) to seek the point of her tortured account, to identify her affective states, or to explore her obvious distress in allowing me to engage her, Mrs. P would abruptly fall silent, or drown us both in her self-depreciation and, in so doing, become fragmented in her thought processes.

When I tried my tactful best to explore her obsessive indecisiveness, to link it to her growing up with a work-absorbed mother and ever-critical father, she invalidated these interventions with contrary new versions that destroyed the significance I had so carefully distilled. Subsequently, I would hear about her worsened depression and binge eating that followed such an impasse. I felt stuck in my inability to help her see, and shaken in my sense of my own competence to see. I was worried for her, for us, and could hear the rising edge of assertiveness in my interventions, made after my lengthy silences spent amassing more data that I hoped would be persuasive should I find a place to intervene. These were clear and compelling indicators that I had fallen into a regressed level of transference of my own, signaling a stalemate that was mine to resolve.

Luckily, I caught sight of a mannerism unusual for me: I repeatedly removed my bifocals during such hours to gaze blankly at the blur of my patient on the couch, and found pleasure, for moments on end, in the soft merging of color masses that were the flowers on my coffee table. The latter gave me a sense of peaceful detachment that I was reluctant to leave in order to observe Mrs. P once more through corrective lenses that did not help me see what I needed to know. Soon after, I heard an unusual intensity as I recounted to new friends an old story of how my childhood visual impairment had finally been discovered when, as a 9-year-old, I had proved an inept caddy for my golfing uncle; how, once behind my glasses, I sighted with delight and expansion a world of immense reach and clarity.

Something fell into place with my linking the storytelling and ritual with my glasses. During my workshop reveries over the ensuing weeks, a darker side of those times drifted into focus, one that I had only touched upon in my previous analyses. I recalled what it had been like to be semiblind and not know it: I had been comfortable enough in the family acceptance of my accustomed bumblings, but had known times of pain and despair, with shamed bewilderment over what was wrong that made my prowess so different from that of the rest of my family. I had accepted my inept lot, and had turned to books and their words to find an authority of meaning that my uncertain visual perceptions could not grasp. The puzzlement and uncertainty of those times drove my need, once I had my glasses, to be accurate and quick to see and say and do it right. These personal strivings found a comfortable fit in the job description of the competent analyst that I accepted. As my work with Mrs. P made clear, I was prone, under her unswerving challenge to my sense of competence, to fall into an exaggerated use of this minimal analytic stance of authoritative knowledge.

What I gradually came to see clearly enough was that Mrs. P's ways of evoking my efforts to reach out to her, then wiping them out with repudiation and altered contexts, had tapped into my old pain of uncertain groping and failing to know. Faced by Mrs. P's very similar distress over her own uncertainty, I had fallen into defensive transference behaviors of excessive assertiveness or silent withdrawal as ways of being rid of the burden of her/our problem. Self-analysis sometimes works in enigmatic ways. In the mirroring of likenesses among differences that breached my defenses, I had come upon fresh sidestreams of familiar transferences, able to feel the surprise of new understanding about old concerns I had thought well enough settled.

What gradually ensued between Mrs. P and me were mainly quiet differences in how things were said between us. On my side there was a greater freedom to float ideas and impressions in a tentative, nondeclamatory fashion, once the old imperatives to say it right could be put aside. Perhaps most importantly, once I discovered and attenuated my old pain of not knowing, I really could hear better the nuances of Mrs. P's manifold distress. It was easier to find more evocative ways to acknowledge the legitimacy of *her* pain that she could not yet risk speaking about, and to grasp better the dynamic nature of her impaired verbal expressiveness.

From Mrs. P's side, her response to my shift showed up rather swiftly, initially in a modest easing of anxiety and greater freedom to challenge and check out my offerings; then a cautiously offered, repetitious, and grudging "I knew *that* all the time," as acknowledgment and dismissal of my offerings. She thus allowed me glimpses of the shame-driven fear and stubborn withholding that lay behind her habitually not saying what she often knew or felt. Especially noteworthy was the gradual diminishing of episodes of confusion and fragmented thought. Her preferred style became for a long time that of disagreeing with whatever I said, then restating these ideas quite articulately in her own words, deepening and extending these ideas in directions of her own that were important for me to acknowledge. It took much longer for her to volunteer that she had quickly noted my changed stance and had tracked it vigilantly for lapse or traps. By this time she was deeply engaged in confronting both of us with the enormity of her feeling herself utterly worthless and unlovable in my eyes.

VERIFICATION OF SELF-ANALYTIC EXPERIENCE

This sketchy clinical sample also captures, or at least touches upon, the cluster of data that I have come to rely upon in trying to assess the authenticity and carrying power of my self-analytic encounters. These experiences have tended to proceed in the following sequence:

An initial uncertain meander from inner tension and groping toward a more relaxed and fuller comprehension plays itself out in varying degrees of pace and emotional impact for me. In this instance I almost literally had to blind myself before I could grope for the connections between this state, my symptomatic behavior with my glasses, and the recital of a bit of family lore. This oft-told tale then

seemed gradually to light up, its familiar dimensions still there, but
their meaning and affective charge vastly transformed and amplified,
as when a hologram shifts, or sets and lighting are changed on the
open stage. This sense of fresh seeing into old aspects of myself came
in an almost leisurely fashion over a period of several weeks, along
with renewed energy and quiet pleasure.

I detail this in order to contrast it with more intense flares of insight
that have occasionally been my lot, these tending to follow upon
jolting, even uncanny, experiences during an analytic hour. One such
instance was triggered by the misassigned dream already described;
another was set off by the almost identical nature of detailed
fantasy-content of analyst and patient, during a shared silence, which
I described in an earlier paper on the analyst's insights (McLaughlin,
1988). In both instances the sense of sudden illumination was itself
startling, along with an intense exhilaration in feeling able, for a
lingering moment, to see to far reaches of one's inner life. This is
rather like experiencing bursts of heat-lightning that light up a
familiar summer landscape with eerie clarity before flickering into a
darkness crackling with the tension of an imminent storm. These
sensory and emotional qualities seem to me to point to the lifting of
old repressions, with the consequences only later to be weighed as
ephemeral, or durable and expanding.

A further verification of the self-analytic experience has to do with
the nature of the effects that new self-observation has upon my ways
of working with a particular patient, both in short range and over the
long haul, and then with my patients in general. In the work with
Mrs. P the sense of an expanded range of seeing and saying, which
I have come to trust as a harbinger of a mutative insight, was quick to
come. Among the later self-perceptions that came over weeks and
months was the rueful recognition of how my investment in verbalizing my perceptions amounted to not listening to Mrs. P, not hearing
her point of view, shutting us off from understanding, and actual-
izing her worst expectations. I was chagrined to realize that I had
defaulted on my commitment to hearing my patient in order to ward
off a revival of an old state of inadequacy, shame, and hopelessness
too resonant with Mrs. P's constant misery.

Yet another criterion of the mutative self-analytic experience lies in
the impact upon my patient, as reflected both in Mrs. P's emotional
and behavioral responses to my altered stance, and acknowledged in
her expressed awareness of the change. Mrs. P was able to find what
she needed that helped her become more articulate, to reveal more of
her hidden concerns, and to have less need to regress to helplessness.
Eventually she could reveal how she had immediately perceived the

change, but had monitored it warily for a long time in order to be sure that it was "real."

The last of my series of clinical indicators of the significant self-perception may be found in the discernible consequences of cumulative change, wrought by self-analytic moments, upon how I am perceived by patients, family, colleagues, and others, and whether these accord with my own perceptions. Here the data are the most problematic, and the most vulnerable to wishful skewing. One large change in my analytic stance, evolving out of years of work with patients in the range Mrs. P exemplifies, has been a commitment to acknowledging and working within the reality view of the patient. The collaborative enhancements of doing so have gradually led me to prefer this as a basic way of relating to all my patients, and to people in general. I take some affirmation of the durability of this attitude from the feedback I get from long-term relationships: family, friends, consultees, and old patients returned for reanalysis; that they experience deeper levels of feeling reached and understood, and see me as more consistently there for them. I know that I convey more my appreciation of the strength and pain in others, and try harder to avoid adding to the pain.

My gradual shift in analytic perspective has been an enduring outcome of the continuing self-inquiry that prolonged work with patients has made both habit and resource for me. Exploring the potential of analysis from within the psychic reality of the patient has been the major preoccupation of my last 15 years as a clinical analyst (McLaughlin, 1981). Reflecting further shaping of my analytic identity, this commitment continues to embody the assets and liabilities of my healing bent. Hence it obviously calls for ongoing self-scrutiny in its own right. In addition, as I have learned this approach and have tried to convey it to those who consult with me, I find its technical challenges difficult and exciting, and inevitably defining of the limits of competence and the need for continuing self-scrutiny.

THE CONSULTATIVE EXPERIENCE AS STIMULUS FOR SELF-ANALYSIS

Here is yet another powerful adjuvant to the self-analytic bent: the stimulation inherent in the consultative process when the analyst knows he or she needs help and is strongly motivated to seek it.

I have benefited from considerable consultation about my clinical work over these many years. None has brought me into so close and illuminating contact with my motives for my ways of working as has the consultation I have sought in my need to enhance my capacities to minimize my own point of view in order to analyze from the patient's perspective. Here I have had recourse to the outstanding proponent of this clinical approach, whose work I have followed closely for more than ten years. Schwaber (1983, 1986, 1992) has pioneered in exploring how much analytic work can be achieved through a committed focus upon both the psychic reality of the patient and the nuances of all the behaviors of the analyst that have become so central to that reality. She has provided a specific technical base and rigorous mode of working by which to seek the patient's view, both conscious and undiscovered, of any aspect of his or her life, and to recognize the dynamic logic of the patient's perspective. A stance that requires close attention to the immediacies of the analytic moment, this may at times include a nonsteering exploration into the patient's experience of the interaction with the analyst. She has demonstrated how powerful and effective this mode can be for analytic inquiry into the patient's intrapsychic processes, and for the therapeutic change it induces.

In consulting about my ongoing work with a patient similar to Mrs. P, I came upon the many ways by which I repeatedly lapsed from this mode of inquiry. In one typical instance, it became clear that I had not picked up enough on the patient's signals of distress over my leaving her for a vacation, accepting too readily the mask of her sturdy self-sufficiency, and her voiced delight in anticipating her freedom as the mouse relieved of the hovering cat. After several repetitions of this theme in varied contexts I felt some of my signal concern, and a need to address my oversight. I came to see a different perspective on my habitual preference for keeping all farewells and partings brief. I often tended to close off separations, leaving and being left, with various disavowals and distancings. One favorite device was to get busy in some solitary activity that gave me pleasure. I had long ago retrieved memories of my childhood distress over my mother's absences, her leave-takings and somber states when I was very young, and had worked through much of what these had meant to me. But I had obviously found no need to connect those experiences of loss with an adaptation I still valued, so ego-syntonic as to leave me with a blind spot of personal values too aligned with the patient's defenses.

On another occasion I did not inquire sufficiently into my patient's hopelessness of ever feeling that I valued her for herself, despite her conviction of my sustained attention and caring. She saw these benign attitudes as being my habitual and generically deployed stance, always there and available to all, a reflection of my superior maturity and inevitable to our tilted relationship. I suddenly realized that I still carried the perspective of my training years on the analytic relationship as indeed inescapably tilted in regard to the relative intensities of need and caring on either side of the couch. Accepting this self-evident truth, I had not held open enough or tried sufficiently to explore what she might be observing in my behavior that allowed her the conviction that mine was a nonspecific benignity having little personally to do with her.

In these two instances what was at stake was not just an exercise in improving technical competence. The flow of the clinical data following my lapses clearly pointed to the patient's sagging into worsened depression, alienation, and hopelessness.

Working so closely to engage all levels of the patient's psychic reality seems inevitably to open the analyst to a heightened appreciation of the patient's affective intensities, and to intensify the depth of his or her own emotional involvement. The impact of seeing and tracking my contribution to these repetitive enactments, up close and in living intensity, indeed had a cumulative and tensional impact that led me to some self-inquiry. The enlarged perspective that gradually lighted up was not startling; I saw better that what was hindering my hearing the patient's pain had to do with my own old and reliable defensive postures. My nonresponsiveness to her masked distress over being left was very similar to my closing off my own sensitivities to partings, and my tacit support of her busy doings was a reflection of my own preferred solutions. Joining her in her quiet hopelessness about the tilt in our relationship manifestly denoted a hard spot in my way of seeing the analytic dyad; that is, accepting a truism of my basic training, and taking refuge in a precept rather than staying with the patient's shame and hurt over being so little and unimportant to me and to the mother of her early years.

Behind both these enactments lay old relationship issues of my own, also having to do with a child's concerns of shame and anger over littleness, helplessness, and need.

I am not sure where to place these recognitions along the spread of self-scrutiny. Their impact is very strong in confronting me with the way in which I cling to familiar ways of seeing and doing. I am inclined to ascribe to them a valid component of self-analysis on the basis of the sense of relaxation, and a freedom to consider other viewpoints, that came with the enlarged perspectives that self-reflective work on these clinical difficulties engendered.

SANCTUARIES OF TRANSFERENCE

This leads to a consideration of the circumstances in which self-analysis takes place, once the stimulus of the clinical occasion has been felt. I would like to single out a particular aspect of self-analysis that has been vital for me and for others who have written about their experiences. In fact, I consider its inclusion, in accounts of such experiences, to be another component of the validating context that I have come to rely upon in assessing self-analytic efforts.

This enhancement has to do with the surround or circumstances in which analysts generate their insights. It seems significant that none of these special contexts is deliberately sought or contrived. Usually some private haven has been discovered without conscious intent, selected for personal dynamic reasons that are vital to the self-analytic enterprise. Here the preconscious can hold sway while familiar routines are played out. Calder (1979) speaks of the "laboratory" of his bathroom shaving, where he could contemplate the "sharp winces" of self-critical remembering. Ticho (1967) tells of lore gleaned from other analysts about their preferred settings of bed, warm bath, or comfortable travel; others have told me of the evocative power of the fishing skiff, trout stream, or park bench. What seems common to all these is the relaxation and freedom for contemplation to be found in desultory thought while anchored in some routine physical activity reinforced by familiar sights, sounds, and smells. I have come to think of these specially sought circumstances as transference sanctuaries.

Shop and yard have been the sanctuaries I still seek. I shuttle back and forth between the two at odd hours, and have learned to trust that I will, without deliberate effort, see ways through the thickets of a patient or paper. As I focus on the immediate woodworking task at hand, I address our tangles with a kind of peripheral awareness, a sidewise looking. Gradually becoming aware of these unobtrusive rituals led me to an appreciation of their importance to my inner balancings.

In my early years after the influenza death of my physician father when I was 6 weeks old, his brother was the single most meaningful male in my life. A master mechanic who was said to have fashioned and sold two horseless carriages, Uncle John spent the summer months of my first 12 years living at our summer place, his son like an older brother to me. Over those years my uncle improved the grounds and cottage in which my mother spent all the remaining summers of her life, her link to the husband she never stopped mourning, and my link to the father I knew through her.

My cousin and I often worked alongside my uncle as he did his improvisational carpentering and plumbing, planting and digging, repairing and building, from rose gardens to septic tanks, from extra bedrooms to rowboats. We also learned from him how to roam with shotgun and fishing rod, how to navigate in fog, to use our peripheral vision to see what we would miss by direct looking.

The smells and tastes of new-cut grass and spaded earth, the pungency of sawed wood, the heft and odor of hand tools, all were part of the nourishment and beckoning provided by a man who was there and available, a man who made me welcome in his world and handed me the tools for being in it. I have never lost my pleasure in, and sense of replenishment from being actively caught up in these pursuits of workshop and yard.

I feel sure that these reliable surrounds and ritual doings have provided me a rich ambience of what were the most sustaining and enhancing relationships of my first 12 years. In these settings I tap into the most positive aspects of my memories of and identifications with the mother and uncle who meant so much to me. It has become evident to me that I needed to spend my adult years living out these likenesses to both, in an immersion in home and grounds and family, as a working toward parity with my parental images. It makes sense that when I sought to do my very best in the intellectual-professional world of my idealized father, I would need the retreat and reassurance of drawing upon evocations of the mother and uncle whom I had known. In these sanctuaries I could be in touch with the complexities of both my mother's feminine nurturing and my uncle's essential masculinity. There I could be reassured by what had sustained me in my parents' world, so full of daunting intimations of a father I could never know.

From all this comes a generalization I have some conviction about: *In the familiar safety of these known places and rituals, these sanctuaries of transference, we draw upon transitional phenomena akin to those experienced in the analytic situation, yet richer in basic sensory qualities. We tap into latent traces of our positive experiences with one or both parental figures, and draw once more upon their nurturing and releasing aspects which had helped us find our earlier way, to gain affirmation and strength to face our present and assimilate our unwanted, conflictual past.*

SUMMARY

There are no conclusions to be drawn from what has been set forth above, just impressions; and perhaps the oxymoron of tentative convictions.

Self-analysis can be real, telling, and lasting in its effects. The strong impulse in the analyst for doing self-analysis lies in those adaptive and reparative necessities alive in him consequent to troubled relations with primary others of early childhood. Clues to the persistence and importance of these necessities lie in the peculiar nature of our work, in the renunciations that it requires in the service of the patient. That the analyst can be caught up with the patient in a tangle of his or her own and shared concerns is evident in the vicissitudes of relating. The persistent return of the analyst to the scene of his or her actions is another clue to the enduring sense of responsibility and commitment to the other whom he has brought close. As he works over time, he first finds in his patient much that is like him and can then go on to find what is unique to the psychic reality of each.

In his need for help with his own tensions, and his need to ease their impact on his patient the analyst turns to further analysis, to consultation with a valued other, or to groups of peers. In each setting he can revive different transference aspects of past relationships, optimally those supporting and honing his capacities.

Most vitally he turns to his own introspective capabilities, particularly as these have been enhanced by his own analysis. His self-inquiry becomes facilitated by his being able to find places and activities whose sameness and familiarity provide a safe haven. In these sanctuaries of transference, resonances of the nurturing and releasing aspects of primary others can be brought alive, as in the analytic relationship itself, and akin to the usages of transitional phenomena.

The self-analytic work that can happen in these sanctuaries has qualities of immediate, affect-laden experience that become recognizable, a kind of first authentication. Other markers of the validity of the self-analytic moment can be sought in observing its effects, in the short term and over time, upon the analyst's work with a particular patient, then with other patients, including those changes remarked upon by the patient(s). The analyst's own noting of changes in himself can find confirmation in their recognition by family, friends, and others who have known him well over an extended period of time.

In all of this is the driving force of analyst's need to heal himself through his striving to help the patient heal him- or herself. In helping our other, we restore and acknowledge our personal past, and those who helped us to shape it.

REFERENCES

Beiser, H. (1984), Example of self analysis. *J. Amer. Psychoanal. Assn.*, 32:3–12.
Calder, K. (1979), An analyst's self-analysis. *J. Amer. Psychoanal. Assn.*, 28:5–20.

Fliess, R. (1942), The metapsychology of the analyst. *Psychoanal. Quart.*, 11:211–227.
Gardner, M. R. (1983), *Self Inquiry.* Boston: Atlantic-Little Brown.
Jacobs, T. (1991), *The Uses of the Self.* Madison, CT: IUP.
McLaughlin, J. (1961), The analyst and the Hippocratic oath. *J. Amer. Psychoanal. Assn.*, 9:106–120.
_____ (1975), The sleepy analyst. *J. Amer. Psychoanal. Assn.*, 23:362–382.
_____ (1981), Transference, psychic reality and countertransference. *Psychoanal. Quart.*, 50:639–664.
_____ (1987), The play of transference: Some reflections on enactment in the psychoanalytic situation. *J. Amer. Psychoanal. Assn.*, 35:557–582.
_____ (1988), The analyst's insights. *Psychoanal. Quart.*, 42:379–389.
_____ (1991), Clinical and theoretical aspects of enactment. *J. Amer. Psychoanal. Assn.*, 39:595–614.
_____ (in press), How the analyst's work shapes the analyst. *Psychoanal. Inq.*
Moore, B. & Fine, B. (1990), *Psychoanalytic Terms and Concepts.* Binghamton, NY: Vail-Ballou Press.
Poland, W. (1992), Self and other in self-analysis. Presented to American Psychological Association, April, 1992.
Schwaber, E. (1983), Psychoanalytic listening and psychic reality. *Internat. Rev. Psycho-Anal.*, 10:379–392.
_____ (1986), Reconstruction and perceptual experience. *J. Amer. Psychoanal. Assn.*, 34:911–932.
_____ (1992), Countertransference: The analyst's retreat from the patient's vantage point. *Internat. J. Psycho-Anal.*, 73:349–362.
Sonnenberg, S. (1991), The analyst's self-analysis and its impact on clinical work. *J. Amer. Psychoanal. Assn.*, 39:687–704.
Ticho, G. (1967), On self-analysis. *Internat. J. Psycho-Anal.*, 48:308–325.
Webster's New International Dictionary of the English Language, 2nd ed., unabridged. Springfield, MA: Merriam Co., 1952.

5

Engagements in Analysis and Their Use in Self-Analysis

Henry F. Smith

When I was a child, a psychoanalyst told me that most people become analysts to learn about themselves. I wasn't sure what he meant. Was it learning from books? Or by studying others? Or the required training analysis I had heard about? Later Elvin Semrad, who taught several generations of residents at the Massachusetts Mental Health Center in Boston, would say the opposite, that candidates lie on the couch thinking it's for training, and it takes them "about two years" to find out they need to be there. Both my surmise about learning from books and Semrad's pointed comment speak to a major obstacle to the analyst's self-learning, his or her own resistance to the work. If Gill (1982) writes cogently and consistently about resistance to the analysis of the patient's transference, we are only beginning to realize the impact of the analyst's parallel and symmetrical resistance to his own self-analysis, including the analysis of his own ongoing transference to the patient.

How analysts learn about themselves is still a mystery, in part because it is one of the areas of our work that we speak about rarely and write about almost never. Although Freud pioneered self-analytic work and described his personal experience in detail, he became skeptical about its results, and while he acknowledged his dependency on his patients for his own self-understanding (Masson, 1985,

A version of this chapter appears in *Psychoanalytic Inquiry* (1993 [13/3], pp. 425–454).

p.281; Loewald, 1960), he rarely described those self-analytic processes embedded in listening to the patient. If the analyzing instrument as it pertains to the patient is difficult enough to illustrate, those
workings of the analyst in the immediacy of the hour that extend the
analyst's self-understanding have been described by only a few
(Gardner, 1983; McLaughlin, 1988; Poland, 1988; Jacobs, 1991), some
of whom are contributors to this volume.

How the analytic work shapes the analyst, how the analyst learns
about him-or herself, or, more broadly, how the analyst experiences
the work, must have as many answers as there are analysts. We are
at this point in the initial stage of description, trying to describe what
we see in what we do, and while, like all description, our vision will
be influenced by what we think we'll find, or what we think we
already know, I would like to try to describe a bit of what I think
shapes me.

But first a generalization: It seems to me the analyst is shaped by
the nature of his or her engagement with the patient's experience and
by the uses the analyst makes of that engagement. I should think the
nature of that engagement varies from analyst to analyst and from
patient to patient, optimally shifting throughout every hour and
always present on multiple levels simultaneously, whether recognized or not. But how that engagement shapes the analyst will
depend in part on how the analyst uses the analytic work, consciously or preconsciously, as part of an ongoing process of "self-
inquiry," in Gardner's (1983) phrase. It will depend on how and to
what degree the analyst experiences the work, not as some form of
altruistic surrender, but as a process of extended self-discovery, as
essential to the analyst's own continued growth as it may be to that of
the patient.

By the analyst's "use of the engagement" I am referring in part to
that area of the work Loewald (1960) describes when he says that the
analyst "in doing his part of the work, experiences the cathartic effect
of 'regression in the service of the ego' and performs a piece of
self-analysis or re-analysis" (p. 243). My interest is in what lies
"beyond catharsis."

In describing the ways in which the analyst may function better in
analyzing than in living, Schafer (1983) speaks of the disinterested
analyst, for whom "less is at stake personally in that the analytic
relationship is not the repository of his or her major personal needs."
Thus, this "disinterested position" allows the analyst to work "sen-
sitively, generously and reliably" (p.38). I agree, but I would argue
that in addition to what Schafer terms disinterest, there is another
aspect of analyzing that allows the analyst to work generously, and

that paradoxically keeps the patient safe from the analyst's own personal needs. I am referring to the fact that the analytic work itself may be for the analyst a source not only of professional satisfaction but of personal growth and development and that inseparable from the analysis of the patient may be a parallel ongoing process of self-analysis, conducted by the analyst and essential to both the patient and the analyst. To view the patient as the stimulus for this self-analytic work does not mean that the patient is the "repository" of the analyst's major personal needs, in Schafer's terms. Nevertheless, for all their differences in function and activity, one of the ways in which patient and analyst function most symmetrically is in their mutual dependence upon the unfolding transference–countertransference field for their own continued growth and development. That interdependence requires each participant, to a degree, to trust the other.

When three of his children were burned by fire, Cotton Mather, the 17th century Puritan cleric, is said to have responded by preaching a sermon entitled, "What Use Ought Parents to Make of Disasters Befallen Their Children" (cited in deMause, 1975, p. 9). Lest my focus appear similarly skewed, let me hasten to add that in describing the use the analyst makes of the patient's experience, I am not suggesting that the work exists primarily for the benefit of the analyst, nor am I speaking of modifications in technique that would alter our intrapsychic focus on the patient.

I am suggesting, however, that the two individuals are involved in an interactive process that lends itself to "reciprocal inquiries," in Gardner's (1983) term; that these inquiries are at times simultaneous, parallel, and symmetrical; and that whatever the analyst's self-inquiry may tell him about the patient, it *will* tell him something about himself if he chooses to listen.

My emphasis here on the immediate, ongoing, and symmetrical is in contrast to the more deliberate end-of-the-day self-analytic activities described by Calder (1980), Sonnenberg (1991; chap. 12), and others. Self-analytic practice and the literature that describes it, include a variety of modes, some more deliberate, conscious, and disciplined, others more involuntary, preconscious, and autonomous. As with the rest of our field, the variations in each analyst's and each patient's self-reflective talents and activities are infinite. My focus is on moments and processes in the hour that may stimulate any of us to self-analyze, each in our own way.

While I will be describing aspects of the work that are normally thought to be useful in finding the patient, called by various terms such as "empathy" and "identification," my emphasis will be on the analyst's experience of them and use of them in finding himself, which may then help him find the patient and thus find himself, and so forth.

The vignettes I have chosen are meant to be garden variety examples, which I intend as readily identifiable to anyone with similar experiences in the work. Except for a few brief examples, they are all drawn from work with psychoanalytic patients, and while I will note some differences for the analyst working in psychotherapy as opposed to analysis, I believe the specific phenomena I am describing can be found in either mode of work. I will use the term "countertransference" interchangeably with the "analyst's transferences," borrowing McLaughlin's (1981) usage and his attention to the symmetry between the patient's and the analyst's transferences.

My emphasis is on the ongoing every day activity of the analytic work not on the more dramatic or discrete aspects of it. In the realm of enactment or potential enactment, for example, my focus will not include the more extraordinary enactments that once discovered lead to breakthrough, benefiting both patient and analyst. My emphasis is on a self-inquiry that stems from the analyst's immersion in the kinetic field of the patient's and the analyst's transferences, and on a listening process that is free-floating and freely responsive, able to encompass multiple simultaneous foci in the patient and the analyst, something we have best described only in metaphor.

Processes that are difficult to observe are sometimes more easily seen when they first begin, or when they end. If the insights of endings are impelled by an affective intensity, beginnings sometimes provide a more dispassionate sharpness of observation, not so encumbered by the force fields of transference soon to fill the room. We are familiar with that first glimpse of the patient and the sense of discovery and surprise that infuses the initial hour, a surprise that we seek to nurture as the work becomes more difficult. We are taught to attend to the details of initial hours and initial dreams, which may communicate much of what is to follow.

My first hour with my first control, my first hour with a patient on the couch, took me by surprise. I could not see her face. I too was deprived of things I usually looked at and so would come to look and to see in a different way. The couch alters the analyst's experience.

I still notice that at the beginning of an hour, especially the first hour of the day, I am more aware than usual of my separateness from my patient. I am not yet immersed in the patient's experience, and I can feel the patient's experience and my experience of being with the patient begin to take me over. Both feelings, that of being outside the patient's experience and of being inside it, are essential to the work as I see it.

Some patients do not like the first hour of the day. One was troubled that I entered the waiting room "trailing" my life behind me. It was tempting to assume he was speaking of the experience I have just described, my separateness from him, not yet immersed in his world. But while there was a symmetry in our experience, for I too felt this as a transitional moment from home to office, his meaning had a specificity of its own in his wish not to intrude on my life, his long-felt fear and longing for attention to himself, and his discomfort that I might be with somebody else.

Although we may try to approach every hour with some sense that it is the first or only hour, the first hour of the day with a familiar patient is very different from the first hour with a new patient. Like returning to a novel we have been reading, but not today, there is a feeling of coming back to something familiar, a familiar world of experience for the analyst, familiar transferences between analyst and patient that have an established fact and place in the analyst's life at the moment. We come to know this world a bit better day by day as we extend that "edge of awareness" (Gardner, 1983) of the patient and ourselves.

Because I suspect that some of these experiences depend upon the number of hours an analyst works clinically, I should note that I see patients more or less full time, and the majority of those hours are analytic hours; this is how I spend the major portion of my day. So at the beginning of the day I notice that the work itself has an orienting function. I know myself through my work, these people whom I see for many years, the transference fields I return to that seem, like dreams, to have a separate existence, and yet not so. I know the sorts of feeling and thoughts they stir in me. While those feelings and thoughts are essential to my understanding of my patients, they also become essential to how I think about myself.

SYMMETRIES OF AFFECT AND EXPERIENCE

If there is a continuity between the analyst's analysis and his or her self-analysis that is triggered by engagement with the patient, it must be that the work not only evokes passively experienced thoughts, feelings, and reflections, but also changes the analyst through an extension of insight or other means "beyond catharsis." As "identification *with* the patient must give way to thinking *about* the patient"

(Arlow, 1981 p. 503), in Beres and Arlow's (1974) definition of empathy, so the analyst's responses stirred by that identification may give way to thinking more or less consciously about those responses. Although Arlow (personal communication, 1992) cautions cogently that excessive emphasis during the hour on the analyst's experience may distract him or her from the patient and thus hinder the analytic process—a condition of true countertransference interference—much of what I am describing seems to happen in an instant, the analyst's mind alive simultaneously in multiple directions.

If we speak seldom about the effect on the analyst of brief or extended identifications with the patient, we speak less about the effect of what the analyst brings with him into any given day or hour of the day, as he trails his life behind him, and yet at some level that too must be part of each analyst's instrument and may be the outer layer of an identification that will take place in that hour and lead simultaneously to the patient and to the analyst. If a patient is describing the pain of separation and I have recently left my child at the airport, those feelings are fresh for me too, and I use them for better or worse to understand my patient. But I may also use my patient to understand my own experience. I am talking about my immediate experience for the moment, not experiences hidden or past. I may even feel my loss less acutely or with less sense of aloneness for focusing on the patient's loss. Such moments are volatile and can indeed pull the work toward the analyst's experience and away from the patient.

I began an hour not so long ago at the end of a trying week. A paper rejected; another to prepare. Into this mix late one afternoon came my patient, silent, looking disconsolate. She had had a recent series of spectacular successes, but now couldn't work, couldn't write. She was late, didn't want to be there. I knew how she felt. She said she was tired of conforming to other people's expectations and felt in great pain over it but also—and here her voice rose in energy— also great pleasure in being defiant. Her defiance made her feel less pain and more pleasure. I felt a surge of energy, too. At her mention of defiance, I was borrowing it for a moment, trying it on. It seemed for a moment a solution to my problem, too. As I was immersed in my trial identification—we'll dignify it with a code word—it occurred to me that my patient was also explaining why she was defiantly silent in my office. Realizing with a note of surprise that her view of me was not my view of us—that surprise that is so essential to our work—I said, "It sounds as if I'm on the side of those who want you to conform." She smiled, reflected, and spoke about her mother's expectations, which were large and burdensome for her. As she spoke I felt myself more and more weighed down by the burden of other people's expectations that I realized then had been plaguing me that week as they had been plaguing her. I said, "I think you have had a toxic dose of other people's expectations." She looked astonished and smiled, her spirits lifting for the first time, "A toxic dose." She laughed. While toxic had a special meaning for her, my intervention had come from a point of common affective experience, a composite of my own experience and my sense of her experience. My comment was in some sense a comment to us both. As it turned out, it was useful to us both.

Notice that the hour moves not only through a common affective experience, a symmetry, but also an asymmetry. She does not see me as I see us. Such shifts from the analyst's perspective to the patient's perspective, which prompt a note of surprise at learning something new, shape our work around transference and resistance.

Staying with the immediate for a moment, sometimes I hear a cautionary tale. A patient speaks of pain and neglect as a child, or neglect of a child, and suddenly there are four children in the room: my patient, his child, myself, and mine. I cannot help it. I will think of it again when I next see my own child, who does not always see me at my best after a long day of listening to others.

Sometimes the impact of what a patient says prompts a visual image that is mine and theirs. A patient, blocked from professional success, described with horror a sudden and gruesome injury to a relative in her family. A musician's finger had been mutilated in a lawnmower. He had to be taken to a provincial hospital, his career surely over. As she spoke the image stirred memories of my own: injuries, fantasies of injury, injuries to my parents, illnesses, injuries to my children, a finger cut short, life cut short. My infant son rushed to a small rural hospital. His later illnesses, the terrors stirred, past and present. And I felt how I had slowly pulled away from him and his frailness, pulled away subtly into my work, a race against time, fearing my own life cut short. I had not seen this in relation to my son before, nor with such affective detail, though I knew it from other sources. My patient, a few months older than I, spoke of her fear and horror, and her own inhibited ambition. Soon it would be too late, she said. I said, "You feel as if time is running out." And she began to cry. Again a comment to us both that hung in the air, as her work habits and mine both seemed to shift in the ensuing months. Her work became dramatically more productive and mine perceptibly less driven.

This is a self-inquiry that takes place during the hour, almost in an instant, unbidden. Does it distract me from my work with the patient? I do not always see so clearly into my own experience during an hour, nor do I try to elicit such self-inquiry, but sometimes both my patient's experience and my own spring sharply into view, simultaneously linked and separate, reciprocal inquiries. At such moments I may be most acutely aware of my patient.

We are familiar with the asymmetries of analysis, most dramatic in the outward differences in activity. Thus Friedman (1991) writes, "*Now* we see a patient complaining of pain to a physician. *Now* we see someone with a companion lost in reverie. At *another* time the treatment is one person teasing another, or one person teaching another, etc." Patients from their own perspectives dwell on these asymmetries, sometimes viewing them as inequities. If we look not from the outside but from the inside, however, I am struck by how similar, how symmetrical, the activity seems to be. My patient's effort at free association is my effort at free attention. What my patient feels and thinks invariably invokes a parallel thought or feeling in me.

A man with a profound fear of abandonment, was fearful of my upcoming vacation. "I am dreadfully afraid I don't have any meaning for you and I'm afraid you'll forget me," he said. "I can't get by that. As if it were imprinted." My patient had been given up for adoption as an infant. I said, "Forget you. That you had no meaning for your mother and that she could easily forget you." And then he made it more specific. "I am terrified if I get lost I don't think I'll get found." I said, "Maybe she wouldn't remember to look for you. If you don't mean anything to me, I won't remember to come back." He said, "I don't really believe you're not going to come back, but I really *believe* you're not going to come back."

In the affective intensity of the transference came the specificity of his words, getting lost and being forgotten. I could feel it too. My best friend playing tricks on me. And deeper fears like his. That fear of getting lost and no one coming to find me. Children play on that fear. Just the other day a child told me they were playing hide-and-seek and his friend left him hiding and went to play with someone else. Before I was born, my grandfather wandered into the woods behind our house and got lost. No one came to find him. He spent the night alone. Our work focused on my patient's experience, but the specificity of his words, "If I get lost, I don't think I'll get found," acted like an interpretation—someone else's words, near enough to my own but importantly not my own—to open or reopen a piece of my experience. I continued to remember my patient's words after the hour, an hour in which *he* felt I would forget him.

Hoffmann (1983) speaks of the patient as interpreter of the analyst's experience. I will return to some specific illustrations and some specific disagreements with his point of view. But in the interplay of the patient's and the analyst's inner worlds, the patient's words and the analyst's words may both function as interpretations of the analyst's experience.

There is a parallel here with the reading of novels or the writing of biography. Moraitis (1979) speaks of transferences stirred in writers of biography and in their readers, and he describes "the power of literary works and other artistic products to provide stimuli comparable to those of analytic interpretations" (p. 100). So as the analyst revisits regressive identifications and transferences with each patient, the patient's words may reach into the analyst's regressive experience, functioning as his or her own analyst's words once did to open new avenues of self-inquiry.

The ground we travel may be familiar to us as analysts, but different patients evoke different aspects of it for analysis or reanalysis, sometimes extending work already done, their words and pieces of experience illuminating long dark or recently darkened turnings.

A patient has been asking me to answer a question that has her feeling cornered, confined. She had left my office furious the previous hour, slamming the door. Now she says, "I want to sit up." I ask, "Can you say more about that?" She adds, "Lying here I feel restrained, tied up." Again I ask about it, and she adds a bit more, "It frightens me to think about it. My mother had this thing to tie my arms and legs in. I wonder if that has anything to do with it." I notice her breathing begins to labor. She asks a question, "What's the difference between that and a strait-jacket?" I say, "Not only tied down but your breathing tied too, constricted." And she, "I hated it. I would have struggled and hurt myself, bouncing your body up and down," and she illustrates, bouncing her body up and down on the couch. Then she notices, "I do feel constrained, and I have a tendency to stop breathing."

I think of my son years ago in his zip-up pajamas, his difficulties breathing, and of another patient and her "trundle bundle"; she too was tied in her crib. And then some dim recollection of myself in a bed sack or a Halloween costume unable to get out. My own difficulties breathing. It is stirred too by the image of this grown woman bouncing up and down with its erotic associations for me, not yet for her. I have come upon a distant not quite remembered image. Another patient speaks of the feeling of the crib, the rail, and I can feel or almost feel the wood under my chin, my foot playing the slats.

Will these moments, reminiscent of reawakenings in my own analysis extend themselves further? Were they once more available

and now gone again? Or are they simply remembrances of the more
recent past, of the experience of being in analysis. I do not yet know
at this point. I do know that by them I am put in touch with
something affectively immediate for my patient both in her history
and in the current moment. It attaches me to the work and to what I
will learn about her and about me. As Freud (Masson, 1985) said in
his letter to Fliess, he did not yet know more about himself because
he had not yet learned it from his patients (p. 281).

My fantasy of me confined is my fantasy not hers, but like all such
fantasies it is stirred in part by my patient, and so, as Gardner says,
in finding her I find myself. It is a tactile and visual image, and the
difference between my fantasy and her fantasy, if I could in fact see
her fantasy, must be the difference between her and me. When
patients tell me their dreams, I often picture the dream clearly. But it
is my picture not theirs. As they fill in their picture, the difference
between theirs and mine and the surprise that accompanies what
they tell me, drives my understanding of the patient a bit farther. I am
left with a clearer picture of myself as distinct from my patient.

A patient speaks of fear and excitement as he approaches a
bedroom through a long dark hallway. I picture the bedroom and the
confinement of the hall. I see it. In speaking of it I call it his parents'
bedroom. He corrects me, "It was *my* bedroom." Suddenly *he* springs
to view, his hallway and bedroom. I had been picturing *my* hallway.
The parents were mine. Finding him I find myself, and finding my
parents I find him and the details of his life more precisely.

In these vignettes I have tried to illustrate the continuity between
the analyst's analysis and the self-analytic work that may continue
after analysis, stirred by the unique stimulation of analytic work. The
analyst is oddly dependent upon his patients for this analytic work to
continue. Sometimes in the termination phase of analysis the analyst
can observe the patient refinding old habits of self-reflection
(Gardner, 1987; Hauser and Smith, 1991). I remember rediscovering
old reading habits, familiar during my adolescence. But I also
remember the beginning of the first analytic hour with a patient
following the termination of my training analysis, and the sense of
relief that I would be able to continue to work within an analytic space
that I had found so usefully familiar, even though the participants
and the actual location would be different. Such moments of transi-
tion, terminations and other life crises, can be critical ones for the
analyst in seeking his own way to keep self-inquiry alive.

Gill (1985) argues that the analysis of transference, which he calls
the "central analytic technique," is "applicable in a broader range of
conditions than is often considered the case" (pp. 87–88). Under

"conditions" he includes frequency of sessions and use of the couch. However much we may debate the necessity of these conditions for the analysis of the patient's transference, my experience is that the continuity and depth of regression fostered by an increased frequency, the freedom granted the analyst's focus of attention by the use of the couch, and the length of contemporary analyses, all significantly benefit the analyst in his self-analytic work, including the analysis of his own transference to the patient. In fact the privacy the analyst enjoys in the analytic setting contributes to an environment in which the analyst's associative drift may be freer than the patient's, a factor which may, for better or worse, influence the choice of modality.

THE PATIENT'S PERCEPTION OF THE ANALYST'S ACTIVITY

If the foregoing vignettes illustrate a symmetry of affect and experience, I am also thinking of an inquiry that places analyst and patient in a more deliberate symmetry. Here the aim, in Schwaber's (1986) words, is to suspend "any notion that we already 'know' " in order to "enter another's psychic world" (p. 930). If at moments we can know ourselves only by what the patient tells us, an inquiry into the patient's world and our own may open to the essence of the work and place both analyst and patient equally at risk (Smith, 1990). In *Learning From the Patient*, Casement (1991) too speaks of the analyst's use of "not-knowing," and thus quotes Bion (1974): "In every consulting room there ought to be two rather frightened people; the patient and the psychoanalyst. If they are not, one wonders why they are bothering to find out what everyone else knows" (p. 8).

An older man, whom I have discussed elsewhere (1990, 1993), had been observing me carefully for months. One day he complained that I was "making him work." "How do I do that?" I asked. He answered, "I feel that you say, 'don't be general, don't withdraw.' " Again I asked, "How do I convey that? What do you notice?" He thought and then said, "You don't exactly say 'don't withdraw,' but you comment on my withdrawal," and then he fine-tuned his perception: "You don't tell me to make observations when I'm feeling things; you make the observations when I'm moving away from it."

Conversely he observed, "There's a change in the quality of your voice when I'm talking about sadness or loneliness; you get a tenderness, I feel, that's not there when you're making observations about my withdrawing, and it is more inviting to me."

The most fundamental ingredients of the analytic process, such as choice of words, timing, and affective tone, have specific meaning to every patient. My patient's view of me meant the fulfillment of a wish for direction and a wish for a man who would help him find the sadness of not having had such a man in his life. But as we began to explore his meanings, his observations gave me pause. My interventions at moments when I saw him shift away from affect were felt by him as directives not to withdraw from the experience. Did I intend them as such? Did I want him to learn to observe these moments? Was it my intent to so encourage an affective deepening? And if so was it for his benefit or mine? And what about my "tenderness?"

His observations of me thus evoked a self-inquiry into my responsiveness to him. What had seemed to me careful defense analysis, he experienced as "making him work," and what I felt was ordinary human feeling, I found was not only fueling an enactment but had important personal roots in my own experiences of safety and risk.

I could easily notice moments when I wanted to "make him work," sometimes through my silence, or in commenting, as he noted, on his own "disappearance" from the work. That wish lurked behind my focus on resistance and was expressed through a somewhat heavy-handed application of what I had borrowed from Schwaber (1986), for example, or Gray (1986).

But my "tenderness" took me further. It took me to hours of devoted listening as Semrad interviewed patients in residency. One day I had interviewed a patient in front of him. The other residents commented on how affectively available this young schizophrenic patient had been. "He had some help," Semrad had said, and then, speaking into his tape recorder, he added curtly but gently, "One day Smith will make it his own." I remembered another supervisor remarking how few analysts truly facilitate the deepening of their patient's affective experience. Semrad had always seemed more at home with sadness than with anger. My patient feared his anger most of all. Was I shying away from it?

If my "tenderness" took me to Semrad it also took me to moments of tenderness in my own childhood and the wish to keep that tenderness alive. My patient had had such moments with his mother. But he had told me in our first meeting that his father had not encouraged such feelings and he wanted to "refind his tears."

So here we had a match. My own wishes and his, joining half-conscious technical intent, shaped by supervisory identifications both recent and remote, ran beneath my responsiveness to create an enactment that might have gone unseen had I not inquired into what he noticed about me.

In what seem to me the relatively minor variations of the way I work from patient to patient, or from one day to the next, I sometimes notice the effect of one or another supervisor, teacher, or analyst. In doing analytic work we revisit and renew old and cherished identifications. The compromise formations that shape our work may not always be as stable as we like to think or to promulgate in our sure-footed literature. As in the above example, our identifications may act collusively with the patient's wishes and fears and our own.

This is not to say that my patient's view of me was identical to my view of myself. The analyst has many potential feelings and responses to the patient, and he may find an approximate match for what the patient perceives about him and for what the patient may wish to evoke; and those matchings may indeed fuel the work. But the patient's view of the analyst is not the same as the analyst's view of himself. The patient and the analyst inhabit different if symmetrical perceptual worlds, and the analysis proceeds on the basis of those differences as well as their symmetries.

In enactments of the sort I have just described, I am not speaking of countertransference errors per se, nor of emergency measures such as countertransference confessions. Such confessions almost always seem to me to destroy what Adler (1989) has called the "essential ambiguity" of the analytic space. With Gardner (1991) I cannot quite picture, no matter how "disinterested" the analyst, a completely enactment-free exchange, nor one that is alive without the sort of reciprocity that I have been describing.

Perhaps "enactment," which implies a discrete event in the analytic process, is a misleading word for the sort of phenomena I am describing. I am speaking first of a level of activity inherent in all we do as analysts and embedded in the derivations of the tools of our trade, namely "interventions," meaning literally "to come between," and "interpretations," meaning "to spread abroad." Our metaphor for listening, "evenly hovering attention," itself conveys a sense of contained activity, a readiness balanced in preparation to swoop, act, or intervene.

I believe Renik (1993) is referring to this level of activity when, conceptualizing a continuum between thought and action, he says, "It seems likely that if we could always closely examine the sequence of events by which an analyst becomes aware of his countertransference motivations, we would find that it *invariably* begins with his noting how he has put them, sometimes almost imperceptibly, into action" (p. 137).

While the analyst may, as Renik suggests, invariably need to put his countertransference into action in order to become aware of it, patients inevitably perceive aspects of the analyst's activity or inactivity as actualizations of their own transference. Again, analyst and patient may give different meanings to the analyst's activity. But beyond these differences, it seems to me there are components of activity on the part of the patient and reactivity on the part of the analyst that are intertwined and inherent to the work. The analyst's timing, phrasing, tone of voice, choice of intervention or decision to remain silent, not to mention facial expression before and after the hour, must to some degree be a response to the patient's stimulus. Just as we have long since foregone the notion of the perfectly analyzed analyst, so at this level there would seem to be no truly enactment-free exchange.

The effort not to so "contaminate" the work leads one analyst to write of the preparation for analysis, "During the interviews I attempted to maintain a constancy of facial expression and posture, without being rigid, and an empathic, but relatively nongratifying, optimally frustrating attitude" (Bernstein, 1983, p. 373). Such an effort might purge my voice of the "tenderness" my patient found, but would it not create yet another action sequence with its own potential enactment? Thus Gardner (1991) writes, "I have a rough idea what an enactment is, but I have no idea what an enactment is not," and Boesky (1989) adds, "It is a bit hard to say what is *not* an enactment."

Surely the form, force, and frequency of the analyst's participation makes a difference, as does the degree to which the analyst is unwittingly abetting the process, as I was to some extent with my "tenderness." But at the level I am describing, enactment would seem to be ubiquitous, a component of transference that results from the interactive aspect of the analytic relationship, or, for that matter, any other relationship.

Rather than discrete moments of enactment, then, we are speaking of ongoing components of enactment throughout the work, and rather than speaking of enactments solely as interference, we might begin to describe multiple functions of enactment within the analytic process, a taxonomy of enactment, if you will. Boesky (1990) has begun to do this in viewing "certain behaviors of the analyst, which actually join in the creation of a 'useful' resistance, as a creative contribution which is necessary only for that analyst to make and would not be necessary for another analyst" (p. 573). He adds, "If the analyst does not get emotionally involved sooner or later in a manner that he had not intended, the analysis will not proceed to a successful conclusion" (see also Bird, 1972).

The question then becomes not the descriptive one, "When is it an enactment," but the dynamic one, "What is its function," and the technical one, "Which enactments are analyzable and which are not." To the extent that the analyst is engaged in the enactment and cannot recognize his or her own participation, that would tend toward an unanalyzable event. Nevertheless, the analyst's goal would seem to be not solely to refrain from enactment, which is an unattainable and "misconceived" technical ideal, in Renik's terms. A driven attempt to do so would inhibit the work, constituting a countertransference interference in its own right. Rather, the goal might be to try to observe the enactments or potential enactments that are taking place at all times and to analyze them. By "analyze them" I am referring to the analysis of the patient's transference and the analyst's private analysis of his or her own transferences as they come into awareness. To what extent the analyst's private self-analysis takes place unbidden during the hour, and to what extent it takes place outside the hour, will vary according to judgment, personal idiosyncrasy, and other involuntary factors. In time we may add descriptively to the taxonomy of enactments and their functions. Toward all of these goals, the examination of the patient's perception of the analyst's behaviors and activities, which Schwaber (1986) and Gill (1982) from separate perspectives have both advocated, would seem to prove useful.

But the analyst may resist such scrutiny. Patients such as the man I have just described, who have been observing me carefully for many years, may finally make their observations known with persistence, intense affect, and considerable detail. Like living with an adolescent, the moment is an opportunity, not always welcome, for new growth.

Searles (1975) speaks of a patient who was trying to cure him (and the patient's depressed mother) of his "characterologic inability to express undisguised, unambivalent enthusiasm for the contribution the other person has made" (p. 389). As if illustrating his difficulty, Searles adds wryly, "Although his therapeutic help had not proved sufficient to enable me appreciably to resolve the problem, he had helped me to confront it much more clearly than I characteristically do" (p. 390). All analysts confront and avoid confronting their own resistances to the analytic work, including whatever characterologic impediments prevent their working optimally, hearing the patient clearly, or interpreting more accurately. Paraphrasing Gill (1982), some of these difficulties stem from the analyst's resistance to the awareness of, or the immediacy of, his or her own transferences. Such resistance may manifest itself as resistance to engagement with the patient or resistance to awareness of the engagement that is ongoing. If the patient resists the analytic work and the encounter with the analyst in the transference, the analyst resists the engagement with the patient's conflicts, the encounter with the patient, and the continued analysis of the analyst's own transferences and resistance.

Sometimes the analyst may sense that he is repeatedly confronting his own resistance. My patient who was sure I would forget her was one of three patients in a row that day who questioned whether they had any meaning for me. To be sure there were external stimuli, a forthcoming interruption, for example, in the schedule. But was there also something I was encouraging, or hearing preferentially? Even when the work is going well, the analyst will continually be confronted with the limitations of his or her own character (as well as its benefits), and patients may explicitly or implicitly call attention to aspects of the analyst's character that limit his capacity to engage, stir his tendency to withdraw, or stimulate him to respond impulsively to their wishes.

THE ANALYSIS OF AN ENACTMENT

In the following vignette I shall describe a more complex but no less symmetrical interaction between patient and analyst. Specifically, I want to demonstrate how the patient and the analyst each perceives what is being enacted between them and how those perceptions then become part of the analysis of the patient's transference and the analyst's own self-inquiry.

My patient, an academic in the fourth year of his analysis, began to talk about wanting to terminate. He noted that money was not the real issue, but he had been having difficulty paying the bill ever since I had raised the fee. "You know there is a reality to this money business," he would say. Each time he returned to the issue of money as if it were "beyond interpretation," I felt annoyed. He had often questioned how he could ever know if I cared about him, since he paid me to do it. I felt he was "torturing" me with this now. Couldn't he see he was angry about the fee increase?

As we traveled these familiar paths, I tried to study my own reactions, and he kept returning to the issue of money. I was anxious about his leaving too soon. Would he have a real termination? I clearly preferred that he continue his analysis. I recognized both my annoyance and my anxiety as familiar "signal" functions that invariably led me to myself and thence back to the patient.

And then I remembered my own termination. How important the "reality" factors had begun to feel, not only as a financial pinch but also and inseparably out of some sense of growth and attachment to my life. What he was telling me sounded similar. Who was I to say how he should leave?

But as he persisted, and as I failed in my attempts at interpretation, or as my patience failed, I began to think about what to do. And so I thought, why not remind him of our agreement that if his circumstances change, the fee can be adjusted in either direction.

At the time I had several minds about this. I noted a hint of triumph: if it was a "reality," deal with it as a reality. More dispassionately I thought it might be useful to disengage the issues of money and termination, so that we could look at them separately. Then I thought, he has such ambivalence about whether I care, how I care, how important money is to me, it may be useful for him to consider the fact that I even bring this up. And then: this was indeed part of our contract, why does he not bring it up?

I was patient, to a degree. I allowed these thoughts and feelings and many others to sift through my mind during and after the hours for several weeks, a familiar background as we tried to analyze his current dilemma and his conflict over his attachment to me.

The month after the fee had been renegotiated he had for the first time paid less than the full amount. Recently he had begun to pay in smaller increments. I wondered aloud if there was meaning to these new payment schedules. He asserted that he had thought about the various ways of coping with his financial constraints and had decided that, rather than waiting until he had the full amount, he would pay me as soon and as much as his own cash flow permitted. Then he wondered whether I, like his father, was unable to accept what he offered and could only engage in criticism of him.

One day, in the midst of such a discussion, I said, "It has seemed more difficult for you to pay the bill since the fee increase. If the increase was unmanageable or if your circumstances should change in the future the fee can be readjusted as we agreed."

There is a character in one of John Le Carré's novels who says, "Sometimes . . . our actions are questions, not answers." That was my intent. But if every intervention has an action component some are more active than others. This was literally an intervening, a "coming between" his linking of money with termination, his use of money as an active issue in the transference. If an enactment was sealed at this point, I want to illustrate what unfolded, how the patient experienced my intervention, and how his experience matched my own and yet remained his own. We might think of analysis (both the analysis of the patient and the analyst's self-analysis) moving forward as patient and analyst work their way into and out of such entanglements, or try to avoid their occurrence.

He responded, "That's nice. Thank you." Then, after commenting again on his cash flow, he paused and said, "I'm waiting for something. I don't know what. Something from you. I felt that was real thoughtful of you, but there is a part that says, 'Oh, he just wants to keep me coming longer.' " Remember I had been anxious about his leaving too soon.

But then he made an interpretation of defense: "I went to that because it was hard to tolerate the feeling that you were doing something for me, giving to me, thinking of me, so I had to find a way to discount it." Or was his interpretation a defense? At any rate here was another of my motives that had led to my intervention, namely that he might explore this issue of my caring.

I asked, "What made it hard to tolerate?" And he elaborated:

> The idea you care about me, care about my situation. Such a concrete way you could be helpful. It makes me realize how helpful you've been to me. I think, why would I want to leave that? I feel like so many times I have to search for ways that you are there, and when it comes in a concrete way, I don't know what to do with it. This felt like an extra.

For a number of weeks we examined the patient's experience of my intervention and the history of that experience in the analysis and in his past, as he remembered and relived it now in the transference. I was struck by how he continued to retrace or to discover specific affective currents that were remarkably similar to those I had felt prior to making my intervention.

He found them in his own terms, his experience not mine. Thus he felt that I must want him to stay, but why would I want *him*? Perhaps, like his parents, I was overly cautious, not wanting him to risk a brave move. This must be my way of saying I did not think he was ready to leave. Or perhaps, like his mother, I wanted him to stay for my own reasons. He had felt obligated to attend to her wishes and her need for him.

I *did* have my own reasons, my own concerns about his analysis and my own attachment to him that resonated with earlier attachments of mine. As he spoke I could sense his parents' caution, his caution, and my own. His father's caution, similar to my father's caution, similar to mine. His mother's attachment, similar to my mother's attachment, similar to mine. As Hoffmann (1983) says, "Because the analyst is human, he is likely to have in his repertoire a blueprint for approximately the emotional response that the patient's transference dictates and that response is likely to be elicited, whether consciously or unconsciously" (p. 413). On the other hand, I have some reservations, to which I will return, about reducing so complex a process to terms like "dictate" and "elicit."

Meanwhile my patient was ambivalent about accepting my "offer." He felt he might owe me some allegiance, as he had with his mother. He wished he could love me as freely as he did a few others in his life. If only loving me didn't make him feel so uncomfortable.

Three weeks after my comment, he decided to continue wrestling with his anxiety over my "kindness" by asking that his fee be reduced, for two months, to the one we had started with at the beginning of the analysis. His request set off a new wave of feelings in me; at first: surprise and annoyance. He had not been speaking of so large a decrease. Why was he asking for more?

When I didn't answer him immediately, his anxiety and distress were palpable. He became annoyed. Perhaps like his father I made offers and then withdrew them. He was afraid he'd done something wrong in not being able to pay. As much as I'd talked about reducing it, I must be resentful. I said, "You've asked for too much?" He said, "Yeah that's my worry, asked for too much, and will I get slapped down?" Again I could feel the pressure to act, and when I finally said, "I can manage the fee you have suggested for two months," his relief was marked: "That's great. That will be an enormous help."

And then a curious thing happened. The anger I had sensed in him began to surface. He yawned and began to feel that he couldn't be as sarcastic and provocative as he would like. He had stifled a "nasty" comment about my clothing because I might get hurt. "Something suggests I'm easily hurt?" I asked, and he answered, "Your gentleness, which is such a great part of who you are . . . Can you be gentle and tough at the same time? I guess I've felt that you are. Do I need to get *to* you in some way?" And he spoke of how polite he had always felt he had to be with me and with his parents.

Now he felt a new wave of misgivings about the fee reduction and his consequent "obligation" to me. Over the next several days he seemed subtly more depressed and passive, less interested in sex or in earning more money. We came back repeatedly to my initial comment about lowering the fee as the precipitant for this change in his mood.

One day I found myself annoyed again; he lay there so needfully, and I thought in the hour and following it of my own parents, my

own father's withdrawal, preoccupations, withholding. How attentive I had been to my own mother's needs. How fearful she had been
of my leaving. How fearful I had been of leaving her. I saw her again,
lying on her death bed. I had been with her the night she died. My
mother in front of me. My patient in front of me. He and his mother,
I and mine. Symmetries, and yet so different. In finding myself again,
I could see him more clearly, separate from me, and it seemed to free
us both. The hour that followed broke new ground in our understanding of the preceding weeks. He led the way.

My patient arrived and said he had been thinking maybe I *had* to
make the offer. Like his father I didn't really want to. I asked if it
made it less threatening to think of it that way, and he said, "Yes.
Less choice on your part, less involvement, less caring. Maybe you
care about me. I don't know what to do with that. I want to run away
from it."

I asked, "What is it about my involvement or caring, I wonder, that
you want to run away from?" He said, "It's a new experience for me.
I have no model for it, for being cared about by a man." And then he
spoke of a dream he had had the previous night about a woman with
whom he had once felt tempted to have an affair. He said, "I wish it
was me *now* instead of me *then*. How did I get off on this? Maybe the
sexual stuff about caring for someone and their thinking of caring for
you. Is that what I'm scared of here?" The "sexual stuff" had long
been a source of conflict for him in his feelings about me.

He spoke of feeling bothered when he felt attracted to "certain
men, still ill at ease." I said, "And these thoughts are prompted by my
involvement and caring?"

He said, "Maybe. It's felt to me like that's something I would have
to go through here, have to experience. This is such an intimate
connection, so why wouldn't it?"

I said, "And something brings it up now, today." His responses
had felt tentative, cautious, "intellectual," as he had put it. I could feel
myself reaching to ground them in the immediate moment, trying to
find a link to the present moment between us. And in response to my
comment he made that link, with a shift that took the previous six
weeks of work to a deeper and more specific level, a specific
perception of my intervention in which he seemed to find me and to
find himself simultaneously. He said, "I think I've been confused
about why I'm having such trouble with your doing something for
me. It feels as if you're doing something *to* me, sticking it to me."

"Sticking it?" I said. He said, "Yeah, ugh. He's doing this, and I've
got to feel I owe him. He's doing this to me, making me feel this
way."

I said, "I wonder what it is exactly that feels like I'm sticking it to you . . . maybe something in the way I suggested it." And he, with great conviction: "I thought I had a way out and you took that away. *Not that I would have left.* But for a while I was thinking, well I can't afford it."

Beyond the confirmatory clarity of his erotic "sticking it to me," I was struck by his perception of that first moment when my "sticking it to him" had been conceived. He was expressing his version of my sense that I had taken away his "excuse" for leaving. But, even more, his corrective, "Not that I would have left," spoke without his being aware of it to my first and primary anxiety about his leaving. At the time when it had seemed inevitable that he would leave, I had felt responsible for seeing that he do it properly, and it had evoked my own anxiety over separation.

I answered, "Yes, I can see that I didn't allow you to use the money to entertain the notion of leaving." He said, "I did for a little bit but not as much as I wanted to. Maybe I would have come to the idea of lowering the fee. But it wasn't my idea it was yours" (this was manifestly true.) "I don't want to leave feeling it was unfinished, but when is it ever finished anyway?" (Remember my thought, "Who am I to say how he should leave?") "I really didn't get to toy with the idea." (I had wanted him to stop toying with *me*.) "I didn't even get to act out a little bit."

In time we explored again the erotic component of "sticking it to" and "toying with," but for now he was somewhere else, and there was a marked relaxation in his posture and voice. He thought of children who misbehave, "driving their mothers crazy," and then wistfully, "I never got to be bad as a kid. I wish I was."

At this level of engagement it is a reciprocal process. Analyst and patient are shaped moment to moment by the work, which then becomes the instrument to shape their own inquiries. I learn about him and from him, and privately I learn about myself.

My patient has found the matrix out of which my intervention had been conceived, but his discoveries have personal meaning and his perceptions of my intervention are different from my perceptions, however similar the affective resonance. Such moments simultaneously clarify elements of the patient's transference, the analyst's transference or countertransference, and the not-quite-conscious agendas each hold for the work.

I had long been aware of feeling pleasure in his freedom to be "bad," to take greater risks, but in this kind of "badness" I was vulnerable, when it came to his "subverting" an analytic termination. Being vulnerable I failed to see that I was subverting his freedom to "toy with the idea" of being bad. As his wish to be bad and his fear of being criticized met my fear of criticism and my wish that he analyze and not act, an enactment was created.

His comment, "Not that I would have left," spoke to a mutual anxiety over separation, uniquely experienced by each of us. We were not done with this aspect of the transference by a long shot. The following week his sense of me as mother still filled the room. He felt I was "helping him stay but not helping him go," and then in a moment that terrified him, he felt held to the couch, pulled through the couch, pulled as if his back would break, an experience that echoed uncannily the details of my own mother's recent death, and my anguish over the loss of her. I realized at that moment with a start the degree to which my attachment and loss loomed over this period of my work with him, helping me find him and his attachment to his mother and to me, and making it difficult for me to let him go (see also Smith, 1992).

We will never know how the sequence I have just described might have unfolded had I not intervened with my offer to lower the fee. As I have already indicated, I believe that every intervention participates in potential or ongoing enactments. The most neutral interpretation, combined with an analyst's wish to have an "effect" on the patient, can be the seed for enactment. The very "rightness" of an intervention and the patient's response to it must be multiply determined and play into multiple potential enactments, inviting similar attention to the patient's and the analyst's experience.

I have tried to illustrate an examination of the patient's perception of the analyst's activity within a transference–countertransference matrix that I find often underlies the work. Every aspect of the patient's transference, including the patient's perception of the analyst's activity, may have a correspondence in the analyst's countertransference, but the analyst's experience and the patient's perception of that experience, however similar, are not the same. Hoffmann's view is akin to this:

> . . . the patient's idea of the interaction of the transference and the countertransference . . . is likely to include a rough approximation of the quality if not the quantity of the actual countertransference. It is in this element of correspondence between the patient's idea of the countertransference and the actual countertransference that the elusive interface of the intrapsychic and the interpersonal lies [p. 413].

But here is also where we differ. If Hoffman's notion of an "actual" countertransference, like Gill's (1982) of the "actual situation," implies that the analyst is in a position to "know" in some absolute sense what is "actual," he attributes a degree of objectivity to the analyst's perspective that may limit inquiry and belie his own assertion of the analyst's sustained uncertainty. I should add that Hoffmann's (1991) recent work, outlining a "social-constructivist" paradigm, moves far beyond this criticism. My experience is more in keeping again with Adler's (1989) essential ambiguity: "Is it I or is it you," and rarely does the question have an answer. As I pursue my experience and my patient's experience, I discover "I *and* you," separately and together.

Nor do I agree with Hoffman's (1983) view that the "analyst's objectivity," as he terms it, "enables the analyst to work to create another kind of interpersonal relationship" (p. 414). It seems to me sufficient that the analyst analyze the transference and whatever transference enactments may be analyzable, toward the further understanding of the patient and of himself. A "new experience" will inevitably result, but one that will differ in important respects from the one the analyst might have "worked to create." The attempt to "create" such an experience must be seen as shaping that very experience, and, like the effort to purge the analyst of all self-revealing responses, such an attempt would inevitably join analyst and patient in another series of resistances and enactments.

In the vignettes I have chosen I have tried to illustrate different sorts of engagements in the analytic work and different uses of those engagements toward extending the analyst's self-analysis. I am not suggesting that one form of engagement is necessarily "better" than another. There are many simultaneous foci for the analyst's attention. If an analyst can be "nimble," as Valenstein (personal communication) puts it, to move from one focus to another, it may allow him to intervene in multiple ways and to use different stimuli for his own self-inquiry.

Nor am I recommending a particular intensity of engagement. Naturally the patient's experience in this regard, as in others, may be quite different from the analyst's experience. One patient finds me "two-dimensional" when I am feeling most responsive, and "three-dimensional" when I am quite peacefully silent.

We customarily imagine that the way we listen shapes what we hear and hence how we intervene. I would suggest that the reverse is also true. How we intervene may determine what we hear and hence how the work shapes us. Thus, if different techniques shape the analyst in different ways, we might speak not only of analysts gravitating to different technical preferences and, therefore, of the influence of the analyst's character on technique, but also of the influence of technique on the analyst's character.

A TERMINATION DREAM

In the preceding vignettes I have described various engagements around symmetries of affect and experience, symmetries of image and fantasy, of experience in the transference field, and a kind of symmetrical methodology that places the analyst's free attention on a parallel with the patient's free association and the analyst's self-analytic work on a parallel with the analysis of the patient's transference.

We are familiar with those moments when the patient's words almost uncannily match the analyst's thought or image. At such moments Simon (1981) sees patient and analyst reaching across some communicative impasse, as my patient and I may have been when he felt as if his back would break. We are familiar with the shared language of analysis (Gedo, 1984; Poland, 1986) that develops as patient and analyst find their own vocabulary. To complete our sweep from beginnings to endings and to illustrate further that reaching across, which may take place more frequently at moments of immediate or impending separation, I want to present one final vignette.

In the termination with my first control we were both, for a time unknown to me, stretching to continue the work with a shared language not yet conscious. I have mentioned her already: my first analytic hour, when I was surprised I could not see her.

Four nights before we were to end, I dreamed that my patient had come for her final appointment and that it was to take place in the living room of a house in an expensive ocean-side suburb. Two men came in and sat with us. While they talked and joked loudly, my patient and I, sitting at a distance from each other, tried to conduct our last meeting face to face. I left the room to ask someone in another part of the house to ask the two men to leave. When I returned they had already left. My patient called me by my nickname and said, "I think I'm getting to like this town." She sounded like Mae West. I went outside and asked another man where my wife was. I was told she was leaving on a boat.

It was a most unusual dream for me. In fact it felt quite unfamiliar to me. Later I came to recognize personal themes embedded in the dream work, but at the time they were well disguised. What made the dream so effective a screen was that it did not feel like my dream at all. It felt like one of my patient's dreams in its imagery and narrative style. In short I felt for the moment as if I had dreamed her dream, not mine at all. It seemed that in separating from her I was taking some of her with me, shaping the narrative style of my dream in imitation of her dreams, not only dreaming *about* her but dreaming as she did.

To my surprise, two days after my "termination dream," as if she were associating to my dream, which of course she knew nothing about, she spoke about staying in touch with me through her dreams, adding that she had done so during previous interruptions.

My patient had been a prolific and creative dreamer. I had long since realized that I would remember her in part for her dreams. But she had never told me the details of those particular dreams of separation; when I had asked, she had "forgotten" them. Now she said they were dreams in which she and I had become friends, so that she might keep me with her. But I was the one who, two nights earlier, had dreamed of her becoming *my* friend. Had I dreamed her missing dream? Now on the next to last day of her analysis, she remembered leaving for college and leaving behind her childhood best friend, "the first person I left that I cared about."

When I reflected on my dream, multiple preconscious and manifest symmetries, stimulated by the affective pressure of termination, came clear. I shall mention only a few for illustration. My patient and I both had a sister with whom we were very close. Coincidentally her sister and mine shared the same first name. We both separated from our sisters when they went to college. For us both it was a painful separation. But for me and my sister the separation brought us closer.

Like my patient I had had a best friend, who when I was 10 had moved away from me to the same oceanside town that now appeared in my dream. Like my patient and her best friend we used to pretend we were twins. He had been my first friend, a friend from age 2, the first person I had lost that I cared about.

At a party many years ago, celebrating child psychiatry residents who were graduating and those like myself just beginning, I had mentioned this lost friend to an analyst who was about to supervise me in my residency. A "latency trauma" he had called it. That analyst was now, many years later, the supervisor of this case. Now I would be losing him too.

There was more. For my patient the theme of seeing and being seen was a dominant conflict in the work. But remember my sense of deprivation at not being able to see her during her first hour on the couch? In my dream we were sitting face to face. That was how we had begun, in our initial evaluation sessions. At that time it was a necessity. As in my dream there was no couch in my office at the time of her evaluation. She was my first control, and my recently purchased couch had not yet arrived. She had noticed and asked, "Am I your first person?"

When I met with my supervisor to discuss the final week of the
analysis I told him my dream. By now the analysis was over. We had
ended it as we had begun, my patient on the couch. But my
supervisor told me that he had suggested that we end face to face. I
had forgotten his advice but followed it in my dream. And while I do
not now, given the choice, terminate analyses face to face, at the time
I was too moved by the termination even to remember his advice. The
truth was, I would have felt too exposed.

Here then was my sense of loss, my difficulty in giving up the
relationship with my patient and with my supervisor, and with others
who had gone before. In my dream I was trying to protect the privacy
of my patient's analysis and yet holding on, however ambivalently, to
our relationship in the face of her termination. We both now seemed
to wish that our relationship would and would not end, would be
something it was not, that our separation might bring us closer.

My dream was a compromise formation that had borrowed some
of the narrative style of her dreams to express my conflicting wishes
and fears, and, strangely, hers. My dream seemed to contain elements of her intrapsychic life and mine, simultaneously intertwined
and yet discrete.

In her first meetings with me she had asked, "Am I your first
person?" Later, she had wanted to be my "first person to stop," so
that I would be sure to remember her. In the transference I had
become her "first person," her mother, her sister, almost a twin, her
best friend. In my associations to my dream she had reminded me of
my sister and of my first friend and of my first loss of a friend I had
loved.

My dream was a signal to me in the final week that allowed me to
allow her more fully to leave and to continue her analysis to the end.
But my dream stayed with me as a continuing stimulus to think about
her, about my work with her, and about myself, three areas of parallel
inquiry that spring from engagements in analysis and their use in
self-analysis.

REFERENCES

Adler, G. (1989), Transitional phenomena, projective identification, and the essential
ambiguity of the psychoanalytic situation. *Psychoanal. Quart.*, 58:81–104.
Arlow, J. A. (1981), Theories of pathogenesis. *Psychoanal. Quart.*, 50:488–514.
Beres, D. & Arlow, J. A. (1974), Fantasy and identification in empathy. *Psychoanal.
Quart.*, 43:26–50.
Bernstein, S. B. (1983), Treatment preparatory to psychoanalysis. *J. Amer. Psychoanal.
Assn.*, 31:363–390.

Bion, W. R. (1974), *Brazilian Lectures, 1.* Rio de Janiero: Imago.

Bird, B. (1972), Notes on transference: Universal phenomenon and the hardest part of psychoanalysis. *J. Amer. Psychoanal. Assn.*, 20:267–301.

Boesky, D. (1989), Enactment, acting out, and considerations of reality. Panel presentation at annual meeting of American Psychoanalytic Association, San Francisco, May 1989.

_____ (1990), The psychoanalytic process and its components. *Psychoanal. Quart.*, 59:550–584.

Calder, K. T. (1980), An analyst's self-analysis. *J. Amer. Psychoanal. Assn.*, 28:5–20.

Casement, P. J. (1991), *Learning from the Patient*. New York: The Guilford Press.

deMause, L. (1975), The evolution of childhood. In: *The History of Childhood*, ed. L. deMause. New York: Harper & Row.

Friedman, L. (1991), Why risk danger? Presented at the Paul G. Myerson Symposium on Psychotherapy, Boston, April 12.

Gardner, M. R. (1983), *Self Inquiry*. Hillsdale, NJ: The Analytic Press, 1988.

_____ (1987), Sexuality, neurosis, and analysis. Panel presentation, annual meeting of American Psychoanalytic Association, Chicago, May 1987.

_____ (1991), A discussion of Dr. Theodore Jacobs' paper, "The Interplay of Enactments." Combined meeting of the Boston Psychoanalytic Institute and Society and the Psychoanalytic Institute of New England, East, Cambridge, MA, January 25.

Gedo, J. E. (1984), Treatment as the development of a shared language. In: *Psychoanalysis and Its Discontents*. New York: The Guilford Press.

Gill, M. M. (1982), *Analysis of Transference*. New York: IUP.

_____ (1985), The interactional aspect of transference: Range of application. In: *Transference in Psychotherapy: Clinical Management*. ed. E. A. Schwaber. New York: IUP, pp. 87–102.

Gray, P. (1986), On helping analysands observe intrapsychic activity. In: *Psychoanalysis: The Science of Mental Conflict*, ed. A. D. Richards & M. S. Willick. Hillsdale, NJ: The Analytic Press, pp. 245–262.

Hauser, S. T. & Smith, H. F. (1991), The development and experience of affect in adolescence. *J. Amer. Psychoanal. Assn.*, 39 (Suppl.):131–165.

Hoffman, I. Z. (1983), The patient as interpreter of the analyst's experience. *Contemporary Psychoanal.*, 19:389–422.

_____ (1991), Discussion: Toward a social-constructivist view of the psychoanalytic situation. *Psychoanal. Dial.*, 1:74–105.

Jacobs, T. J. (1991), *The Use of the Self*. Madison, CT: IUP.

Loewald, H. W. (1960), On the therapeutic action of psychoanalysis. In: *Papers on Psychoanalysis*. New Haven, CT: Yale University Press, 1980, pp. 221–256.

Masson, J., ed. (1985), *The Complete Letters of Sigmund Freud to Wilhelm Fliess, 1887–1904*. Cambridge, MA: Harvard University Press.

McLaughlin, J. T. (1981), Transference, psychic reality, and countertransference. *Psychoanal. Quart.*, 50:639–664.

_____ (1988), The analyst's insights. *Psychoanal. Quart.*, 57:370–388.

Moraitis, G. (1979), A psychoanalyst's journey into a historian's world: An experiment in collaboration. In: *Introspection in Biography*, ed. S. H. Baron & C. Pletsch. Hillsdale, NJ: The Analytic Press, 1985.

Poland. W. S. (1986), The analyst's words. *Psychoanal. Quart.*, 55:244–272.

_____ (1988), Insight and the analytic dyad. *Psychoanal. Quart.*, 57:341–369.

Renik, O. (1993), Countertransference enactment and the psychoanalytic process. In: *Psychic Structure and Psychic Change*, ed. M. Horowitz, O. Kernberg & E. Weinshel. Madison, CT: IUP, pp. 135–158.

Schafer, R. (1983), The psychoanalyst's empathic activity. In: *The Analytic Attitude*. New York: Basic Books.

Schwaber, E. A. (1986), Reconstruction and perceptual experience: Further thoughts on psychoanalytic listening. *J. Amer. Psychoanal. Assn.*, 34:911–932.

Searles, H. F. (1975), The patient as therapist to his analyst. In: *Countertransference and Related Subjects*. New York: IUP, 1979, pp. 380–459.

Simon, B. (1981), Confluence of visual image between patient and analyst: Communication of failed communication. *Psychoanal. Inq.*, 1:471–488.

Smith, H. F. (1990), Cues: The perceptual edge of the transference. *Internat. J. Psycho-Anal.*, 71:219–228.

――― (1992), Analytic listening and the experience of surprise. Panel Presentation, annual meeting of American Psychoanalytic Association, Washington, DC, May 1992.

――― (1993), The analytic surface and the discovery of enactment. *The Annual of Psychoanalysis*, Vol. 21. Hillsdale, NJ: The Analytic Press, pp. 243–255.

Sonnenberg, S. M. (1991), The analyst's self-analysis and its impact on clinical work: A comment on the sources and importance of personal insights. *J. Amer. Psychoanal. Assn.*, 39:687–704.

III

MODES OF SELF-ANALYTIC ACTIVITY

Wolf comments on the perpetuation among present-day analysts of Freud's life-long ambivalence about the efficacy of self-analysis. "More than half a century after Freud's death we are still gripped by the same ambivalence: we pay lip service to the great value of self-analytic endeavors but we rarely report the data that would justify our faith." Wolf attempts to provide such data from his self-analysis of a taboo.

Following Kramer's conceptualization, Wolf distinguishes between two modes of self-analysis: deliberate, conscious attempts (such as Freud's systematic analysis of his dreams) versus spontaneous, unconsciously initiated self-analytic activity (such as Wolf's response to the eruption of surprising symptomatic behavior).

The inhibitions and intense anxiety occurred when Wolf, a German-born Jew who fled to the United States during the Holocaust, returned to Germany 27 years later (see Eifermann, chap. 9). As his self-analysis proceeds, he gradually becomes aware of the relationship between his symptoms and the existence within himself and his friends of a taboo against talking candidly about what happened to them during the Nazi era.

Wolf's narrative suggests the interplay of self as experiencer and self as observer. He oscillates between experience-near, phenomenological description and experience-distant, abstract conceptualization growing out of a self-psychological perspective. His self-analysis,

guided by his assumptions (see Bernardi and de León, chap. 2), leads
to his fuller awareness of the selfobject functions served by Germany
and the Germans, of the self pathology that resulted from the
traumatic disruption of those functions, and of their role in the
creation of the "German taboo."

Wolf's self-analysis leads further in his associations to the arche-
typal incest taboo. He wonders whether he has displaced anxiety
related to the incest taboo onto his German taboo, but concludes
otherwise. Again demonstrating the interplay of experiencing, observing (and theorizing), he states:

> . . . my self-analytic exploration of my (and others') taboo about
> discussing what happened to me (or them) during the Nazi era reveals
> not a displacement of an incest taboo rooted in the Oedipus complex
> but a displacement of my fragmentation anxiety resulting from a fear of
> disconnectedness.

In his discussion, Wolf comments on the relationship between
self-analysis and self-revelation in doing and writing about analytic
work. He feels that analysts have been excessively concerned about
anonymity, and also slow to recognize "the subtle power of the
patient's subjective experience of the analyst." Nevertheless he
advocates a cautious approach and expresses the hope that analysts
may become "less afraid of being somewhat more self-revealing."

Wolf suggests that we accept the impossibility of being a blank
screen.

> From a practical pragmatic point of view the analysand will always
> make observations of his or her analyst that will somehow skew the
> transference at least a little. Therefore, since the exposure of the analyst
> to the analysand cannot be avoided altogether, it seems more reason-
> able to accept and regulate it than to totally deny its occurrence.

Implicit in Wolf's comments is the view of transference as largely
emanating from within the patient, although subject to being
"skewed" by the analyst's countertransference. Wolf's conceptualization takes a narrower view of countertransference, and differs in
emphasis from that of several other contributors to this volume (e.g.,
McLaughlin, chap. 4, Smith, chap 5, Poland, chap. 11) who explore
aspects of the transference as joint creations (enactments) of patient
and analyst. Wolf recognizes that further conceptualization "of the
intra-analytic interaction between analyst and analysand is required

for a rational approach to self-revealing discussions of countertransference reactions as well as self-analytic events."

As is the case with Wolf, Gedo finds that he does not actively
initiate his most intense self-analytic experiences. Whereas Sonnenberg (chap. 12) engages in a more deliberate, systematic form of
self-inquiry, Gedo's more impactful experiences are "auto-analytic,"
to use Kramer's term, and come unbidden. They are set in motion by
significant personal stresses or crises which challenge his previous
adaptations.

> . . . they go into operation only in case of dire necessity. Whenever I
> have tried to evoke them as a matter of conscious volition, the nature of
> the subsequent psychological processes was utterly different—not
> necessarily less useful, but lacking in the automaticity and unbroken
> impetus that characterize the more crucial episodes.

Unlike Margulies, McLaughlin, and Smith, who find analytic work
to be a major stimulus of their ongoing self-analyses, Gedo discovers
that for him transference–countertransference dilemmas and resulting enactments lead to more routine forms of self-analysis (compared to emergent personal circumstances). He notes that these less
affectively charged episodes provide insufficient motivation for the
sustained self-analysis necessary to overcome strong resistances. He
adds that the analyst's self-analytic efforts, while he or she is engaged
with the patient, are necessarily limited and circumscribed in order to
maintain the proper focus on the patient's inner world. Gedo does
not, however, refer to the equivalent of "transference sanctuaries"
(McLaughlin) outside of the analytic situation during which the
analyst can pursue his or her self-inquiry.

In speaking of the relationship of self-analysis to self-revelation in
the analytic situation, he warns against the analyst's inappropriately
or prematurely sharing the fruits of his or her self-analytic labors with
the patient: ". . . one should have the conclusions of a piece of self-
inquiry ready-to-hand before attempting to communicate them to a
patient." Other analysts (e.g., Margulies, chap. 3, McLaughlin, chap.
4, Gardner chap. 8), in this volume emphasize the tentative nature of
the analyst's "conclusions" which may be at considerable variance with
the patient's perceptions and experiences of the analyst.

Modifying Isakower's phrase, the "analytic instrument" Gedo
speaks of the "self-analytic instrument" as a capacity developed in the
course of his personal analysis. Furthermore he suggests that attaining such a capacity should be the primary goal of analytic
treatment.

While being enthusiastic about the possibilities of self-analysis, Gedo is also mindful of its limitations. He points to the difficulty of proceeding in self-analysis without some form of consensual validation (which he discovered in the writings of Gardner). He reminds us of the utility of consulting with colleagues, and of the necessity of returning to treatment when at an impasse in dealing with more archaic issues, but concludes:

> Despite these caveats, the cumulative results of continuing self-inquiry can be far-reaching. In my own case, I suspect that I have changed more decisively in the decades since I terminated my personal analysis than I did during that treatment. Yet, as I have already stated, it was the experience of the analysis that made subsequent self-analysis possible for me.

Gardner takes issue with the very term "self-analysis" which he feels connotes a misleading identity or similarity with dyadic analysis. He prefers instead the term "self inquiry" which means for him "something different from, and somewhere in between, some aspects of psychoanalysis and ordinary introspection."

Both self-analysis and self-inquiry are abstractions, generic terms encompassing various approaches to self-understanding. Our necessary attempt to put these approaches into words sometimes makes static and reifies what is an ongoing process. In his description of the vicissitudes of his visual impressions as they shape and are shaped by shifts in his internal world, Gardner succeeds in conveying an alive sense of that process. As was the case with Winnicott, Gardner feels that self-inquiry proceeds best in an atmosphere of play.

Gardner identifies different points of entry into his self-inquires. One is the auto-analytic. "Often . . . some current event catches my attention, and seems unaccountably and irresistibly to demand consideration. As a rule, through no conscious plan, I seem strongly to prefer as a starting point these conditions of the immediate, the inadvertent, and the demanding." Another is more systematic and relies on journal-keeping, although in a somewhat passive–receptive mode, rather than a more active conscious effort to focus on dreams, daydreams, or conflicts. He records "whatever is most vividly on my mind or, as it sometimes seems, whatever is hardest to get off my mind." Frequently the starting point is some strong visual impression. The third point of entry is the stimulus of doing analytic work. In contrast to Gedo, Gardner finds what he experiences in the analytic encounter as providing "the most consistently fruitful" material for his self-analytic efforts.

No matter how the process begins, Gardner finds that it proceeds from something primarily visual, an inchoate, rapidly changing mix of images and words to something that is still mixed but becomes more verbal-ideational to something that he tries more actively to make sense of. This last stage is primarily, but not exclusively, verbal. Gardner is aware that this scheme, while useful in helping us think about stages and boundaries, does violence to the fluidity of the process. He emphasizes that there is no final interpretative resting place. Today's interpretations are tomorrow's associations, and vice versa.

His description of this self-analytic process does bear many similarities to the demands of the dyadic analytic process, with patient and analyst involved in a complex interplay of experiencing and observing. The self-analytic process involves similar shifts. As Gedo emphasizes, a reasonably successful experience in analysis, partly through identification with the analyst and internalization of the "analyzing instrument," enables us to make those shifts more reliably and nimbly. Because of these multiple identifications, as Gardner points out, even in self-analysis we are not solitary. "I can't escape the impression that in self-analysis, as in other moments of talking to ourselves, we're rarely if ever alone. Of talkers and listeners there are many."

Just as Bernardi and de León (chap. 2) explore the ways in which our unexamined assumptions (including our customary modes of processing sensory information) may facilitate or inhibit our self-analytic inquiries, Gardner looks at the effects of what we think we know on our ability to discover something new about ourselves. How do we forget what we know? Is such forgetting possible? His playing with the idea of forgetting leads him spatially to the image of placing knowledge in the back of his head and temporally to the memory of being a child running ahead of his parents, but all the time knowing they were there watching over him. He suggests that we reenact this drama of separation and rapprochement and create a kind of transitional space when we allow ourselves to forget (i.e., to let our knowledge and customary way of seeing recede) so that we can see in a new way, without losing our way altogether.

As Gardner indicates, self-analysis takes place slowly, when it takes place at all, depending on the ebb and flow of our defenses. Gardner, like Gedo, emphasizes both the limitations and the value of self-analysis. He acknowledges its utility in unraveling countertransference complexities, but is unimpressed by its self-therapeutic potential. He appreciates its pleasure-giving qualities as it sharpens our awareness of our subjectivities and their relationship to the creativity of everyday life. Gardner suggests that the ultimate value of self-analysis may lie in its "search of the relation between observer and observed" and by extension between self and other.

6

Self-Analysis of a Taboo

Ernest S. Wolf

"Because we practice our virtues mostly with conscious intent but are taken unawares by our failures, the former rarely give us real pleasure while the latter constantly keep us in need and torment. Herein lies the most difficult moment of self recognition, making it almost impossible" (Goethe, 1812-13, p. 523, my translation). Goethe's sentiments about the difficulties in confronting oneself are mirrored by Freud writing to Fliess in 1897:

> My self-analysis is still interrupted. I have now seen why. I can only analyze myself with objectively acquired knowledge (as if I were a stranger); self-analysis is really impossible; otherwise there would be no illness. As I have come across some puzzles in my own case, it is bound to hold up the self-analysis" [Freud, 1887–1902, pp. 234–235].

Freud (1935) repeated his self-analytic skepticism near the end of his life: "But in self-analysis the danger of incompleteness is particularly great. One is too soon satisfied with a part explanation, behind which resistance may easily be keeping back something that is more important perhaps" (p. 234).

Yet for all these warnings, Freud's (1914) ambivalence about the value of self-analysis manifested as a kind of cautious recommendation: "[self-analysis] may suffice for anyone who is a good dreamer and not too abnormal" (p. 20).

And he recommended:

> One learns psycho-analysis on oneself, by studying one's own person-
> ality. This is not quite the same thing as what is called self-observa-
> tion . . . Nevertheless, there are definite limits to progress by this
> method. One advances much further if one is analysed oneself by a
> practiced analyst [Freud, 1915–1916, p. 19].

More than half a century after Freud's death we are still gripped by
the same ambivalence: we pay lip service to the great value of
self-analytic endeavors but we rarely report the data that would
justify our faith.

Self-analysis has been defined by Laplanche and Pontalis (1973, p.
413) as the investigation of oneself by oneself, conducted in a more or
less systematic fashion and utilizing certain techniques of the psychoanalytic method, such as free association, dream analysis, and the
interpretation of behavior. Such a definition carries with it all the
uncertainties and controversies that have developed regarding the
appropriate theories and methods that can properly be called psychoanalytic. Leaving aside such controversies, however, we must distinguish between two quite different processes that have both been
described by analysts as self-analytic. One such process is the
conscious and deliberate attempt to analyze oneself when one has
discovered one's own symptoms as either recurring or, as may
happen at times, when the discovered symptoms are seemingly being
created de novo. Perhaps, the most frequent occasion for an analyst
to seek recourse to such self-analytic activity is the unpleasant finding
of some countertransference attitude that interferes with the proper
conduct of the analytic work. Freud used such deliberate self-analytic
techniques in developing the theories that created psychoanalysis,
especially when trying to fathom the meaning of his dreams and
methods for their interpretation. "I soon saw the necessity of carrying
out a self-analysis, and this I did with the help of a series of my own
dreams which led me back through all the events of my childhood"
(Freud, 1914, p. 20)

There is, however, a second, and apparently therapeutically more
effective self-analytic method that does not depend on the deliberate
and conscious efforts of the analyst. This second type of self-analytic
activity is initiated unconsciously and occurs spontaneously. It
catches the analyst by surprise, so to speak, though it occurs only
when the analyst has been well analyzed already and is chronically in
a state of unconscious but alert readiness for self-observations. I

believe Freud (1910) was referring to this type of self-analysis when he stated: ". . . we have noticed that no psycho-analyst goes further than his own complexes and internal resistances permit; and we consequently require that he shall begin his activity with a self-analysis and continually carry it deeper while he is making his observations on his patients" (p. 145).

Twenty-seven years later Freud (1937) was still able to say, in spite of much expressed caution about the efficacy of self-analysis: ". . . but we reckon on the stimuli that he has received in his own analysis not ceasing when it ends and on the process of remodeling the ego continuing spontaneously in the analyzed subject and making use of all subsequent experiences in this newly acquired sense" (p. 249).

Reik (1948) similarly observed spontaneously received insights. Kramer (1959) showed that such nonvolitional processes of spontaneous self-observation do indeed occur and she designated the self-analytic function thus described as "autoanalytic":

". . . the capacity to integrate unconscious conflicts in the form of insight can become an independent ego function, which for purposes of this communication I shall call autoanalytic. . . . The non-volitional nature of the autoanalytic function was demonstrated to me repeatedly by the emergence of analytic insights when I was not actively seeking them" [p. 18].

Kramer contrasted conscious and deliberate efforts at postanalytic self-analysis:

In self-analysis, the analytic understanding of such reactions [e.g., transference feelings] can be accomplished, as in the analytic situation, by self-interpretation. . . . In identification with the analyst in his capacity as interpreter, the same procedure is followed as during the analysis, with the important difference of being patient and analyst at the same time. For example, when I tried to interpret a dream or a counter-transference reaction, I used free association, interpreted defenses, and often arrived at an understanding of the dream, counter-transference reaction, or whatever else I was trying to analyze. . . . The process described applies to all situations where resistances can be overcome by the methods enumerated. . . . [Superego promptings] to continue the analytic efforts lead to further awareness of the frustrating power of resistances. One often has to admit defeat. . . . There also occurred quite different, seemingly spontaneous experiences. . . [p. 18-19].

Kramer then proceeded to elaborate an extensive discussion of the latter, the spontaneously generated autoanalytic function. In my discussion of the self-analytic functions I shall follow the usage introduced by Kramer in designating the deliberate and conscious attempts to analyze oneself as "self-interpretation" while designating the unconscious and spontaneous occurrence of self-revealing insight or behavior as "autoanalytic."

Generally it seems to be assumed that all self-analysis, whether self-interpretative or autoanalytic, can take place only after the usually customary formal analytic situation has ended. This assumption, however, bears closer examination and, perhaps, some modification. It is true, of course, that an analysand during the usual analytic session is not likely to take over from the analyst and begin to follow his or her own associations to dreams, parapraxes, or other self-observations. Yet, we cannot make this an absolute statement because some analysts might well encourage such self-analytic activity in preparation for postanalytic life. As the planned termination of the regular analysis approaches, some analysts will try to facilitate the development of the analysand's self-analytic function, especially if the analysand is a future analyst. Thus some analysands will be helped to get into the habit of self-interpretation of dreams and other self-observations. Furthermore, and this is of greater importance, one can expect that a successful analytic experience will have altered the structure of the self to result in a more cohesive and stronger self as well as in diminished defensiveness. Consequently, the self will be more open to formerly repressed or disavowed aspects of the self that now will be more efficacious in exerting their influence on the self's behavior and self-experience, but without necessarily reaching self-awareness. The spontaneous discovery by an analysand of a sudden new freedom of action and a deepening feeling, together with the recognition of the dynamic factors that brought about the change, must be called autoanalytic whether it comes about during or after an analytic hour. I realize that some analysts would claim that such changes occur only as a consequence of the analyst's analytic activity in the analysis and could not have occurred without the analysis. But even granting that, I would insist that not all the dynamic changes occurring in an analysis are solely the result of the analyst's actions. Indeed, even in the face of my conviction that all dynamic events require the active participation of both analyst and analysand, it must be granted that for some of the intrapsychic as well as the interpersonal events the initiator is clearly the analysand. In these latter cases we must therefore speak of self-analytic events.

SELF-ANALYSIS OF A TABOO

Having emigrated from Germany just before World War II because of the increasing threats of anti-Semitic violence, and because of other unconscious factors that are the subject of this essay, I felt a fearful and angry reluctance to ever set foot on German soil again. This reluctance became an overwhelming anathema when, after the war, the full extent of the Holocaust that I had barely escaped was revealed. Naturally, and in retrospect naïvely, I ascribed my Germany-shunning attitude to the Nazi horrors that had taken place there and from which any decent human being would want to distance himself, both figuratively and literally. In my new home, the United States, I had become an American in every respect, but it was not, of course, my birthplace. Propelled by ambition and by family tradition—a great uncle and a cousin had been admired physicians— I aimed to follow a medical-academic career and, during the fourth decade of my life, found myself in analytic training. I had become a physician, then a psychiatrist, and finally a psychoanalyst. Twenty-seven years after leaving Germany I made my first trip back to Europe and had planned to include a brief five-day excursion to the city in Germany where I had grown up. Consciously, the reason for this brief German journey was that I wanted to show my American wife where my family had lived, where I had gone to school, and what the city and countryside looked like. I remembered the beauty of the woods and mountains and rivers as clearly as I remembered the ugly behavior of my high-school classmates. Nor could I forget the deathly panic and fright that I might be arrested and sent to a concentration camp. There had been the terror of Krystallnacht, when I saw our synagogue burned to the ground and close relatives beaten and sent to concentration camps. A panicky anxiety had hung over me constantly during those last few months until the moment that the train carried me across the Belgian border into Western Europe on my way to America.

So, here it was 27 years later. For decades now there had been peace, and our former enemies had become valued allies. While planning our trip I was aware of a certain ambivalence, a mixture of curiosity and the old detestation, but, I reassured myself, surely I had nothing to fear now. I was driving a rented car as we were approaching the German border from Holland when suddenly I could not drive anymore. I could see the border post with its barriers. The border police were stopping cars and questioning the people inside before letting them through. I was paralyzed. I told myself that I must be afraid of the police, of any possible contact with them. I speculated on the reason for my paralyzing fear, wondering whether I was afraid, perhaps in the unlikely event that I might commit a traffic offense, that I would have to talk to a German policeman. That thought was totally unnerving. I could not drive in Germany. I moved over and my wife drove. Under the circumstances there was no denying that my fear leading to my inability to drive in Germany was a neurotic symptom. There was no real danger. I explained the symptom to myself and to her as being an expression in the here-and-now of a recurrence of the old fear of the Nazi police. That seemed reasonable enough. But there were other symptoms. When ordering a meal in a restaurant I suddenly could not get myself to speak German and could speak only English. I explained that to myself as my not wanting to be identified as anyone but an American. In the light of past history that also seemed reasonable enough. However, our whole visit was less than satisfying, and by leaving Germany the next day we cut short the planned five-day sojourn. I breathed a sigh of relief as I again crossed the border going west.

The symptoms did not recur during subsequent visits to Germany, which primarily involved attending professional conferences and giving lectures. I should have wondered about this "cure" of my fears but I did not. I got to know a number of German colleagues and some became real friends. I did notice, however, that though I lectured in German and though it was obviously known to everybody that I had been born and had lived in Germany, no one asked me anything about that. Questions such as "Where did you live?" or "How did you get out?" were never asked. It seemed as if there were an unwritten taboo that did not permit any mentioning of my German background or, indeed, any personal questions. I did not notice then that I seemed to obey the same taboo, that in conversation with my German friends I never mentioned anything pertaining to my personal history before emigrating. Evidently, my fear of driving in Germany and of speaking German had become displaced onto a taboo that forbade talking about my German past.

A case presentation at one of these professional meetings proved to be a decisive stimulus to my becoming aware of my peculiar self-imposed reticence. Central to the neurotic symptoms of the patient being presented was an upsetting absence of information, an ignorance in the patient's mind about his father's doings and where-abouts during the war. The patient suspected something terrible because the children were definitely not allowed to ask questions about the parent's activities during the Hitler era. How the parents comported themselves during the Hitler years was as taboo for the children as the parents' sex life. In the course of the treatment it then was revealed that the father (or maybe it was the grandfather, I cannot recall clearly) had indeed been a Nazi general. The psychological trauma to the patient, however, it seemed to me, was more linked to the all-encompassing family ambience of secrecy and taboo that interfered with easy communication between parents and children than to the possibly frightening content of the withheld information per se. In the discussion following the case presentation it emerged that this type of suppression of personal information about the role of family members during the Nazi era apparently was very common and not infrequently was thought to lead to neurosis.

As I was listening to the presentation and discussion of this case, I suddenly and unexpectedly became aware of the very similar structure of an aspect of my relationship to my German friends: apparently we all obeyed the same taboo forbidding talk about the Nazi era either by them or by me. What were they afraid of? Were they ashamed to reveal that, indeed, they had participated in perpetrating the Holocaust? I could not believe that, particularly since most of them were small children or not even born at the time. And what about me? Was I afraid to find out that they were Nazis or Nazi sympathizers? That also seemed unlikely. The self-analytic process had been started. I did not make it a deliberate task to observe slips and parapraxes nor did I make a particular effort to analyze my dreams. But I became consciously aware, gradually, of a yearning to be closer, more intimate with my German colleagues while at the same time feeling ashamed of this longing. As I thought about my unconscious motivation to do away with the taboo about talking of the Nazi era, it occurred to me that it was I who had chosen the word "taboo" to characterize this phenomenon, and in a deliberate self-analytic inquiry I immediately associated to the incest taboo. As I will discuss more extensively below, I see the incest taboo as only partially referring to a prohibition of intergenerational sexuality. It also is manifested by a taboo on asking parents about their sexual life, especially the sexual activity they have with each other. I believe that the more important trauma for the child is not the castration anxiety in connection with oedipal wishes nor the frustration and humiliation because the parents forbid or ridicule the child's sexuality. The psychic trauma arises from the parents' unwillingness or even violent rejection of the child's longing to participate in the parents' most intimate moments of closeness. The child is not even permitted to ask or talk about the parent's intimate sex life. When parents close the door to their bedroom they are not frustrating their youngsters sexually nor threatening them with castration, but they may be depriving them of needed selfobject experiences that confirm the child's self as securely belonging to the family. Children need and long for the affirmation of being part of the family group. Lichtenberg (1989, p. 116–24) distinguishes attachment, the selfobject experience of being affirmed by individuals, from affiliation, the selfobject experience that emanates from being part of a family:

> The motivation for attachment involves the experience of pleasure in intimacy, . . . The motivation for affiliation is, I believe, precisely the same. The experience of pleasure in intimacy that begins with mother, father, or both at some point has as its corollary a pleasure in intimacy with the family [Lichtenberg, 1989, p. 118].

> The psychoanalytic studies that bear on affiliation generally approach it from its negative or pathological aspect, whereas I regard the motivation for affiliation to be as integral to development and as universal in its occurrence as that of attachment. I believe that a latent value judgment in favor of individuality has led to a negative twist that psychoanalytic theorists have given to belonging [Lichtenberg, 1989, p. 117].

Lichtenberg calls attention to the central importance of affiliation experiences during self-development and I am in full agreement with that, and I would emphasize particularly the need for such experiences for organizing and structuring the self. The experience of belongingness appears to be a fundamental selfobject experience. On further self-analysis, therefore, my thoughts and feelings were suggestive of my experiencing my German colleagues as if I were a child and they were parents who lived in a longed-for different and secret world that was forbidden to me to enter or even to know about. Unconsciously, Germany was my parent's bedroom and all Germans had become parental transference figures. In childhood being excluded was felt traumatically as being deprived of the kind of needed experiences that confirm one's identity and one's right to belong. No wonder then that I had to deny any unconscious aspirations to belong to Germany for fear of being humiliatingly rejected again, and had to assert loudly and proudly my new identity as an American to the point of not being able to speak German.

Now, in retrospect, I could also understand my initial inability to drive into Germany as an expression of my fear of entering the parent's exclusively intimate privacy. An intense need to be affirmed as belonging was overcome by an even greater need to avoid the experience of rejection and fragmentation that comes with being ejected by the needed parental selfobjects. By institutionalizing the protective avoidance one creates a taboo. It is not an unusual phenomenon to displace to a group or to a country the very powerful transferences that initially arise from the experiences that one has with one's parents. The fact that many people refer to their country of origin and its language as "my fatherland" or "my motherland" and "my mother-tongue" testifies to the ubiquity of this transference experience. Yet, when writing this paper, I was surprised to realize that I rarely ever use these terms, certainly not in connection to myself and, like Eifermann (1987, p. 250) may refer to German as "my first language" but never as "my mother tongue." Here again a taboo on using a seemingly innocuous word indicates my denial of a longing for an intimate selfobject experience.

I want to mention here the experience of continuity in time as one further selfobject experience because I believe, as Kohut did, that it is of crucial importance in the establishment and maintenance of a cohesive sense of self.

> We search for the continuity. "How was I when I was a little boy?" "How were you when you were a little girl?" "What did you do?" "Tell me about me," we ask. "Did I really say clever things? Was I bad sometimes?" It doesn't matter what the questions are exactly. The importance of these questions is not so much to investigate the past because of old conflicts that have become unconscious and still bother you, but to establish the continuity of the self via the reflecting eyes of the selfobject. The excitement of such questions is not an object-instinctual one, i.e., "I love you mom and once wanted to sleep with you." The excitement is the knowledge of me, me, me. You saw me, you held me. Tell me about it. It's the me that's the important issue, and that I was important to you and that you remember that and that you can tell me about it. Groups likewise need that sense of connectedness along the time axis . . ." [Kohut, 1985, p. 236].

The time axis that Kohut talks about here does not start at birth but extends way beyond one's own individual lifetime into the past and also into the future. My emigration had disturbed to the point of denial one aspect of my roots into the past, the German aspect of my roots. No longer could I proudly feel that Goethe and Schiller, that Bach and Beethoven were a part of me also. Yes, I still could admire these cultural heroes at a distance, but I could no longer feel that intimate connectedness that one has with one's family. And it was not fear of an unforeseeable persecution and Holocaust, but precisely that I could no longer feel that my self had a future as a German self that, as a 15-year-old, I decided to emigrate. The very intimate connection between that decision and my sense of self, recognized by me only decades later, made my first postwar visit to Germany in

1966 a particularly poignant and potentially pathogenetic event. Thus to my unconscious yearning to again belong and be connected must be added the urge to overcome a discontinuity in my self and to reestablish a continuous time axis for my self, into the distant past and into the unfathomable future, that included not only my roots and destiny as an American Jew but also my roots and destiny as a German. It must have been a very fragile self, precariously balanced on the threshold of an unknown and unknowable future, that protected its cohesion by suddenly not being able to drive into the fatherland or to speak its mother tongue. It is interesting to note that in a recent paper Eifermann (1987), who also was a German-Jewish refugee, had made analogous discoveries during a period of self-analysis following a visit to Germany. Using the language of object-relations, she says:

> . . . I first discovered, and later on, in the course of my self-analysis rediscovered, that I had been relating to Germany and Germans in ways that largely correspond to transference relationships as they occur in the analytic situation, and that my ways of relating were unconsciously driven by deep ambivalences. My self-analysis revealed that I had, to a large extent, unconsciously regarded my Munich audience – and in fact everybody and everything German – not in terms of who or what they are, but rather in terms of unconscious fantasies related to "good" and "bad" aspects of my internalized love objects and their derivatives [Eifermann, 1987, pp. 246–247].

The evidence presented here for the displacement to one's country of origin and its people of parental transferences will probably not arouse much question though my particular self-psychologically based self-analytic formulation of the dynamics may not be as easily accepted. Therefore, I will elaborate briefly:

The self-sustaining functions of selfobject experiences are needed for life but the form of these experiences changes age-appropriately. Thus the neonate's or infant's need to be held and soothed as a confirmation of its self will take a different form during adulthood (Wolf, 1988, pp. 53–54). Similarly, the child's need for confirmation may at times be satisfied by the experience of belonging to the source of most selfobject experiences, namely, the family. The family as a group may substitute for missing or faulty selfobject experiences with individuals, for example, with a parent or a sibling.[1] In the adult the

---

[1]The experience of belonging to one's family, of having a secure place within the constellation of father, mother, siblings, and other members of a family, all of whom

need for this type of confirmation is no longer dependent on the most intimate group, the family, but may be satisfied by the experience of belonging to more distantly valued groups, such as, for example, one's professional organization, or one's religious community, or, of course, one's country and people. An intense emotional involvement with certain groups is usually explained by the attraction that is held by the ideas of the group and by the values it stands for. Rarely does the individual get a glimpse into the mostly unconscious yearnings for needed selfobject experiences provided by the group. It is only when the needed selfobject experience is missing that symptoms, often very puzzling symptoms associated with such a state of disconnectedness from one's selfobjects, call attention to the fact that not all is well in the emotional household. Eifermann (1987, p. 247) describes this disconnected state very well when she recalls her symptomatic difficulties in reading to her German audience. She read very slowly, tripped over the text, mispronounced, struggled to decipher words, put the emphasis on the wrong place in some sentences, was hardly able to look at the audience. She finally self-analyzed and explained it to herself as an acting out of being a little girl. Indeed, I would add, a little girl with a fragmented self, feeling discomfort and embarrassment (Eifermann, 1986, p. 248).

I can imagine many colleagues going along with my self-psychological self-analysis of my symptoms but then thinking that I had not gone far enough. They might propose that I have resisted facing up to the oedipal-libidinal aspects of my collusion with the German taboo that forbids talking candidly about the Nazi era. I would have to admit that my own self-analytic association to the incest taboo and the associated taboo on discussing one's parents' sex life with them suggests the need to take a closer look at the incest taboo.

Freud (1887–1902; letter to Fliess of May 31, 1897, Draft N) had mentioned that the "horror of incest . . . is based on the fact that, as a result of community of sexual life (even in childhood), the members of a family hold together permanently and become incapable of contact with strangers. Thus incest is anti-social—civilization consists in this progressive renunciation" (pp. 209–10).

---

accept each other as unquestionably belonging in spite of other differences, may be one of the normally needed early developmental experiences without which a cohesive self cannot become established. Such a belongingness selfobject experience contains elements of mirroring and elements of alter-ego selfobject experiences but deserves to be mentioned separately.

And again, in 1905 in the *Three Essays on Sexuality,* he wrote:

No doubt the simplest course for the child would be to choose as his sexual objects the same persons whom, since childhood, he has loved with what may be described as damped-down libido. But by postponing of sexual maturation, time has been gained in which the child can erect, among other restraints on sexuality, the barrier against incest, and can thus take up into himself the moral precepts which expressly exclude from his object choice, as being blood relations, the persons whom he has loved in his childhood. Respect for this barrier is essentially a cultural demand made by society. . . . Psychoanalytic investigation shows, however, how intensely the individual struggles with the temptation to incest during his period of growth and how frequently the barrier is transgressed in fantasies and even in reality [p. 225f].

Freud's last mention of the incest taboo was in 1939 shortly before his death: "The first form of a social organization came about with a renunciation of instinct, . . . Thus the taboo on incest . . . came about" (p. 82).

Freud believed consistently that the oedipal impulse was a most powerful one and that only the strongest prohibitions could hold it in check. Anxiety, whether from fear of castration or from superego punishment was held to be an ever-present threat that was needed to keep the oedipal impulse from transgressing into forbidden actions. The incest taboo in this conceptualization is rooted in the social threat of castration followed by the renunciation of the forbidden oedipal desire. So unshakable was Freud's belief in the dominance of the infantile sexual desire that he overlooked clinical evidence that he himself had presented, evidence for the overriding importance of the needed presence of others who by their soothing demeanor command the child's love. Only a short page away from his description of the "struggle with temptation to incest," he had noted in a footnote

. . . a three-year-old boy whom I once heard calling out of a dark room: "Auntie, speak to me! I'm frightened because it's so dark." His aunt answered him: "What good would that do? You can't see me." "That doesn't matter," replied the child, "if anyone speaks, it gets light." Thus what he was afraid of was not the dark, but the absence of someone he loved; and he could feel sure of being soothed as soon as he had evidence of that person's presence [Freud, 1905,p. 224f].

Today I would conceptualize that the boy clearly indicated the need for the presence of a soothing other who by her very presence would provide him with a selfobject experience that was needed for the continued cohesion of his fragile self. I think Freud apparently realized later that this little vignette did not show anything about the boy's sexual desires having led to his anxiety, for in 1920 he added the following to the footnote:

> One of the most important results of psychoanalytic research is this discovery that neurotic anxiety arises out of libido, that it is the product of a transformation of it, and that it is thus related to it in the same kind of way as vinegar is to wine. A further discussion of this problem will be found in my Introductory Lectures on Psycho-Analysis (1916–17), Lecture xxv, though even there, it must be confessed, the question is not finally cleared up [Freud, 1905, p. 224f].

Indeed, it seems that the question was never finally cleared up. It is with these considerations in mind, then, that I must restate what is revealed by my self-analytic exploration of my own (and others') taboo about discussing what happened to me (or them) during the Nazi era. It is not a displacement of an incest taboo rooted in the Oedipus complex that is revealed but a displacement of my fragmentation anxiety resulting from a fear of disconnectedness.

DISCUSSION

Freud's self-analysis was the most important in the history of psychoanalysis. It led him to have those deep and perhaps poignant experiences that became the fundamental insights out of which psychoanalysis was constructed. Clearly, self-analysis is not only a therapeutic activity for the self but also remains a fountain of creativeness as well as a testing ground where the new ideas may prove themselves. Considering the essential role of self-analysis in the initiation and continuing development of the psychoanalytic enterprise, the analytic literature on self-analysis is meager. There are good reasons for this scarcity. In their capacity as clinical psychotherapists, analysts need to maintain a high degree of anonymity in order to facilitate the emergence and the detection of transference phenomena. In this respect the analyst optimally resembles a Rorschach inkblot: the more ambiguous the image, the more revealing the description projected onto it. In their effort to remain hidden, therefore, self-revelations by psychoanalysts to their analysands or through their written contributions via the psychoanalytic literature, are thought of as poor technique, or worse, as countertransference acting out, and have become unacceptable.

These concerns have contributed to the relative scarcity of psycho-analytic literature dealing with such a central topic. The same considerations discourage the publication of self-revealing observa-tions of countertransference reactions. Quite aside from a reluctance to expose oneself, particularly when the circumstances favor a less than flattering view of oneself, there are also weighty objections on theoretical and clinical grounds against lifting the veil that protects the analyst's relative anonymity. I will argue here that such analytic anonymity has been overdone even though I know that there exist serious dangers of contaminating the purity of the clinical transfer-ence. From a practical pragmatic point of view the analysand will always make observations of his or her analyst that will somehow skew the transference at least a little. Therefore, since the exposure of the analyst to the analysand cannot be avoided altogether, it seems more reasonable to accept and regulate it than to totally deny its occurrence. Some conceptualization of the intra-analytic interaction between analyst and analysand is required for a rational approach to self-revealing discussions of both countertransference reactions as well as self-analytic events. Only with such a conceptualization of what has occurred is it possible to estimate the impact on the analysand and on the course of the analysis. It has been my experience that a rigidly principled anonymity of the analyst—such as refusal to answer some personal questions or the omission of average socially expectable behavior, for example, congratulations on the occasion of major achievements, is easily perceived or misperceived by the analysand. Let it be understood, however, that advocating a less rigidly anonymous response constitutes no license to do or say anything that pleases the analyst in the false belief that it can all be analyzed away later.

It is only in recent years that Kohutian ideas have sensitized analysts to the subtle power of the patient's subjective experience of the analyst per se. The inevitability of the analysand's experiencing not only transferences from the past but also reactions to the reality of the analyst in the here-and-now brings the anonymity of the analyst dangerously close to being experienced as a disruptive nonrespon-siveness. It is to be hoped that the influence of Kohutian self psychology will make analysts less afraid of being somewhat more self-revealing, both in the privacy of their consulting rooms as well as in print. We should follow Freud's good example.

The fruitfulness of self-analytic work has been commented on by Kohut (1966). He recalled that

> Freud described his famous self-analysis as a veering back and forth
> between alternating phases of insight concerning himself and of

comprehensions concerning his patients. "We see . . ." said Ernst Kris in his introduction to Freud's Letters to Wilhelm Fliess (Freud, 1887–1902), "how he [Freud] went on to use the insights gained in his self-analysis in the analysis of his patients: and how in turn he applied what he learned from his patients to further his understanding of his own pre-history [p. 419].

Kohut believed that the self-analytic function was so important to the clinical practice of psychoanalysis that he made a special point of bringing this insight to his students:

Since no training analysis can ever approach completeness . . . the self-analytic function of the student must be observed and their autonomy must be evaluated. During this phase, there is also a chance for the removal of endopsychic obstacles that stand in the way of continuing self-analysis, as, for example, through the demonstration of persistent infantile reliance on the training analyst as the sole interpreter of neurotic disturbances [pp. 421–422].

In the spirit of Freud's construction of psychoanalysis out of self-analytic experiences and insights, it should be an accepted task of all analysts to carry on self-analytic activities with the aim of further developing and modifying the structure that Freud built. In this spirit, Kohut's self-analytic experiences and insights, gained throughout his life as an analyst, but especially during periods of narcissistic vulnerability, allowed him to add some new rooms to the building started by Freud.

CAPACITY FOR SELF-ANALYSIS

An essential element of all analytic work consists of expanding the realm of consciousness. Specifically, clinical psychoanalysis augments conscious awareness at the expense of unconscious content that is made accessible after having been hidden behind defenses. The more an analyst is able to shed defensive attitudes, particularly regarding himself or herself (i.e., his self or her self), the more the unconscious becomes available for an exploration by the self-analytic function. Self-analytic capacity, therefore, depends on the reduction of one's defensive armor which in turn has come about by successful analytic work. The point of all this apparently circular reasoning is the old truism: the most effective analyses of self or of others are performed by the best analyzed analysts. Age and experience are important factors. As an analyst goes about doing the daily analytic work with analysands, a certain amount of more or less conscious self-analytic activity is a regular by-product. Thus, over the years, as the analyst's own analysis proceeds, the defensiveness ameliorates and the unconscious becomes increasingly available. At the same time, the analyst is probably becoming more secure professionally and socially, and more self-assertive. All this translates into being less afraid to take an honest look at one's self.

REFERENCES

Eifermann, R. R. (1986), "Germany" and "Germans": Acting out fantasies, and their discovery in self-analysis. *Internat. Rev. Psycho-Anal.*, 14:245–262.

Freud, S. (1887–1902) *The Origins of Psychoanalysis: Letters to Wilhelm Fliess, Drafts and Notes: 1887–1902.* New York: Basic Books, 1954.

_____ (1905), Three essays on sexuality. *Standard Edition*, 7:135–243. London: Hogarth Press, 1953.

_____ (1910), The future prospects of psycho-analytic therapy. *Standard Edition*, 11:141–151. London: Hogarth Press, 1957.

_____ (1914) On the history of the psycho-analytic movement. *Standard Edition*, 14:7–66. London: Hogarth Press, 1957.

_____ (1915–1916), Introductory lectures on psycho-analysis. *Standard Edition*, 15–16. London: Hogarth Press, 1963.

_____ (1935), The subtleties of faulty action. *Standard Edition*, 22:233–235. London: Hogarth Press, 1964.

_____ (1937), Analysis terminable and interminable. *Standard Edition*, 23:216–253. London: Hogarth Press, 1964.

_____ (1939), Moses and monotheism. *Standard Edition*, 23:7–137. London: Hogarth Press, 1964.

Goethe, J. W. (1812–13), Dichtung und Wahrheit. In: *Werke*, Vol. 5, part 3, 13th book. Frankfurt: Insel.

Kohut, H. (1966), Discussion of "Termination of Training Analysis" by L. G. de Alvarez de Toledo, Leon Grinberg & Marie Langer. In: *The Search for the Self*, Vol. 1, ed. P. Ornstein. New York: IUP, pp. 409–422.

_____ (1985), *Self Psychology and the Humanities*, ed. C. Strozier. New York: Norton.

Kramer, M. (1959), On the continuation of the analytic process after psycho-analysis. *Internat. J. Psycho-Anal.* 40:17–25.

Laplanche, J. & Pontalis, J.-B. (1973), *The Language of Psychoanalysis*. New York: Norton.

Lichtenberg, J. D. (1989), *Psychoanalysis and Motivation*. Hillsdale, NJ: The Analytic Press.

Reik, T. (1948), *Listening with the Third Ear*. New York: Farrar, Straus.

Wolf, E. S. (1988), *Treating the Self*. New York: Guilford Press.

7

On Fastball Pitching, Astronomical Clocks, and Self-Cognition

John E. Gedo

Some years ago, I was invited to deliver a Radó Lecture to the Columbia University Institute for Psychoanalytic Training and Research. This event was scheduled to take place at the New York Academy of Medicine, and my hosts insisted that I wear a tuxedo for the occasion. The night before I left for New York, I had a dream that struck me as so fitting that I decided to share it with the audience at the start of my presentation. After the lecture, more than one person complimented me on the clever joke in the form of a pseudodream they thought I had concocted. Of course, I knew that these misperceptions were trivial—I had, indeed, created the manifest dream—but I found it difficult to grasp how anyone could see these matters as comic.

In my dream, I was at Yankee Stadium. I was wearing a baseball uniform and warming up in preparation for the start of the World Series. I realized that I was the pitcher Ron Guidry, who was supposed to lead the New York Yankees to the championship. A number of sportswriters approached me, and one of them asked, "Is it true that you have the best fastball in the business?" I gave the inquiry careful consideration but remained puzzled; finally, I answered, "I don't know. We'll see. We'll see." This answer gave me enormous pleasure.

More than a decade has passed; I suppose I can now forgive those who found my discomfort laughable. Perhaps one cannot expect people to empathize with a successful person who has reached a pivotal moment in his life. At the time, I was totally preoccupied with the dream; it was beyond my control to disavow its significance or to stop the process of trying to discern its meaning—after all, I had even continued the effort to decipher it in the course of my lecture. It is not irrelevant that the topic of the presentation was the problem of "the choice of symptom," so that I experienced this message from the inner depths as a unique marker of my own compromises in adaptation—a key to the issues left unresolved in my personal analysis.

I do not mean to imply that I ever reached a definitive or fully satisfactory understanding of the dream; after all, it is self-evident that at this time I feel the need to review its significance once again. Although my willingness to share some of the results of my intro-spection with my readers is a consequence of a certain degree of confidence I have gained about understanding myself—and the belief that others will empathize with such self-inquiry (as the French say, "Tout comprendre, c'est tout pardonner")—I do not plan to share the putative infantile determinants of the intense ambition articulated in the manifest content of the dream. First, I do not wish to claim more self-knowledge than I in fact possess; second, about certain matters I do not intend to surrender my privacy.

I did not know, I said, whether I was then the "best in the business," but my current assignment led me to take the possibility very seriously, indeed. I once lived in New York for a decade and attended medical school there; during those years, the New York Academy of Medicine assumed for me the aura of The Castle in Kafka's fiction. My father attended medical school in Prague and practiced in New York for many years. Yankee Stadium, Hradčany Castle, and the Academy of Medicine, where I was now a welcome personage, were inaccessible to him, a perpetual exile. Perhaps I had achieved this competitive success because my father, poor man, never gave himself the opportunity to have a psychoanalysis, and his introspective efforts—he tried, he really did!—were defeated. At any rate, a dozen years ago, Ron Guidry really did have the best fastball in the majors . . .

I suspect that people were amused by the lame pun on my name involved in identifying with the Yankee player. For me, of course, other less obvious associations were more important. I did not wish to be taken for an invader from Chicago, with its inept baseball teams; or, if you will, my psychoanalytic loyalties were with the Eastern establishment. I was still a Yankee fan, almost 30 years after accustoming myself to spoken English by listening to radio broadcasts of the Yankees' 1941 championship season. The star of 1941 had been Joe diMaggio, a son of recent immigrants; Guidry himself was a francophone Cajun from Louisiana, and I arrived in New York from French North Africa.

I do not report these details at this juncture because they matter in themselves; I am merely trying to illustrate the kinds of thoughts that were crowding in upon me following the occurrence of the dream. Suffice it to say now that the sum of these associations pointed in the direction that I had always desired to be the very best, that nothing had thus far occurred to disabuse me with regard to these hopes, and that I was still in painful suspense about how to evaluate my performance. This was much as I had been as a 15-year-old green-horn, when I applied for admission to Columbia College. (I was somewhat bitter then about being rejected, although subsequently I came to realize that an Ivy League college full of prospective Navy officers [V-12] would have been a bewildering place for a child of political refugees. Perhaps the college authorities did understand that I would not fit in.) Was it arrogant of me to think that there is special merit in finishing high school that early, or in articulating a new theoretical proposal for psychoanalysis in the 1970s? We'll see; we'll see. In the meantime, one cannot allow Radó Lectures, tuxedos, or reporters or pychoanalytic meetings to turn one's head. (Or, I might now add, to discourage one: the reporter of my presentation utterly misunderstood it and wrote an offensively hostile commentary. Sometimes "Kill the umpire!" is really the only proper attitude one can take!)

At any rate, the pleasure I experienced in my dream seemed to be connected to the long-delayed and still tenuous mastery of the propensity to yield to complacency or self-satisfaction. Fastball pitchers are so likely to ruin their arms—this was to be the fate of Ron Guidry within a few years—and the proponents of theoretical schemata in psychoanalysis generally gather a cult following devoted to glorifying the leader. I had recently witnessed the fall of a colleague I had greatly admired as a consequence of such a failure of self-criticism. As another great Yankee, Yogi Berra, always said, "It ain't over 'til it's over!"

In the course of my 35 years of self-inquiry (Gardner, 1983), the number of experiences as illuminating as the dream of the World Series could be counted on the fingers of one hand. As I recall, in every instance of that kind, some insight was attained as a result of a process set in motion without my conscious volition. Some mental content—perhaps a dream, a daydream, sometimes a parapraxis— would come back as if to haunt me, even if at first I made no effort to pay attention to it. When I had further associations to such material, they flowed easily, with a mounting sense of excitement and discovery.

If one can refer to the mental operations involved as an "apparatus," this equipment was automatically triggered, and, once the process started, it appeared to have a certain momentum that carried it to a more or less satisfying conclusion. In no case was the conclusion an end point: I am discussing matters of life-long significance that do not admit of any permanent solution. In the early stages of these experiences, I was aware that the associations that arose into consciousness represented only the tip of an iceberg of mental activity. Preoccupation with the underlying problem was continuous and absorbed as much capacity as other requirements of living allowed me to spare.

I should perhaps specify that I never experienced such an episode prior to the termination of my analysis, or, for that matter, while that treatment was in progress. I have therefore concluded that this new functional capacity was one (invaluable!) benefit gained from analytic treatment—the acquisition of previously unavailable psychological skills as a consequence of new learning (Gedo, 1988, Epilogue). Although I am aware that the term has been used in a slightly different sense, I believe that Isakower's famous but unpublished concept of an "analytic instrument," the availability to an analyst of certain unusual cognitive skills, may be applicable to the phenomena I have in mind. Perhaps we might call it the "self-analytic instrument." I suspect that certain cognitive operations, initiated in the course of a therapeutic analysis, are facilitated through practice and then become automatized as a consequence of the adaptive advantages they confer on the individual. From the viewpoint of cognitive psychology, the relevant skills have been described by Bucci (in press), who calls them "referential schemata" that connect verbal and nonverbal representations. The attainment of such capacities should be the primary goal of every psychoanalytic treatment.

It is also worth noting that these capacities are not available to me as a matter of choice; they go into operation only in case of dire necessity. Whenever I have tried to evoke them as a matter of conscious volition, the nature of the subsequent psychological processes was utterly different—not necessarily less useful, but lacking in the automaticity and unbroken impetus that characterize the more crucial episodes. The latter almost always arose in the context of fundamental problems in adaptation and not in performing the responsibilities of a psychoanalytic clinician. To cite an example that might well apply to many other people, the first time one of my children married produced an emergent need to reexamine my sense of "self-in-the-world." In comparison, the desirability of analyzing a parapraxis committed while doing analytic work pales in significance.

All that is not to say that career issues are less likely to arouse adaptive emergencies than are family matters—after all, the illustration with which I began this essay deals with a turning point in professional life. In fact, the very first time I experienced the availability of the processes in question was toward the end of my candidacy at the Chicago Institute, when a bitter confrontation I had with a supervisor led the powers-that-be to urge that I resume a personal analysis. In the face of this pressure (and the implicit threat of penalties for noncompliance), the yield of the self-analytic process emboldened me to assert that accepting the opinion of someone else in such a situation would have amounted to a self-betrayal. It is people who are unable to stand their ground who need therapeutic assistance.

On that occasion, in the very middle of my preoccupation with this dilemma, I did consult my ex-analyst, and it was his inability to add anything to my own thinking about the problem that convinced me that interpreting the meanings of one's associations is best performed for oneself. It was entirely clear to me that I was the only one who had at his disposal the full range of associations to my associations, so that no other person, however professionally skillful, was equally positioned to formulate the requisite interpretations. My conviction in this regard did not find confirmation in the analytic world until Robert Gardner showed me early drafts of his crucial study of this question, *Self Inquiry* (1983).

Thus the problem of self-analysis is not the difficulty of discerning the proper interpretation, however novel that insight may be; it is the scarcity of affectively charged associative material in circumstances less emergent than are the crucial turning points I have discussed thus far. Another way to put this is that one must be strongly motivated to deal with one's routine resistance to self-inquiry, and it is strong affect, particularly *unpleasant* affect, that is most likely to provide the necessary motivation to engage in productive self-analysis. For matters of everyday significance, Freud recommended the process he wittily called doing one's "analytic toilette"; as his phrase implies, this is not a pressing need.

I must admit that, on weekends and holidays, whenever I plan to stay at home, I am likely to skip shaving. I have been no more diligent about my analytic toilette—I suspect most of us regard it as a terrible nuisance, and one seldom hears about colleagues who pursue it systematically. In this regard, Calder (1980) represents the most notable contemporary exception. I require some incentive to focus my attention on poorly understood psychological issues, something like an untoward event in my consulting room or a dream charged with sufficient affect to become memorable. I do not think that the manner in which I endeavor to work on such puzzles is in any way unusual, and I shall say no more about it here: Freud's analysis of his Signorelli parapraxis (1898) may serve as the ideal prototype for such work.

What I would like to focus on, instead, is my impression that, exactly contrary to the situation with regard to more pressing personal issues, these matters from the psychopathology of everyday life tend to involve vicissitudes in managing transference crises in the course of doing analytic work. To be more precise, in my experience, incidents that require self-analytic attention tend to arise when, in a way more subtle and insidious than usual, an analysand creates a transference enactment wherein the role of his or her childhood self is assigned to me while that of the original parent is assumed by the patient. Whenever such a constellation goes undetected for a while, one is likely to respond (countertransferentially) with complementary attitudes or activities, without realizing that one has accepted a role extrinsic to one's usual motivations. The crux of the self-analytic task in such contingencies is to differentiate what is authentically one's own desire from behaviors that comply with the desires of the analysand.

To give a brief example of a temporary confusion about such matters: Some time ago, I was forced to make a slight change in my schedule, so that my appointment with a certain analysand was to begin and end 10 minutes later than previously. Shortly thereafter, I realized one day that I had terminated his session 6 minutes early, under the sway of an illusion that I had kept him 4 minutes overtime. When I asked the patient whether he had noticed my error, he replied that he had only perceived that he had felt confused about when his session should have ended. I then made it clear that the error was entirely mine and that I did not yet understand its significance or even whether it had a bearing on his analysis. There matters rested for a few days, until I made an identical parapraxis. Before the patient's next session, I made a good-faith effort to take care of my "analytic toilette," and I realized that I was enacting my analysand's habitually cavalier attitude about our schedule. I began the next session by telling him that, by reversing our roles, I was sending the nonverbal message he had repeatedly sent me: that it is intolerable to be at another person's mercy with regard to that person's availability. When he perceived that he had the power to cause me the kind of discomfort he found so difficult to bear, this patient's need to convey his feelings through nonverbal channels was replaced by syntactically encoded messages. In parallel, I regained my customary ability for precision about my handling of time.

As a consultant, I have had the opportunity to observe that even colleagues with adequate self-analytic capacities tend to have particular difficulty in preventing patients from perpetuating enactments wherein the analyst is sadistically abused. Similarly, it took me many years to trust my own sense of outrage whenever I felt misused in the analytic situation—to understand such a reaction as a signal of a potentially fruitful transference–countertransference development (such as the parapraxes about time I have just described) rather than seeing it as an unmanageable reality. Yet, of course, each and every occurrence of this kind must call forth fresh self-analytic efforts, lest one fall from the frying pan of masochism into the fire of unempathic rigidity.

What is most difficult about handling these matters via self-analysis is the lack of opportunity to get consensual validation for one's conclusions. Perhaps the solution most frequently available to analysts to overcome this problem is to seek consultation with a trusted colleague, either formally or on an informal basis. My own experience has been confined to the arena of informal exchanges with friends. When I have been consulted by colleagues, generally of a younger generation, they have very seldom shared with me detailed personal material; if they talked about countertransference feelings or a temporary identification with a patient, they tended to state their self-diagnosis tersely, without citing their thinking in reaching it.

The dilemma of needing validation induced Ferenczi (1932, pp. 71–73) to experiment with mutual analysis—reportedly with a patient who was also a colleague. Obviously, the experiment only proved that such a procedure is unworkable. In my experience, however, it is on rare occasions quite effective to share the results of a bit of self-analysis with analysands, particularly those who have good reason to mistrust their caretakers' capacity for honest self-inquiry. (Whenever I have tried such a procedure, I have been as careful to balance the need for candor with the desirability of preserving my privacy as I have tried to be in writing this essay.) Clearly, there is no time for serious self-analytic efforts in the course of performing an analysis for someone else, so that one should have the conclusions of a piece of self-inquiry ready-to-hand before attempting to communicate them to a patient.

In these circumstances, it should be possible to determine in advance the appropriate limits of the self-revelations one is willing to make. With my patients, I have seldom mentioned any details of my personal history or my current private life, and (in exact parallel with my policy in writing this essay) I have only shared aspects of my inner life insofar as I felt entirely comfortable about these. But as I have grown older and better established as an analyst, I have become comfortable about more and more aspects of our common humanity.

Obviously, the useful range of self-analysis may have its limits. It is important to be able to determine when it would be preferable to seek either consultation (about a clinical impasse) or further personal treatment. On theoretical grounds, I would expect that it would be extremely difficult (perhaps impossible) to deal with archaic issues against which more or less successful defenses were erected in childhood without setting in motion a systematic regressive process in a context conducive to the evocation of transferences. This is particularly true if the relevant issues have been split-off from the part of the personality that came into focus in a therapeutic analysis. In other words, self-inquiry is most likely to be fruitful if one's defenses are neither too rigid nor completely unfamiliar—or, if you will, when one has overcome one's propensity to avoid threats of potential traumatization (Freud, 1926).

Obviously, none of us gets immunized against potential traumata through personal analysis, so that self-analysis remains a limited instrument for us all. I have found that I have been unable to profit from it when, in the context of some meaningful relationship, someone repeats with me those behaviors of my parents (particularly the mother-of-attachment) that proved to be traumatic in the past. In some instances, the old wounds have reopened and were only healed by the passage of time. On other occasions, I could see the traumatic potential before it reached me, and I withdrew from the situation—something I had been unable to do as a child. It is probably worth noting that neither waiting out a traumatic state nor withdrawal qualifies as self-analytic activity.

Despite these caveats, the cumulative results of continuing self-inquiry can be far-reaching. In my own case, I suspect that I have changed more decisively in the decades since I terminated my personal analysis than I did during that treatment. Yet, as I have already stated, it was the experience of the analysis that made subsequent self-analysis possible for me. In some instances, I have come to believe that certain issues were misunderstood when they emerged in the analytic transference. I shall here offer only one relatively innocuous example of such an error.

A pattern of slight tardiness for analytic sessions was interpreted by my analyst as an expression of depreciation for my elders and betters. This inexact interpretation temporarily eliminated the symptom which then recurred after termination. It was permanently overcome following a casual remark by a colleague who witnessed my distress on an occasion when I was afraid of being tardy. This casual acquaintance bluntly stated that my discomfort was entirely self-induced. Confrontation with this self-evident truth enabled me to review the transference meaning of having come late for analytic sessions. I believe it represented ambivalence about longing for maternal involvement in regulating time-related activities. (My analyst was perfectly correct in sensing my hostility but absolutely wrong in seeing this bit of behavior as depreciating—I believe I had been trying to fend off a wish to submit to his overwhelming influence.) I have never since become disorganized in carrying out my schedule. I assume that such a correction of an inaccurate interpretation was only possible because the defenses against experiencing unjustifiable hostility had been loosened, and the entire sequence of transference reactions continued to be affectively available for reprocessing.

Perhaps the effects of dealing with issues that failed to emerge in the course of analysis have been still more striking than that of correcting minor errors of commission. In my own case, I now consider the most important omission to have been a failure to examine carefully the meanings of a commitment to a healing profession—although, to be sure, we did consider such obvious determinants of this choice as my identification with a physician father. At least, this omission is the one I have thus far found to be most regrettable; needless to say, I have no way of identifying other sleeping dogs that subsequent events have still failed to waken, to use the metaphor Freud (1937) invented to characterize this issue.

Interestingly enough, I have been very slow to come to grips with the unconscious motives for becoming a clinician, despite my lifelong preference for the humanities (I should have become a historian of medieval Europe!) and a marked scholarly bent. Needless to say, this problem does not tend to occupy the forefront as long as clinical work is going well; to put it differently, the secondary gains of being a successful clinician generally silence all objections. Thus I did not confront this issue until I also encountered it in family life, in terms of what I found I expected from my grown children in return for having been a conscientious (and relatively successful) caretaker.

The fact that I expected more than one could realistically hope for was gradually clarified, in large measure through sharing my feelings with friends at the same stage of life, many of them analysts. (I do not mean to suggest that my attitudes were significantly different from those of my peers: we all had to come to terms with the fact that adequate parenting is, in retrospect, simply taken for granted.) In the process of renouncing unwarranted expectations, I experienced moments of bitterness, and these eventually focused on some of my professional disappointments as well. In particular, I began to feel that my local colleagues did not adequately reciprocate my efforts on behalf of the analytic community. This idea was concretized in my mind in the form of the metonym that I was being used in the same way as the famous astronomical clock of Strasbourg, which goes through amazing gyrations at an appointed time, for the delectation of assembled multitudes. I was so taken with this image that I began to write a "memoir" around it, at first without realizing that the impulse to make art was taking the place of self-inquiry.

After a while, I became sufficiently aware that I was engaging in symptomatic behaviors to mention my preoccupation to a respected, older colleague, who, not at all coincidentally, reminded me of my father. We were in an informal setting, and my friend wisely fended off my communication with a joke. I mention this detail merely to suggest that the temptation to reestablish a father transference alerted me to the fact that I was struggling with archaic issues – that the culprits were neither my children nor my indifferent fellow analysts. This was the only occasion, I believe, when my effort to seek validation for my self-analytic attempts took the form of turning to a transference figure rather than an alter ego. It was also the sole instance of not finding a receptive ear when I shared something private with a fellow analyst.

At any rate, I began to pay closer attention to the fantasy of the astronomical clock as a potentially analyzable derivative of the underlying issues. I trust it will be understood that I prefer not to spell out their details in their entirety. Suffice it to say that Strasbourg is connected with my mother, some of whose forebears were Alsatian, and that it was for her that I had first attempted to perform wonderful but dehumanizing feats. In this sense, all analysts are used, appropriately, as one makes use of scientific measuring devices. In our professional capacity, we cannot expect reciprocation on a human level. All those who have paid the price of admission may take advantage of our services without giving us credit or even feeling gratitude. A person with childhood experiences such as mine should think three times before embarking on an analytic career. I have now thought about it twice, and I decided to cut my clinical responsibilities to a minimum. It has been a salutary change!

I trust that I have now provided a fair sampling of bits of my self-analysis and that these vignettes suffice to demonstrate that, albeit this process of self-inquiry appears haphazard when observed in terms of its overt (i.e., conscious) manifestations, in reality it amounts to a continuous (and therefore essentially seamless or holistic) monitoring of one's status as an individual within a specific milieu. Doubtless most of the time this process is automatized and can yield effective results without gaining conscious representation. The manner in which a skilled driver operates an automobile may be roughly analogous to the operation of routine self-analytic activities: only when confronted with sudden and previously unfamiliar contingencies does it become necessary to pay conscious attention to such matters.

Viewed from this perspective, the new psychological skill one is enabled to acquire in the course of a personal analysis is that of systematic reliance on the process of free association. Clearly, when one resorts to this, the process of self-inquiry has been elevated to the level of consciousness. Endopsychic resistance to facing the truth about oneself in "one's own mind" perforce must take the form of breaking off the work of associating before it succeeds in linking words and affects. (It is true that certain matters of archaic origin may never have been verbally encoded and consequently may emerge not in the form of a symbolically represented "thought" but in that of pure affect or some other bodily event. However, it is just as feasible to observe such phenomena and draw verbally encoded conclusions about them in the course of self-analysis as it is to discuss them in discursive language in a dyadic analytic setting.) In sum, the most important gain of a personal analysis proves to be the conviction one should gain about the unfailing power of Freud's procedure, that of paying minute attention to the yield of the free-associative effort, to produce increments of self-understanding. One must learn to damn the torpedoes and think full speed ahead.

If, by means of reaching rational, symbolically encoded conclusions concerning one's self-monitoring, it becomes possible to make reasoned decisions about one's future conduct, this acquired skill— the all but unique outcome of mastering the analytic method—should provide greater effectiveness in choosing optimal adaptive solutions. As the frequent necessity for resuming therapeutic analyses demonstrates, all too often analysands fail to master this skill during their initial exposure to the analytic situation. I believe it is worth discussing some possible reasons for this kind of failure.

My experience in performing second (or third, or fourth!) analyses has given me the impression that a certain attitude of laissez-faire has become prevalent about making certain that the method of free association is in fact followed by analysands. On the one hand, it is often falsely assumed that, as long as patients keep talking, they are adhering to Freud's technical prescriptions—this laxity may lead to the neglect of associative links that are not topically related. On the other hand, it is nowadays quite common to condone the triumph of resistances vis-à-vis the obligation to report all mental activities—as if the anxiety or shame attendant on total candor were more than analysands can be expected to bear. The result of such complaisance is the encouragement of irresponsibility about the analytic task. Analytic delinquents will not acquire self-analytic skills.

One of the principal pieces of evidence that will convince me that a reanalysis is needed, if I am consulted by someone who was previously analyzed, is the report that, instead of attempts to achieve self-understanding by engaging in free association, the patient tries to fit his or her behavior into certain (more or less familiar) formulations. These formulations may be either those heard in the analysis or (in the case of mental health professionals) certain intellectualizations that may have come into fashion more recently. Although such a result may come about in a number of different ways, it is quite likely that such persons had analyses characterized by excessive interpretive activity on the part of the therapist. Moreover, the interpretations seem often to have been chosen on an arbitrary basis: analytic formulae used as magical incantations.

Am I implying that, if all analyses were properly conducted and completed, their outcomes would obviate the need for reanalysis because sufficient self-analytic capacity would invariably develop to deal with all subsequent adaptive challenges? I am tempted to think that this statement approaches the truth—although, to be sure, perfection in human affairs is unattainable, and it is never to be expected that any analysis will be concluded without serious flaws. There is, however, one particular constellation of circumstances that may leave an analysand unprepared to cope with future contingencies through self-analysis, however "properly" the initial treatment may have been performed. I have in mind the possibility that certain potential difficulties may be masked through the provision of symbiotic assistance by family or friends, so that the developmental deficits in question never come up for scrutiny in the first analysis. In such a case, later loss of the symbiotic mode of adaptation will leave the person unable to cope—however capable of self-inquiry he or she may be. This is another way of saying that the loss of symbiosis reveals potentialities for traumatization that were previously warded off by the assistance of the symbiotic partner.

In this regard, it is relevant to recall that Kohut (1984) ultimately came to believe that the very effort to engage in self-analytic activities is a pathological disavowal of our eternal need for "selfobjects" (i.e., that it is healthier to turn for assistance to another person than it is to attempt to cope by using one's own resources!). I hope it is clear that such an opinion reflects assumptions about the human condition that I do not share. No stigma should be attached to the need for several periods of analysis to deal with different sets of pathological deficits. In principle, however, the primary task of every analysis is to enable the analysand to conduct effective self-inquiry, thus freeing the person of the necessity to use therapeutic assistance. Incidentally, when Kohut first communicated his clinical discoveries about what he called "narcissistic" transferences, he proudly shared with his friends his conviction that they were the fruits of his self-analytic activities. Pathological or not, the process of self-inquiry may be fruitful!

In a celebrated letter to Wilhelm Fliess, Freud (Masson, 1985, p. 281) stated that self-analysis is actually not feasible—that in his own case, he only succeeded in applying the insights accumulated in his analytic work with his patients to the material of his associations. My personal experience has been different. Although it is ever tempting to resist self-understanding by falling back on intellectualizations, in the manner Freud mentioned, for me such defensive operations obstruct self-inquiry only when I am going through the motions, pro forma. It must not be forgotten that Freud made his pessimistic assessment without the benefit of a personal analysis—or, if you will, at a time when systematic ego analysis was more than a generation away. Once an analysand has learned to identify his or her defensive operations and consequently masters the capacity volitionally to forego using these capacities in the service of resisting self-cognition, some measure of self-inquiry does become feasible.

If the results of self-analysis tend to be underplayed, nonetheless, I suspect that this prejudice may stem from the widespread conviction that personality change is most likely to take place as a consequence of transference interpretation. Whenever the problem represents a transference repetition of more or less archaic behavior patterns, it is, of course, quite true that transference interpretation is most likely to lead to insight, and such circumstances are unlikely to arise in a self-analytic context.[1] It is quite erroneous, however, to assume that useful self-knowledge can be gained only about transference repetitions. In my experience (Gedo, 1988, chaps. 11–12), it is equally crucial to gain insight into the precise limits of one's psychological skills, thereby enabling oneself to fill the lacunae in one's

---

[1]Such contingencies are by no means unknown. One colleague shared with me his experience of developing a crucially meaningful transference to the analyst of his spouse—a process he was able to turn to good account through self-analytic efforts.

repertory. In the realm of overcoming one's apraxic deficits, the potentialities of self-analysis are limitless.

REFERENCES

Bucci, W. (in press), The development of emotional meaning in free association: A multiple code theory. In: *Hierarchical Conceptions in Psychoanalysis*, ed. A. Wilson & J. Gedo. New York: Guilford.

Calder, K. (1980), An analyst's self-analysis. *J. Amer. Psychoanal. Assn.*, 28:5–20.

Ferenczi, S. (1932), *The Clinical Diary of Sándor Ferenczi*, ed. J. Dupont (trans. M. Balint & N. Z. Jackson). Cambridge, MA: Harvard University Press, 1988.

Freud, S. (1898), The psychical mechanism of forgetfulness. *Standard Edition*, 3:287–300. London: Hogarth Press, 1962.

———— (1926), Inhibitions, symptoms, and anxiety. *Standard Edition*, 20:77–172. London: Hogarth Press, 1959.

———— (1937), Analysis terminable and interminable. *Standard Edition*, 23:216–253. London: Hogarth Press, 1964.

Gardner, R. (1983), *Self Inquiry*. Hillsdale, NJ: The Analytic Press, 1987.

Gedo, J. (1988), *The Mind in Disorder*. Hillsdale, NJ: The Analytic Press.

Kohut, H. (1984), *How Does Analysis Cure?* ed. A. Goldberg & P. Stepansky. Chicago: University of Chicago Press.

Masson, J., ed. (1985), *The Complete Letters of Sigmund Freud to Wilhelm Fliess, 1887–1904*. Cambridge, MA: Belknap Press/Harvard University Press.

8

On Talking to Ourselves
Some Self-Analytical Reflections on Self-Analysis

Robert Gardner

PART 1

One day, a friend said of the unsettled weather:
"It looks as if it's going to clear."
"Yes," I said, "but it's been trying all morning to clear and each time it's failed."
Hours later I was struck—though I'd not been before—that I'd talked of the weather as if the weather had a will. And having noted my animism, I said to myself, in some way or other, "I wonder who is it who's been trying all morning to clear?" (I say "some way or other" because private conversations go mainly in zigzags, not reportorial lines.)
Though my question might seem to have implied the answer, I needed a few moments to catch up.
One thing led to another and another—word, image, feeling—till I realized at last that all morning long I'd been "under the weather" and I'd been trying to clear my dampened spirits. Understanding that, I noticed an unrecognized reason for my unrecognized distress and felt a quick relief from the distress I'd not realized I was trying to relieve.
Several hours later, "It's been trying to clear" came back to my mind and with it an incident I'd several months earlier put in my journal and forgot. On that earlier occasion, seated before a window, looking out at the gray wintry sky, I'd been wondering, if I were to

paint it, how I might catch its varied and varying tones. Though the sky at first seemed a strangely uniform blue-gray, one small section was slowly lightening, and, almost imperceptibly, taking on, in turn, one warmer hue and another.

Musing about these idiosyncrasies of the sky, and the problems they might present in painting, and having set down those musings in my journal, I turned to something else. I was startled, therefore, when almost a half-hour later, the entire sky took a turn for the better and seemed to confer on my earlier observations the status of an unrecognized prediction of improvements to come.

I'd wondered then whether similar, though unrecognized, views of slight brightenings of the sky might have been what had made me able on other occasions unaccountably to predict the coming of sunnier weather and to do so considerably before the appearance of those favorable signs of which I was aware of being aware (changes in humidity, wind, behavior of the birds). I noted and put down these wonderings with no further comment, and, till the moment at hand, no further thought.

But looking back at that earlier moment of sky gazing, looking back, that is, in the light of the current incident of the weather "trying to clear," I realized that on both occasions I'd not, as I'd first thought, observed casually, but rather searched diligently, for those brightenings of the sky. I wondered then how widespread my habit might be of searching in this way first for gloomy skies and then for my favorite harbingers of what the English call "sunny intervals."

My thoughts turned from one thing to another and then to a familiar pattern of my outlook I'd long been accustomed to call "looking for silver linings." I realized at once, as I'd not before, that to speak of my inclination to look for silver linings was to tell not only a metaphorical truth but a literal truth about the conditions of the sky upon which, as I'd now seen, I tended to fasten attention. I realized, too, that such vivifying of ossified metaphors comes always as a surprise, which includes the surprise that the obvious should be a surprise.

In talking to oneself it seems possible, though hard to say how, to say more than one thing at once. Or almost at once. When I thought of the literality of my search for silver linings, it struck me simultaneously as quite understandable that I like to paint skyscapes, especially the contrasts between lights and darks, and am partial to the use of watercolors, a medium so suited to capturing the vagaries of light and to creating illusions that a static picture is changing from one fluid state to another.

On the darker side, my associations took a sudden turn toward the past, and wandered back by a long path to my much earlier years. I recalled at last, and was startled to recall, a custom of my childhood, one I could not recall being aware of before, of tempering sadness by seeking comfort in "Mother Nature." I remembered most vividly that in a place well known for its gloomy weather, at a time of special reason for my being under the weather, I'd gone off from time to time to a secret nook, stared gloomily at the gloomy skies, and then felt a special delight in watching the skies clear.

I say I "recalled" those moments long past but I think it truer to say that for an instant I "stepped back." (Or as we like to put it in our Latinate way: I re-gressed.) And I re-called too, or in my mind's re-viewed, a moment in the same time and space when, sitting quietly in my private nook, I observed joyfully the winter suddenly give way to spring.

Proclivity becomes perception becomes memory becomes metaphor becomes proclivity becomes perception becomes memory and on and on and back and forth in endless exchange. It seems safe to say that my perception of brightening skies was no idle perception (if there is any such thing as an idle perception). Looking back at my climatic associations, I surmised that at such moments as had now come to my attention, I first blurred carefully the distinction between my gloom and nature's—making the sky, so to speak, a large parabolic mirror—and then cheered myself by finding a bright spot to reflect, abet, and magnify a brightening of my inner nature.

This over view—dare I say these insights?—and a rush of thoughts about the probable effects of a known challenge in my still earlier years, struck me with peculiar force, and in the manner of a good-enough interpretation, or series of interpretations, impressed me as new and convincing, stirred a sense of understanding and a feeling of satisfaction, and rapidly brought to my mind what I perceived to be related events, thoughts, images, and feelings, some of which, as far as I could recall, had previously been unavailable, and others, though available, had previously seemed unrelated.

For months after, I experienced fresh bursts of resonant associations which, with further exploration, enlarged my views of several times and places of my past and several current events. To put the matter another way, my representations of the two weather incidents have been and remain highly evocative. I believe that even now, if I were to associate anew, my associations would lead me in still other directions. I want to mention this matter of the evocative power of particular configurations—genres—for one person and another and come back to it.

Of the intimacies of these weather incidents—of the oedipal, preoedipal, and postoedipal lights in the dark—I'll say no more. Public confession suffers a double difficulty: whoever confesses, faces a loss of privacy; whoever listens is made to bear uneasy witness to events whose recounting runs the all too narrow path between candor and sentimentality. (I shall only add that I believe one contemporary spur to my long search for the light in the dark was my reaching the age of 60, an event made more complicated by my having moved so speedily to 60 from 16.)

What shall we call such perambulations of the mind? Self-analysis? I don't know. I don't like the term. It seems to me to carry misleading connotations of a similarity, perhaps identity, between what we ordinarily call psychoanalysis and what we call self-analysis. I prefer to reserve the terms psychoanalysis and analysis for the special circumstances and possibilities of the two-party situation and to refer to the climate and procedures of the solo endeavor as self-inquiry, a term that, whatever its limitations, means for me something different from, and somewhere between, some aspects of psychoanalysis and ordinary introspection. But with that objection stated, and since the term is so entrenched in our literature and everyday parlance, I shall refer in these remarks to "self-analysis."

PART 2

Self-analyzers, it seems, have strangely stringent requirements for the gathering of self-analytical materials, the kinds of materials they gather, and the ways in which, and conditions under which, they customarily proceed. What works best for each is arrived at by long trial and error. For the serious self-analyzer, these idiosyncratic necessities change again and again through more trial and error. I gather that what is called self-analysis by one person may be very different from what is called self-analysis by another. So, when we discuss self-analysis—perhaps even more than when we discuss psychoanalysis—we may be discussing approaches more different than alike.

My own self-analytical efforts begin mainly in one of three ways:

a) Often, as in the case of the clearing weather, some current event catches my attention, and seems unaccountably and irresistably to demand consideration. As a rule, through no conscious plan, I seem strongly to prefer as a starting point these conditions of the immediate, the inadvertent, and the demanding.

More often than not, when self-analysis begins so, I have a sense of it being "despite" myself. My self-analysis, that is, seems to go better in the face of a slight but surmountable resistance: strong enough so I disavow active seeking but not so strong that I reject the seemingly unsolicited invitation. (I imagine that Freud, in those letters to Fliess in which he tells of ideas "dawning" upon him, or of "waiting" for ideas to come, is not indulging in romantic excess but trying to describe a similar mix of resistance and receptivity.)

b) For more systematic efforts at self-analysis, I've found it handy to keep a journal where I set down from time to time—daily when I can manage it—whatever is most vividly on my mind or, as it sometimes seems, whatever is hardest to get off my mind. Whether that takes the form of an image, a word, a phrase, or a full-blown essay, it seems most often to begin with and frequently to return to something I've seen: actually seen or visualized. Most often in the writing, when things go best, I have the curious illusion that what I'm writing has nothing whatever to do with me but refers only to some "external event" that has inescapably caught my eye. (In the midst, therefore, of the activity of "keeping" a journal is the passivity of a conscious surrender of choice of subject: an intercourse, so to speak, between the more active and the more passive.)

It's one thing to know abstractly that all I write has much to do with me, it's another to know it in the act of writing. When things go best, I don't at first know that what I write, and how I write, is about me— indeed, is me. At least, I manage for a while not to know that I know it.

I find it necessary, or at least favorable, for my self-analysis not to regard particular materials—whether dreams or anything else—as something I "should" or "must" explore. I know that some self-analyzers find it routinely fruitful to analyze their dreams or something else. I do not. Rather, I stick strictly to the policy of exploring whatever grips me, whatever form it takes, and no matter how trivial or promising it may at first seem. I've learned that if, in advance, I tip off my resistances (and other self-analytical saboteurs) that I plan automatically and routinely to analyze my dreams or anything else, they pile up so many obstacles to self-analysis—a pastime sorely limited at best—that I discover little or nothing I did not know before. I find I must catch myself by surprise if I am to learn anything surprising.

I believe there's another matter at stake. I've found that my self-analysis goes better in a climate I experience as play rather than work. In self-analysis, as in all arts, some practitioners prefer to stress play and to address in passing the necessities of work; others prefer to stress work and to address in passing the necessities of play. It seems reasonable to suppose that there must always be a mix of play and work or the end is not art but license on one hand or drudgery on the other. Few practitioners seem to create the same mix, however, or to go about their mixing the same way.

c) Beyond wool-gathering and journal-keeping, my third common source of material for self-analysis—I believe it's the most consistently fruitful—is what I experience in the psychoanalytical situation. I seem to learn most about myself when I try to learn something about someone else. Having described those events elsewhere, especially the visual images I see in those circumstances, I shall not dwell further on them here (see Gardner, 1983). I want only to say that in the psychoanalytical situation, as elsewhere, I've found that direct introspection is not my best route to new findings. I need to look outward in order to look inward; I need, that is, to look outward to find ways in which looking outward is looking inward, and looking inward, outward.

Whether my self-analytical efforts begin from one source or the other, I find they generally move along this way: First, having been caught up in the subject at hand, I seem to spin off in unspoken drifts that in contrast to spoken associations trip along more erratically, and, in particular, show richer mixes of visual images and metaphors and quicker shifts back and forth from one to the other and from these to other ways of picturing. Second, ideas emerge in what I experience as a counterpoint to the first: again with a mix of words and images, but this time with a shift toward more words and fewer images.

Third, I find myself trying to make sense of some piece or of the whole. This phase is much wordier but not always exclusively wordy.

Sometimes, the boundaries between the one phase and the other are clear, sometimes not. Sometimes the substance of the third—the sense-making—seems suddenly no longer a logical conclusion but simply a fresh association that triggers the whole sequence again. In one mood, that is, I feel inclined to regard my interpretations as interpretations, and in another, as associations. In the latter circumstances, I find my interpretations more revealing of the interpreter than the interpreted.

I think it's correct, if odd, to say that often I have the sense that I'm first someone free associating, then someone associating to the associating person's associations, and then the same second someone, in a different and more deliberate mood, considering his (or the other's) associations and the play of the one with the other. There seem to be two someones present and one someone is first in one state and then another. If one supposes this imagined dialogue might in some ways repeat the arrangements of the psychoanalytical situation—both those in which I've been the analysand and those in which I've been the analyst—I suppose that might be right, but the conversations I've been able to hear usually involve a larger cast of characters. I can't escape the impression that in self-analysis, as in other moments of talking to ourselves, we're rarely if ever alone. Of talkers and listeners there are many.

Hearing many voices over many years, many voices of the observed and observer, hearing who is talking to whom about what, in which style, idiom, grammar, accent, tone, and rhythm, has led me to the view that each of these matters is worth fuller study. I've found it fruitful in self-analysis, as in the analysis of others, to watch for moments of an abrupt change of voice: for example, changes in who is talking, changes in ways of talking, changes in what is being talked about, and changes in the imagined nature of the person talked to.

I've come especially to watch for those moments when all or many of these changes take place at once. For solo self inquiry and for assisting the inquiries of others (I call the latter psychoanalysis), I find these moments of multiple change to be moments of the fullest opportunity.

PART 3

Exploring the incidents of the weather "trying to clear," I was struck repeatedly by the strength of my urges to drag in once fresh but now stale insights from my earlier self-analysis and still earlier psycho-analysis. This led me in turn to muse at some length about the ways in which over and over, liberating ideas—perhaps especially the most liberating ideas—become enslaving. We see it in art. We see it in music. We see it in literature. We see it in politics. We see it in the hard sciences. We see it in psychology.

Going on in this vein, I found it ironic that we must struggle so hard to learn what needs learning and then in the practice of our art must find a way to "forget" yesterday's truths in order to find today's. Painters know there's no great harm and even some value in learning that the foliage of trees is green. They also know that if they want to paint a picture of a tree today, if they want to catch it as it as it is in today's light, they must forget that trees are green. If they can manage that feat, they will find no tree always green, no tree entirely green, and some trees never green. The beginning of the painter's art, as of all art, lies in the difficult task of forgetting how things looked in yesterday's light. Evenly hovering attention, the toleration of uncertainty, the tempering of what Keats called "irritable reaching for fact and reason," all ask a finely tuned capacity to forget.

Having for some time found myself going on in these and other ways in loose if heavy dissertation about the importance of forgetting, I wondered at last if I might unconsciously be claiming that by performing such sleight of mind, I could avoid the effects of prior experiences, beliefs, biases, frames of reference, and other letters of my alphabet. Indeed, if such clearing of the psychic slate were possible, what would it profit me if, in losing my biases, I lost my bearings?

Surely by "forget" I could not mean forget. What I must mean, I told myself, is that we must learn somehow to act as if we've forgotten. Otherwise, we come only upon what we expected to come upon. What I must mean is that when, in the act of seeing, we make our prior knowledge less directly available—when we somehow "redistribute" it from center-of-awareness to edge—we prepare ourselves to come upon fresh examples of what our knowledge had prepared us to find, and even on some occasions, to transcend some limits of that knowledge. Old knowledge, though the friend of the new, is at best an ambivalent friend; and sometimes, having such a friend, to paraphrase the old saying, new knowledge doesn't need an enemy.

Having at last noted that in this monologue I'd changed my way of talking, and having noted in particular that I'd swapped "forget" for "redistribute," I wondered at last why I'd jumped from the clearly paradoxical to the opaquely precise? Did I fancy myself on firmer ground by speaking a geographical and Latinate lingo? If by my shift I meant to do something more than comfort myself, did I mean "redistribution of knowledge" as analogy or more? (When Isakower was asked if he meant "analyzing instrument" as analogy or more, he replied: "Somewhere between the one and the other.")

I don't know if what I shall now report will reveal more the advantages or the disadvantages of the chasing of analogy. But I ask the reader to go with me through a concatenation of thoughts which, though I know it confounds the abstract with the concrete, and otherwise violates several canons both of science and ordinary logic, is nevertheless the route upon which my associations insisted.

Faced repeatedly with the question: "Where does knowledge go when you redistribute it?", I found myself of the repeated and decided conviction that it goes "to the back of my head." Taking this location as seriously as I could, I observed that it pertained to a very different "edge-of-awareness" from the one I'd long been accustomed to imagine.

My customary images of edge-of-awareness experience were of

things off to the side, peripheral visions as it were. Yet clearly in my present representation of putting knowledge aside, I was imagining that aside as not to the side but to the back.

Having thus settled the matter of location, I asked myself, on another day, "What is this idea of putting knowledge to the back of your head? Just how do you do that?" The tone of these questions reflected another of those changes of voice I mentioned before. This was no longer a proper self-analytical tone. It was cynical. In that tone—I know several persons I've come to regard as its prototypical bearers—my questions were meant not as the questions they purported to be but as question-stoppers. These pseudoquestions loudly proclaimed by their tone: Stop it! You're going off the deep end with this reifying of spatial analogies.

To my regret, I talk to myself that way sometimes though I know that nothing kills my self-analysis quicker—and means to, I gather—than this mix of oppressive cynicism and reason. That knowledge notwithstanding, being sorely afflicted at the moment by an uncontrollable fit of rigor, I was happy to drop precipitously my uneasy elaborations of topography.

With not even a parenthetical wondering about yet another change of voice, I simply translated my thoughts into other abstractions—"attention cathexes," and the like—and let it go at that.

I was startled therefore when on still another occasion, the dismissed question gently, though firmly, returned: How do you put knowledge in the back of your head?

Soon after, as if in reply, I observed myself and have observed myself since, in the visual midst of a curious fantasy: curious in form, and having as its subject, I take it, the exercise of curiosity.

In one of those edge-of-awareness images that come and go in a flash, I saw myself as a wide-eyed child, running happily ahead, followed by my parents, sometimes father, sometimes mother. (I've not been able to tell when the one or the other though I imagine it depends on the subject of my inquiry.)

It struck me then that here was how I "redistributed knowledge to the back of my head." I imagined that knowledge no longer my own but the knowledge of my parents behind me, in back of my head, so to speak. By virtue of that imagined division of knowledge, and head, I felt myself freer to run about and to look with a fresh eye.

My associations to this transformation into child peripatetic observer—walker or runner and seer—have led me back on one occasion and another to joyful moments of childhood in which I rush ahead to find things and then back to my parents to report my findings and to benefit from their enthusiasm and knowledgeable commentary. (I persist in the belief that, in the main, my parents entered into those exploratory exchanges with as much excitement as my own.)

Probably you've noticed that in the overall sweep of my remarks, my images have gone from recent sky searchings for lights in the dark, to a solitary child seeking similar lights in the dark, to adult self-analytical searchings for light in the inner dark (moments of opportunity), to imagined redistribution of knowledge, to the child-of-separation seeking other enlightenment with benefit of parent-in-back, and so on and on in full spirals of distressing darks and pleasing lights.

I did not, of course, consciously plan these details of my itinerary. Rather, they reflect, I think, the strength of the regressive and progressive forces that shape and reshape not only our associative drifts but all our perception, cognition, action, and other activities.

They reflect, I think, the evocative and organizing effects of the special configurations one recovers, wants to recover, and can't help but recover in particular states of self-analysis: configurations formed and reformed in dreamlike states, recalled or otherwise reexperienced in dreamlike states, and in the recall or reexperiencing, evocative of fresh dreamlike states. I mean, of course, slightly dreamlike states.

PART 4

If I've created the impression that I've found my self-analytical efforts always—or even usually—fruitful, I want now to correct that miscreation. I find self-analysis a most uneven procedure. Often my thoughts seem to lumber along and go nowhere in particular: at least, nowhere in particular I can recognize. Indeed, "nowhere in particular" and "no feelings in particular" are among the most familiar landmarks.

Even when self-analytical efforts seem to go without a hitch, a second glance reveals many. When, for example, my images of the weather trying to clear and my analytical afterimages took place, I regarded them as relatively moving bits of self-analysis, moving me and moving rapidly; but what impresses me looking back is how slowly each step advanced, and once taken, how quickly and often it was reversed. I'm struck by the scope of what I missed and by the narrowness of my associations and interpretations. The sense in the thick of things of proceeding rapidly and the retrospective sense of slowness and incompleteness seem ubiquitous.

What's more, anyone else's report of self-analysis often strikes me as much ado about nothing: or to put it more cautiously, usually leaves me with a similar impression that self-analysis progresses exceedingly slowly and small piece by small piece, if it progresses at all.

What seems surprising is not that self-analysis progresses slowly but that self-analysis progresses at all. Two aspects of our natures seem to favor this occasional, though limited, progress.

First is the fortunate circumstance that defenses and other resistances are neither so consistent nor solid as we sometimes imagine. In the abstract, we may conceive of structures as relatively abiding configurations; but in practice it's all too easy to forget the "relatively." A self-analyzer finds and needs often to refind that defenses and other resistances—like all structures, psychological and physical—have their hidden fluidities. We find and need to refind what we thought we knew: Nothing in nature is static.

If sufficiently patient and persistent, we can sometimes catch our resistances—especially our defenses—at ebb tide rather than flood. Self-analysis blocked at one hour often moves a bit at another.

A defense, or its derivative, completely obstructive at one point, becomes bypassable at another; a defense, invisible at one point, becomes visible and occasionally self-analyzable at another. Self-analysis has helped me sometimes to rediscover and explore the defenses I'd earlier discovered in my psychoanalysis and sometimes to explore defenses I'd not earlier discovered either in myself or in others.

Along with the fluidities of our defenses and of other resistances, and the resulting chances of observing their workings, there comes to our aid in self-analysis, however quietly that obscure phenomenon we call the thrust toward development. In advancing my own self-analytical efforts and in assisting the self-analytical efforts of others (i.e., as analyst to myself and to others), and in examining other spoken and unspoken flights of imagination, I've been struck how elaborately and persistently the thrust toward development expresses itself in edge-of-awareness self-analytical efforts, or what I prefer to call edge-of-awareness inquiries. I have the impression that conscious self-analysis, when most effective, joins forces with those on-going, leading edge, half-hidden, or latent inquiries essential to our development.

In my view, those edge-of-awareness inquiries, those questions both universal and particular, are always expressed and disguised in highly individual codes; and those questions and those codes always shape and are shaped by both reactionary and progressive intentions.

Assuming it is in some regards possible, of what value is self-analysis? Even a cursory review of the literature reveals the expectable divergence of views. Self-analysis is lauded as promising the

most remarkable possibilities and scorned as, by definition, impossible. Arguments are particularly sharp over the therapeutic possibilities of self-analysis. These extremes are familiar, I'll not discuss them
now. But I do want to say of our expectations that there seems to be
a ditch on both sides of the road—expecting too much and expecting
too little.

Most psychoanalysts would agree that the line is thin between
self-analysis and self-deception. I know some who maintain that
there is no line. To those who say self-analysis is impossible, I can
only reply that if we gave up all activities we know to be impossible,
life would be impossibly impoverished.

I suppose we might learn more about the therapeutic value of
self-analysis when and if we have the benefit of many samples of the
efforts of many persons over short runs and long, and when and if we
have a satisfactory way to explore how these persons have or have
not changed. We shall then face the knotty problem of assessing how
our method of assessing has or has not changed what we're assessing.

I imagine we'll sooner come to the view that in matters of such
complexity, it's highly unlikely there are simple sequences deserving
consideration as cause and effect. We are after all, almost in the 21st
century.

In my own case, I believe that the long and fanatical pursuit of
self-analysis has brought about no discernable improvements in my
character, and no more than occasional small gains in tension
management, in selfobject differentiation, in solidifying self-esteem,
in resolution of intrapsychic conflicts, and in advancing homespun
creative capabilities.

Even if therapeutic gains were considerably greater, I see no reason
to confine self-analytical endeavors to the therapeutic, nor to confine
them to the alchemic conversion of countertransference burdens into
useful insights, nor even to the maintaining and advancing of evenly
hovering attention, all of which might reasonably be touted by and
for those analysts of a utilitarian turn of mind. In my view, for
involvement in so conspicuously inefficient and demanding a procedure as self-analysis, the best justification is that it's fun. To paraphrase George Bernard Shaw's review of a play: this is an activity that
will be liked by those who like this sort of activity.

Yet I want now to depart sufficiently from this hedonistic position to
say something more about the potential advantages of self-analysis. If
we follow my weather images and my fantasies of redistribution of
knowledge one way, they reflect, in both content and form, specific

old and on-going disturbances of my nature. But followed another way, it seems to me, these images and fantasies reflect efforts each of us makes, in ways specific to each, to re-create conditions, real and imagined that each finds salutory for many ends.

My fantasy of "redistribution of knowledge" seems both a way to "forget" and a way not to "forget," a way to let go, and a way not to let go. Of course. Freud said it all along. We never really let go. We only find, when we can, new forms for the old. Others have said the same. Everything changes; but all remains the same. Nothing changes but all is different.

My "redistribution of knowledge" seems one of those efforts to have things both ways: to throw out neither the baby nor the bath, neither, that is, the baby nor its supportive surround. My imagined division of cognition between self and parents creates in my mind a mind-clearing illusion of "forgetting," an illusion that assures me, all in the same moment, that the knowledge still guides me—won't let me get lost—and if and when needed will be available on request. (Request, in this dialect, is surely a euphemism for demand.)

I find over and over my visions of pleasurable childhood comings and goings, separations and returns (and other pleasurable findings of light in the dark), seem to soothe the pains of separation from familiar knowledge, especially personified knowledge, to which I'd previously clung. I find over and over these visions soothe the pains of other separations and other changes of orientation, present and past, inner and outer, shallow and deep. I find over and over visions of painful partings from persons, places, and things delicately balanced by visions of pleasing partings and returns. I find as often that my very ways of letting go are my ways of holding on. Each object, each function I glimpse, proves a bridge from there to here, from past to present, from inner to outer.

I find that I seek and find comfort and challenge in imagining or seeing today's lights in the dark; I find comfort and challenge in my particular ways of imagining and seeing (favorite colors, shapes, tonal juxtapositions). In visual play, in general, and with lights and darks, in particular, I find my mind most frisky and most exploratory. I find that in the look of a ray of sunlight on an old stone wall, in the twinkle of colors in the shadow of a dune, in the tension between a gleam in the eye and a dark scowl, my mind leaps about and seems to find apparent connections between the seemingly limited microcosm of current visual impression and the seemingly endless preoccupations—conflicts, interests, and other occupants of my mind—that press for expression.

Proceeding from the assumption that what I've observed of myself is not entirely idiosyncratic, let me try now to frame some generalizations. As we go back and forth in time and space, each has preferred ways of touching home base. When in slightly dreamlike states, we suspend some functions and sharpen others, when we turn our worlds upside down and in the turning, enlighten and frighten ourselves, each has his or her own ways of making the unfamiliar familiar.

In these epiphanies — Wordsworth called them "spots of time" — we go home again both by what we conjure and by our very ways of conjuring. Having organized our first self-other worlds in our own idiosyncratic ways of seeing, hearing, thinking, and other ways of figuring, we expand those worlds from the most familiar to other and larger worlds — from mother, for example, to Mother Nature. The very exercise of these familiar functions then helps each of us to find, that is, to construct, in the face of extraordinary change, an extraordinary array of constancies and continuities. In this sense, we can and always do go home again. We cannot go forward without going back.

To put the matter another way, we go home not simply through what we perceive in the world away from home, but by perceiving in those familiar ways we once exercised solely at home, which is to say, by our familiar and highly individual ways of perceiving. All this, I imagine, forever creates new versions of the child immigrant to new worlds.

We find the worlds we seek and we find them in the favorite ways we seek to find them. As John Berger (1980) once put it, "The field that you are standing before appears to have the same proportions as your own life" (p. 198).

If we could and would associate freely to all our everyday perceptions, we could and would find that in many regards those perceptions are as much a dream as those dreams we dream asleep. If every dream is full of day residues, every perception is full of dream residues.

I take it that this ordinary interdigitation — this interpenetration, this endless conversion of inner to outer to inner to outer — is even more complex in those special worlds of perception in which each of us most fully chooses, and cannot help choosing, to live. To those who make their worlds most rich by what they touch and by what they are touched, one such perception, memory, metaphor, or other image of touching, is more touching than a thousand perceptions, memories, metaphors, or other images otherwise figured. Let Proust have the smell of his madeleines; they will have the touch.

When once we know these favorite experiential codes of ourselves or another, we know where in our self-analyses or in our analyses of others to attend most carefully in order to grasp what most moves us or the other. We know, too, the tongue in which we must talk in order to talk most movingly to ourselves or another.

Some people have confided that in their reveries, and other progressive regressions (for example, in states of evenly hovering attention), they routinely see things; others that they hear things; others that they feel things. Only one person has spoken of smelling things. No one has yet told me of tasting things.

One woman revealed that she not only customarily feels things but that she feels them in what she takes to be a particular part of her gut. When she has a "gut feeling" about something, it's really a gut feeling. I know a man who feels things mainly in his large muscles. I know another who gets his messages most richly in proprioceptive sensations.

One man revealed a consistent series of visual images in which I was able to discern a special sensitivity to an extraordinary range of details of perspective, and of the complex relations of near objects to those far off. Another heard things in ways that put special stress— described though unrecognized—on nuances of volume and pitch, especially on subtle contrasts of volume and pitch, in particular quick and slight juxtapositions of louds and softs, highs and lows. He fathomed what people meant as much or more from these musical particulars as from the content of their words.

I've been struck by how often the preference for a particular perceptual system is matched by a preference for metaphors constructed of the materials of that system, and within it, of preferred subsytems. I've been struck by how often the boundaries between the preferred perception and preferred metaphor are unclear. When some persons say, "I see what you mean," they mean what they say. They are not talking metaphor; they are talking actuality.

We know of this phenomenon in psychotics and even in those we say have a vivid imagination, are visual thinkers, or who use eidetic imagery. But I suspect these experiences are more common to the rest of us than we know. And I wonder what kinds of confusion result when the person who hears things and the one who feels things talk to each other and each thinks the other is talking metaphor when the other is not.

I believe—which means I have a hunch—that in self-analysis, as in other arts, when we descend into those states in which our preferred metaphors, images, and perceptions shift most fluidly from the one to the other, we are most where for us "the action is." Which is also to say, I suspect that, for most of us, creativity is liveliest where the boundary narrows most between creativity and confusion. We cannot choose the terms of our creativity. We must, as the old Texas saying has it, "dance with what brung us."

Though I agree with those analysts who've said that our most adaptive functions tend to be most silent and therefore most difficult to observe, I wonder if those functions would seem quite so silent if in listening to ourselves, and to others, we were tuned less selectively to the sounds of malady. If in our states of what we hope to be regressive progression, we were to observe more carefully the contents of our preferred means and conditions of perception and representation, if we were to pursue those observations more vigorously, take them more seriously, and share them more candidly, I wonder if self-analysis might make a more consistent, recognizable, and valuable contribution to the variegated fields of adult observation.

I wonder, especially, if a fuller sharing of our preferences for perception and representation, and of our accompanying fantasies, might tell us more about those functions, about the intricacies of separation and restitution, and about the elusive workings of the creativity of everyday life. I refer to the earliest creativities of our childhood and to those later creativities that repeat, elaborate, and transcend the earlier.

In self-analysis, I believe, some aspects of our common functioning, that is, of our functioning in common, become, through different quirks of our natures, more visible to some of us and other aspects to others. We have, one might say, different holes in our heads; and these permit different looks inward at what, in one form or another, may pertain to us all. If we could bear telling more and hearing more, it seems plausible to expect an advance in our common knowledge.

Even if I'm mistaken in these expectations of general advance, I believe such pursuits of self-inquiry might have the individual benefit of sharpening our sensitivities to the endless subjectivities in what we ordinarily regard as objectivities. If nothing else, the expanded search of the relation between the observer and the observed (i.e., between ourselves and what we observe) might help us to achieve a laudable, if limited, increase of humility.

In this regard, however, we are forewarned by Benjamin Franklin, who, in the conclusion to his discussion of "self examination" in his *Autobiography* says that the reader can now see what a struggle he, Mr. Franklin, has waged to achieve a proper humility. But the trouble, he adds, is that it's so easy to become inordinately proud of one's humility.

REFERENCE

Berger, J. (1980), *About Looking*. New York: Pantheon.
Franklin, B. (1791), *Autobiography*. New York: Heritage Press, 1951.
Gardner, R. (1983), *Self Inquiry*. Hillsdale, NJ: The Analytic Press, 1987.

IV

The Role of the Other in Self-Analysis

As Gardner pointed out in the previous chapter, we are not alone when we engage in self-analysis, but are involved in complex relationships with our internal objects: "Of talkers and listeners there are many." Others, real and imagined, play a significant role in our self-analyses.

Eifermann explores the interplay between inner and outer worlds, past and present, self and other in the course of her ongoing self-analysis. In a burst of creative output over a brief four-year period, she wrote a remarkable series of six self-analytic papers. In her chapter for this volume, she looks back over the unfolding process of writing, publishing, and presenting those papers, as that process leads to her progressive discovery of the impact of real and fantasized audiences on her self-analysis.

She becomes aware of strong transferential connections between her experiences of the audience and her early internal objects (see Wolf, chap. 6). Her working through of those transferences (and the complex, conscious–unconscious dialogues associated with them) become the central task of both her writing and her self-analysis, as well as her exploration of their dynamic mutual influence.

Her initial modes of private self-analytic inquiry included analysis of her interactions with patients, self-reflection regarding events in her personal life, and examination of her associations to dreams or spontaneous preoccupations. "All these self-analyses, while they were initiated by design, always led in quite unpredicted directions that brought in their wake unanticipated recollections, thoughts, and emotions, often deeply disturbing."

Her written record of these psychic activities provided added raw material for her self-analysis. The writing, like a fixative in a photographic darkroom, granted a degree of permanence to the otherwise fleeting, elusive mix of thoughts, images, and feelings. Also, as suggested by Sonnenberg and Anzieu (chaps. 12 and 13), the writing creates a certain distance and lends a quality of "otherness" to our psychic productions, and therefore facilitates the splitting of our ego into experiencer and observer, so necessary to both the dyadic and the self-analytic process.

Although she did not initially plan to make aspects of her self-analysis public, she found that her published articles, her earlier drafts and notes, and her reactions to the very process of writing and presenting publicly, became rich sources of data for her self-analysis, which, in turn became the focus of her professional writing.

> Thus my audience, fantasized and real, took form and gradually became a constant presence. Indeed, unanticipated discoveries concerning the unconscious role the audience played, or served, in the course of writing, turned out again and again to be integral to the subject of the paper I was writing.

Unifying both her self-analysis and her writing is Eifermann's dedicated search for the "child within" the adult. Her ongoing self-analysis is her "within search" method for evoking the child and "for studying the child's experiences and their unconscious meanings."

More explicitly than most other psychoanalytic writers, Eifermann describes the fears and hesitations encountered as she moves from reserving self-analysis as a private activity to publicly sharing important aspects of the process and content of her self-analytic efforts. She becomes increasingly aware of the extent to which she experiences the audience as a threat which mobilizes defensive reactions. In particular, she focuses on the fear of the audience regarding her as crazy (and on the childhood origins of that fear). She goes on to explore the relationships among self-analysis, creativity, and madness, as well as the risks and benefits of sharing our "crazy" ideas with others.

Eifermann approvingly quotes Anzieu who concludes his study of Freud's self-analysis with the comment: "There can be no proper self-analysis unless it is communicated to someone else." But Eifermann grapples with the questions of how much and in what form to share the results of her self-analysis. Her articulation of her dilemma helps us think about our dialogues with our inner objects, and our relationships to our audiences, real and fantasized, as we proceed with our self-analytic efforts. She illuminates the anxieties and conflicting motivations all of us confront when we attempt to share our fragments of self-analytic understanding.

Freud's interest in treatment was secondary to his passion for theory building and scientific investigation. In contrast, Sandor Ferenczi, who was analyzed by Freud and who developed a complex, conflictual friendship and collaboration with him, was drawn more to the therapeutic potential of psychoanalysis and to experimentation with technique to enhance the efficacy of treatment. Ferenczi's experiments raised questions that we still struggle with today. In what form and under what conditions are the analyst's abstinence and neutrality helpful to the patient? When do they lead to a retraumatization of the patient? To what extent and under what conditions should the analyst reveal to the patient aspects of his or her inner world, including thoughts and feelings about the patient? What is the role of insight in producing therapeutic change? What is the role of experience, particularly the patient's experience of the relationship with the analyst? How is the analytic relationship the same as or different from an "ordinary" relationship? How does the analyst understand and make use of the patient's perceptions and interpretations of the treatment relationship? To what extent is mutuality possible in the analytic relationship?

Ernest Jones's (1957) negative portrayal of Ferenczi in his biography of Freud, as well as the actual disagreements and conflicts between Ferenczi and Freud, led to a neglect of Ferenczi's ideas, particularly in the United States until recent times. Also contributing to that neglect was the reaction to the heavy-handed, manipulative quality of later technical experiments, in particular those of Alexander's (1946) "corrective emotional experience." But the fundamental questions that Ferenczi raised about the nature of therapeutic action and about the centrality of the relationship in treatment remain.

Growing out of their friendship, professional collaboration, and shared interest in the questions raised by Ferenczi's work, Harris and Ragen are experimenting with a technique which they refer to as mutual supervision. Their innovations enable them to explore their countertransferences more fully (without burdening their patients as Ferenczi did in his experiment with mutual analysis) and to advance their self-analytic understanding.

Harris and Ragen also innovate in their mode of organizing and presenting the material for this volume. They offer excerpts from an

interlocking set of dialogues between patient and analyst and between analyst and supervisory colleague "in an attempt to evoke the
complexity and richness of the multiple transferences and countertransferences."

They carefully structure their mutual supervisory sessions to focus
on their countertransference reactions to their patients. Each has the
opportunity to seek help from the other, and each has the opportunity to provide help. This shifting of function and perspective
involves moving fluidly across internal and external boundaries and
across a variety of emotional polarities. Such a process makes
considerable personal and professional demands on both members of
the mutual supervisory dyad and obviously requires deep respect and
trust.

Like Ferenczi, Harris and Ragen are interested in making use of
what they learn about themselves in their mutual supervision for the
benefit of their patients. In particular, they struggle to be fully
engaged and to make optimal use of their relationships with their
patients. Conceptually they split the relationship into "transferential"
and "real" elements. In their view, analysis of transference distortions
contributes to the patient's sense of who the analyst isn't, but not who
the analyst is.

> The question then becomes, if this is not who the analyst is, who is she
> or he? Analyzing the transference leaves the patient to build a picture
> of the analyst by implication and inference. In contrast, when the
> analyst also at times presents herself or himself as a real other who is
> genuinely affected by and has authentic personal responses to the
> patient, the patient has a different kind of experience. She or he
> discovers and engages a new object and out of this builds a new psychic
> structure.

Conceptually splitting the treatment relationship in this way can be
problematic. Who is to judge what is real and what is transferential?
If patient and analyst disagree, who is the arbiter?

When transference is viewed from a different perspective, as an
interaction of patient's and analyst's subjectivities, and therefore as a
joint creation of patient and analyst, then analysis of the transference
necessarily reveals aspects of the psychic realities of both participants.
Such a perspective may extricate us from the dilemma of determining
what is "real" and "genuine." Nevertheless the challenge of making
optimal use of the treatment relationship remains.

The data generated by Harris' and Ragen's model of mutual
supervision will help us simultaneously to investigate the treatment

relationship and to deepen our understanding of the self-analytic process. Their approach vividly demonstrates the importance of the "other" in advancing our self-analytic efforts.

Poland begins his exploration of the role of the other in self-analysis by comparing the self-analytic and dyadic-analytic situations. The most obvious difference, the absence or presence of another person, may obscure underlying similarities. We are not as alone as we may believe in the self-analytic situation nor as connected to the other as we may believe in the dyadic situation. A variety of others — some in our awareness, others hidden — engage with us in helpful or not so helpful ways in our self-analyses. In the dyadic situation, both patient and analyst are immersed in their own subjective experiences and struggle to become more fully aware (and to remain unaware) of the separateness of the other.

> The search for knowledge of the inner workings of one person's mind is the ultimate similarity between self-analysis and clinical analysis. Behind that similarity lies an essential difference. The paradox that discomforts our usually ordered way of thinking is that one's inner emotional experience is unique and internal even when one is sharing a moment with an other, and at the same time one lives within the network of human connection even when one appears to be alone. The seemingly self-evident difference of solitude of self-analysis and shared intimacy in two-person clinical work is not so simple as at first appears.

Poland reminds us of Anna Freud's (1981) distinction of the different kinds of knowing of self and other. She spoke of "insight" to describe knowledge gained from within our self-experience and of "understanding" to describe knowledge gained of another's internal experience. The two kinds of knowledge are not the same. We try to bridge the difference through our empathic identification with the other. In the self-analytic situation, how do we go about providing the "empathy with ourselves" (to use Margulies' phrase), or the "other eyes" (to use Poland's terms), so that we can be experiencer and observer and can attempt to look at ourselves, as Poland suggests, "with ruthless candor"?

He goes on to describe the ways in which we take in the eyes of supportive, challenging, and interpretive others:

> The seemingly lonely task of self-analysis opens within the matrix of connection to others in the world, others known and not known to be known, others as close at hand as one's spouse and children and friends and enemies, and as far removed as the presences hidden in the inner lives of other people and their works.

Even with the aid of "other eyes" our self-analyses proceed slowly, incrementally, that is, when they proceed at all. Poland distinguishes between self-analytic gains in understanding of a segment of our inner life (e.g., illuminating a delimited countertransference enactment) and self-analytic contributions to understanding and modifying aspects of our character. Confronted with ongoing resistance and the enduring power of the repetition compulsion, we find those characterological changes harder to come by, as is also the case in a dyadic analysis. With benevolent skepticism, Poland concludes, "We await multiple longitudinal studies which could demonstrate clear alteration in character beyond repeated small steps."

REFERENCES

Alexander, F., French, T.M., et al. (1946), *Psychoanalytic Therapy: Principles and Applications*. NY: Ronald Press.

Freud, A. (1981), Insight: Its presence and absence as a factor in normal development. *The Psychoanalytic Study of the Child*, 36:241-249. New Haven, CT: Yale University Press.

Jones, E. (1957), *The Life and Work of Sigmund Freud, Vol. 3*, pp. 176–177. NY. Basic Books.

9

The Discovery of Real and Fantasized Audiences for Self-Analysis

Rivka R. Eifermann

ON MAKING SELF-ANALYSIS PUBLIC

Self-analysis is a private, personal undertaking. This at least in part explains the scarcity of publications describing self-analytic processes outside the context of the analysis of countertransference. But from Freud onward, psychoanalysts have acknowledged that self-analysis can be effectively applied to the exploration of various psychological phenomena. Thus, when I applied my self-analytic work to issues of general interest, I had an interest in making it public. In consequence, the public audience with whom I would share my self-analytic material began to come into my awareness. Awareness of this audience developed in various directions. I came to know of other audiences that were accompanying me in the course of my self-analytic work and were influencing the form it would take as well as its content. My self-analysis of the process I underwent as I contemplated making pieces of my self-analysis public, and struggled with my reactions to the fact of doing so, led to the discovery of audiences

The writing of this paper was supported by a grant from the Breuninger Stiftung Gmbh, Essen, Germany.

I would like to acknowledge the essential contributions of Erich Gumbel, Regine Haesler, and Rachel Blass to my self-analytic writing. Since their contributions can be understood only in the context of what I say regarding "private audiences," I postpone further elaboration to the final section of this chapter.

both real and fantasied and the complex role they play in the private process of self-analysis.

My own self-analysis was exclusively private until a few years ago. It has come to include analysis of clinical interactions as well as occasional self-reflection regarding personal matters. In periods of more focused self-analytic work, the method I use is to put down in writing associations to whatever is preoccupying me (often it is a dream). These associative notes frequently include some spontaneous reflections on whatever comes to my mind as well as unanticipated observations and even new insights. This "basic material" then serves as "raw data" for my self-analysis. I begin working on it right away or some hours, or even days, later; at times I return repeatedly to the material as it accumulates. This work includes putting down in writing new ideas and associations that occur as I go over the material. But in periods of intensive self-analysis most of my new insights, even breakthroughs, happen while I am not actively "at work," but primarily when I am dozing, or as I wake up at night or in the morning. It is the intense commitment to, and deep involvement with self-analysis during such periods that inevitably, in my experience, sooner or later lead to new discoveries. The method is described in some detail in Eifermann, 1987b. Applying the same method in working on childhood recollections of events, tales, and games that have been "encapsulated" since childhood, I have often successfully evoked "the child within me." In my published writings two kinds of material are used as my self-analytic data: encapsulated childhood material and, in addition, my publications and their earlier drafts and notes. That is, the process of writing and making it public, became a new source of data for self-analysis, although this was never planned. Because the data are available in written form, they provide a frame of reference to which I can keep returning.

Not all pieces of self-analysis that I made public were originally conducted with such a purpose in mind. This is the case in particular with my 1987c paper, which is based on an analysis motivated by the deep distress that I felt following the presentation of an earlier paper (Eifermann, 1987b). Other papers are based on self-analyses that began as a means of studying specific issues, such as the exploration of unanticipated and fleeting or "slippery" phenomena, parapraxes, momentary fantasies and the like, for which this "within" search method seemed to me extraordinarily suitable. Regarding these issues one's own self is the most available, "on the spot," for the exploration. My paper on the "eureka" experience (Eifermann, 1989a) belongs to this category. The "within" search method is also effective for studying a child's experiences and their unconscious meanings.

Children may have great difficulty simultaneously experiencing and observing themselves "from the outside," let alone verbalizing their observations and then analyzing them. By using self-analysis as a search method, it is possible to evoke the "child within" and as an adult articulate and analyze the experiencing child. Several of my other papers are based on this view.

All these self-analyses, while they were initiated by design, always led in quite unpredicted directions that brought in their wake unanticipated recollections, thoughts, and emotions, often deeply disturbing. Thus, questions always emerged, in one form or another, in the course of writing such as: Do I wish to make this material public? Is it appropriate to do so? Does what I have to say justify the risks I would be taking? Why do I want to take such risks? My audience, fantasized and real, took form and gradually became a constant presence. Indeed, unanticipated discoveries concerning the unconscious role the audience played, or served, in the course of writing, turned out again and again to be integral to the subject of the paper I was writing.

In this chapter I discuss aspects of my analysis of the processes I underwent in relationship to my audiences. While the relationship was multidimensional and complex, it is possible nevertheless to trace a line of development that runs through the evolving interactions. It traversed a difficult path from my first recognition of the audience's meaningful presence for me, through the unfolding of various significances that my audiences represented and my attempts to defend against their emergence and the recognition of their significance. I had the opportunity to work through my relationship with my audiences, to discover their inner representations and elucidate the nature of my dialogues with them. Of special import was a dialogue concerning the creativity—or perhaps, was it the craziness—of my writing and public performance. While this analysis resulted in important developments of personal significance, its significance extends beyond. It reveals some of the forces inevitably involved in the course of making self-analysis public. But in a larger sense it contributes to the understanding of the dialogues that all persons have to some extent, with private and fantasied audiences in the course of their self-analysis.

What follows in this chapter deals with seven recent papers of mine. Since the order in which these papers were written is relevant, yet not apparent from the order of the manuscripts' publication, I clarify the following. Six of the seven papers discussed, all written in the years 1985–1987, are based primarily on self-analytic material. The one exception is an analysis of the fairy tale *Little Red Riding Hood* and of interactions between mothers and daughters in the course of reading it. Written in 1985, it was published in a book that appeared only four years later, and is hence referred to as Eifermann, 1989b. In the same year (1985) I analyzed this analysis of *Little Red Riding Hood*. This paper, published in 1987, was my first self-analytic paper, and although written following 1989b, it is referred to as 1987a. There followed Eifermann 1987b – a more extensive self-analysis concerning "my" internalized Little Red Riding Hood, an analysis that was the basis of a discussion of psychoanalytic approaches to fairy tales. The presentation of that 1987b paper at a symposium in Germany evoked powerful inner reactions that eventually led to the writing of the third paper of the self-analytic "series," 1987c, on insights gained following that presentation, concerning my internalized "Germany" and "the Germans." In the fourth paper of the "series," 1987d, I presented my "within (re)search method," by means of an analysis of a recon- structed childhood game, and in the same year I wrote the fifth paper, applying the method to a self-analysis of the occurrence of the "eureka" and related phenomena. This paper was published two years later and is referred to as 1989a. It was followed by the sixth and final paper of the "series," Eifermann, 1987e, that appeared in print in German translation only. It is a sequel to the 1987c "Germany" paper, and they will be discussed consecutively.

THE SELF-ANALYTIC "SERIES"

My Initial Discovery of the Audience in Self-Analysis

Already in the course of writing my first self-analytic paper (Eifer- mann, 1987a), I could not help but recognize the significant role that my prospective audience (or potential readers)[1] had taken in shaping the paper's content as well as its form.

The main argument of the paper, entitled "Interactions Between Textual Analysis and Related Self-Analysis," was that "self-analysis can contribute to textual analysis, as the latter can evoke and enrich the former" (p. 39). For purposes of illustration I presented a piece of self-analysis on my own text of an earlier paper (Eifermann, 1989b), in which I had presented an analysis of the tale *Little Red Riding Hood*. In my reported self-analysis of my 1989b text, two childhood recollec- tions related to myself and my internalized mother emerged as

---

[1]While throughout the chapter I refer to "audiences," what I have to say applies broadly to readers as well, despite the fact that they remain nonspecific to me.

connecting links with my earlier analysis of Little Red Riding Hood
and her mother, who had (also) been depicted as wanting as a
protecting figure.

In that first paper I communicated this realization and the insight
to which it had led, as follows:

> As I was putting down the above, with considerable feeling of
> discomfort and increasing doubts as to whether I would ever so crudely
> and unfairly expose my (internalized) mother in public, I was suddenly
> shocked by the realization that precisely this has been the unconscious
> driving force behind the enterprise. At that time the angry, hurt,
> vengeful child within me still wished to do something through which I
> would expose my mother to shame, just as she had exposed me to my
> whole (rather new) class of school-children. But I would overcome my
> pain and disgrace actively by telling my tale rather than being a passive
> victim. And in so doing I would place the blame where it was due!
> [Eifermann, 1987a, p. 49; italics added].

My first impulse upon discovering my unconscious motive in
"telling on" my mother "by telling my tale" but not as a victim was to
stop with that paper. Instead, however, I undertook a further stretch
of self-analysis, which then led me to continue writing it, sharing my
new realization, as just quoted. I then explained that "with further
processing I have gradually become more in touch with the child
within me, the child to whom the shock of awareness, the accompanying shame and guilt—and the vengeful intentions—belonged" (p.
50); and that moreover, as my stance had changed:

> I have come to realize that a rare opportunity has come my way in the
> process of writing this paper. For I have inadvertently, "before your
> very eyes," while creating a text—and this time an analysis of a textual
> analysis—reached an unanticipated inner realization. This has driven
> me to a stretch of self-analysis, which has affected my self-experience
> and, in turn, the direction and fate of my text. That such a process
> exists, and that it can be reciprocally enriching, is the main thesis of my
> paper! [p. 50].

The fact that my fantasized acting out toward my internalized
mother in the here-and-now of my presentation ("before your very
eyes") was integral to the theme of the paper, helped to alleviate my
further doubts, as well as to partly deny them, and thus enabled me
to proceed to the second paper of the series. My experience in writing
the first (1987a) self-analytic paper convinced me, as I argued in the
second (1987b), that "the context of fairy tales, encapsulated, preserved and untouched as it often remains since childhood, tends to

provide a particularly productive source of rediscovering the child within the adult" (Eifermann, 1987b, p. 60). Hence, when invited to a symposium in Munich on psychoanalytic views on fairy tales, I chose to continue the self-analysis of my internalized tale of Little Red Riding Hood and present it to my audience using the presentation as an illustration of my views regarding two issues concerning fairy tales. I argued that although the "narratives" constructed by psychoanalysts in their various attempts to interpret fairy tales can often serve as useful general paradigms or prototypes, such interpretations nevertheless seldom overlap with the personal significance and meanings of fairy tales for the individual for whom the tales have many idiosyncratic associations and meanings, which no general statement can ever encompass. I also argued that there is an almost exclusive emphasis in these interpretations on the meanings of fairy tales to *children* and that my intention was to counterbalance this bias to some extent through my presentation:

> In my direct and indirect experience . . . fairy tales remain preserved (albeit in an often condensed and distorted form), loaded with (descriptively) unconscious meanings in adults who have been exposed to them as children. For re-exposure in adulthood evokes, with particular facility and strength, conflicts and defenses that belong to the child within the adult [p. 52].

In my particular case, this re-exposure also meant public exposure. Indeed, although I failed to refer to this fact in the just quoted introduction to the paper, I once again became keenly aware of its role in my writing as my self-analysis unfolded in its course. For I became aware that I was not just reporting on "the child within," but was partly guided by that "child within" in the manner of my exposition. In a section of that same paper headed "Revealing [in public] the Embarrassed Child Within" (p. 72), I described how as I reread the final section of its original draft, it seemed to me that the section describing childhood recollections about my grandfather had been written very unevenly. I wrote:

> [I]n part I sense the child within coming across directly—excited and involved; in part, remote and distant, rather boring, the anxiety and fascination, let alone the (almost) explicit sexuality, hardly coming across. . . . Only some time after I had written this description of my games with my grandfather, did it become clearer to me just how hesitant and cautious I had been in writing it, and how much the child within—still excited, scared, and terribly guilty—was guiding what I said and what I had left out. As in analysis when one sometimes suddenly feels extremely uncomfortable or even completely unable to

say things one would have no difficulty saying under less regressive circumstances, so I found myself, for example, leaving out the word "sexual" when I described the pleasures of sitting on my grandpa's knees ("I don't quite recall that," I thought, trying to be as accurate as I could in my description) [1987b, pp. 72–73].

At the time I wrote that description, I was not clearly in touch with the part of the child within me that, notwithstanding embarrassment, guilt, and anxiety, nevertheless chose to expose her oedipal triumph for all to see.

The Audience Emerges as Transference Object

The first hint of an awareness that the role my audience served for me was that of a *transference object* is expressed in the foregoing quoted section; I say that the feelings that were evoked in me as I was writing about my experiences were similar to those that may occur in analysis. Rather than pursue the issue of transference I continued with my preoccupation with "the child within me," and this helped me, once again, to deny my discomfort regarding my self-revelation. And it turned out that while this internal strategy regarding my self-revelations served to relax my disconcerting feelings in the course of working on the paper, as well as upon presenting it, the strategy broke down immediately following the presentation. Notwithstanding the paper's positive reception at the Munich symposium on psychoanalytic views on fairy tales, my doubts and anxieties increased following its presentation to the point where they threatened to overwhelm me; and I then undertook an intensive stretch of self-analysis in an attempt to deal with my distress.

Eventually, this effort turned in part into the paper that followed, " 'Germany' and 'the Germans': Acting Out Fantasies, and Their Discovery in Self-Analysis" (Eifermann, 1987c). In the introduction I explained:

> When I wrote the final version of my recent paper, *"Fairy tales—A royal road to the child within the adult"* . . . to be presented in *Munich* at an international symposium on psychoanalytic views of fairy tales, I referred to everything written in my notes and draft for that paper, since my reflections on them had turned out to be a major aspect of the paper. There was, however, one section of the notes that I left untouched, "for future reference": what I had written in that section about *"Germany"* and the *"Germans"* as *"transference objects"*—although of great interest to me—was, at the same time, very upsetting. Besides, I thought (and commented in my notes), I could not include it in my paper anyway, since it would open up an issue which, although related

to the paper's main theme, would make it too long. Yet it turned out that this exclusion had extraordinary significance for me, and some consequence. For, what I had put off elaborating and working through in the words I was writing, I acted out, unaware, towards my Munich audience upon presenting it [p. 245; italics added].

This acting out was closely related to my having been born in Germany and having left it in early childhood. I, being Jewish, emigrated, together with my family, with the rise of the Nazis, not to return, except briefly for a conference in 1960 and again in 1985 in quick succession for the International Psychoanalytic Conference in Hamburg and for the symposium on fairy tales in Munich. I had written the paper in English, and it was translated into German, which I could barely read. Hence my reading was slow and rather clumsy:

I found my finger running along the lines as I struggled from one word or phrase to the next. I felt dependent on my host . . . who . . . quietly read the "difficult" words for me to repeat after him. . . . I only later gradually realized [that these were signs that] I was performing as would a little girl: not quite up to the difficult task at hand, and yet determined to make it to the end—all the long way" [p. 247].

Later it dawned on me, that

by reading my paper as if I "were" in the *here* and *now*, the little girl who had left Germany at less than 3 years of age, hardly able to read/ cope . . . I . . . realized, that [what] was (at least in part) responsible for my feeling so upset, as though something was wrong, when my audience applauded . . . [was that] I was telling "the Germans": "See, and experience with me what you have done to me, driving me out, inadequately prepared. . . . The 'German' part of me has remained a little girl. I am hardly able to cope/read, express my own feelings and thoughts in my-your mother tongue. I am agonized while doing it because it is so difficult. But, bright and determined little girl that I am, I carry on persistently, in spite of you. And I will make certain that you, who are the cause of all this agony, will agonize with me, all the long way" [pp. 249–250].

Summarizing the ambivalent manner in which I had presented the paper, I wrote:

I had returned to my mother tongue, that of "the Germans," I had also revealed my associative processes and shared some very personal tales and deep emotions with "them". Nonetheless, I had remained remote, up on the podium, reading into a microphone, so engaged in my task that I had almost no contact with the people listening to me. Moreover, I made it quite clear and explicit that what I was reading was not quite my own, because it was in German [p. 252].

In terms of the paper's latent content, "I was struck, amazed, and also shocked, at the parts of my paper that came to my mind; they seemed blatantly directed toward my transference 'object' " (p. 249)— the Germans. In the self-analysis that followed I became aware that behind my vague apprehension that my German-speaking audience was international, there were unconscious fantasies about that audience as "the Germans." Moreover, in unconscious fantasy "the Germans" represented, and were represented by, persons of special significance to me from my early life.

Creativity or Craziness: Entering a Threatening Self-Analytic Dialogue with the Audience

Recognizing the Audience's Threat. Through a gradual process, mostly unconscious, I reached an important discovery regarding my intensive involvement in self-analysis at that time. I found that my preoccupation with latent meanings of the content of my paper kept me from attending to what it emotionally meant to me to present the manifest; that my focus on latent meanings of that third paper, on " 'Germany' and 'the Germans'," kept me from "knowing" about the continuing threat that exposing the manifest content of that paper to my audience held for me. The awareness that the audience did pose such a threat after all, and that I was defending against being in touch with the threat, became more explicit while I was preparing a public lecture on "close listening to the *manifest*." In the course of preparing that lecture there returned a "thought/feeling" that had taken hold of me briefly following my presentation in Germany, before I began to delve into the latent meanings of the content of that paper. That thought/feeling, however, was only further articulated three self-analytic papers later, in a paper on "craziness,"[2] the sixth and last of the "series." There I wrote:

Following my presentation [in Munich] I was struck with the thought/ feeling . . . that I was "crazy" to have presented such a manifestly personal paper to an audience of complete strangers. Along with the

---

[2]"Craziness" denotes a wide spectrum of emotional and ideational states ranging from "wild," "absurd," and "inappropriate," to dangerous sources of inspiration. This ambiguity is reflected in my varying use of quotation marks.

thought came very short waves of acute embarrassment, "pangs of panic," which seem to have acted as signals. For the feelings were soon totally covered up and replaced by the nagging questions, "What was I doing?" "Why did I do it?" which focused on the length of my presentation, due to my having read it in German, which I can barely do. It was these feelings—evoked through my general feeling of distress—that led me to explore . . . latent meanings. . . . It seems that, rather than remain with the helpless feeling that threatened to sweep over me when I "recognized," too late, that I had acted "crazy" quite openly, I engaged myself instead in the active, self-analytic search for the unconscious meanings of my presentation [Eifermann, 1987e, p. 24; in German].

Facing the Threat: Confrontation and Defense. From the start I had doubts about making this paper on "craziness" public. In part these doubts had precursors: during and following the presentation of my earlier papers I was concerned with how I could, expose/reveal in this way or even whether it was appropriate to do so. Now, however, I was directly facing my internal fear of being considered crazy. I was no longer isolating what it meant to me to expose/reveal this personal material in public. And yet I knew that I wanted to do so nevertheless. Now my concern was less how or should I expose, but why I wanted to do so. Here, as before, my preoccupation with thoughts and fantasies about presenting led to insights and now necessitated major modification of the paper. I knew that I was going to present this paper once again in Germany, and I sensed that matters deep and unfinished, relating to the Germans,[3] were continuing to play an important part. At this point my thoughts and fantasies led me to the realization of the nature of these matters: *that I was in the midst of a vocal yet unspoken dialogue with the Germans, and the topic was craziness and the freeing of creative forces.* This dialogue took center stage in the modified paper. While I was telling the Germans what I still had left to say to them, I was trying to draw them into a dialogue with me. The original draft remained as the middle section of the paper, but it was now preceded and followed by sections that placed it in the wider context, pertaining to Germany. I recognized once again the unconscious connection that I had formed between my audience and my early internal objects. Once this connection again reached consciousness, I was free to use it to suggest an analogy between my

---

[3]My inconsistent and varying use of quotation marks in this context is meaningful in that it reflects variations in the degree to which I recognized that I was using the Germans as a transference object.

internalized family and the German "family," and thus I told my German audience:

> The more inner freedom we have to "free associate," the more likely we are to reach the genius (*gaon* [in Hebrew]) but also the "madness" (*she' gaon* [in Hebrew]) within us. And those of us who have known *she' gaon* in their "family (member)" may be consciously or unconsciously frightened of being in touch with the "spark of genius" within, lest what they encounter and expose turn out to be their "madness," or "psychotic core" [Eifermann, 1987e, p. 26; in German).

Following my presentation of this modified paper in Frankfurt and Tübingen, my agreement to have it published (in German translation) in the *German Psychoanalytic Bulletin* was requested. I was reluctant. The distressing and difficult aspects of self-disclosure prevailed. The paper finally did appear.[4]

The conflictual nature of my invitation of my audience to engage in a dialogue is quite explicit in the comprehensive version of my paper. I said to my audience (of psychoanalysts):

> Even after completing the draft of this paper, which contained a description of how my latent and manifest preoccupation with "madness," and the embarrassment that my revealing it here would evoke — I still doubted whether it was suitable for presentation in public. For I knew that the fact that what I had written was quite outside of the conventions of current psychoanalytic presentations, might well lead my audience to consider the paper either unnecessary, or, indeed inappropriate. And I knew that if this did happen, my audience would then feel imposed upon, captive in the upsetting situation of someone exposing him or herself overmuch; in other words, an unwilling, embarrassed witness to inadequate behavior [p. 20; in German].

I then further explored the inner processes that had led me to the decision to present the paper, notwithstanding my many doubts:

> It was only as I came more and more in touch with how very embarrassed I had been by my experience of the "psychotic" aspects of

---

[4]I later submitted the manuscript for presentation at a conference in the United States, this time in its original form. The referees felt that something was missing that made the paper incomplete. It was as if they knew that what I was giving them had been pulled out of its context. Did they sense that it was the partner to my dialogue that was removed? Was I drawing them into a substitute dialogue with me in which they were put in the role of demanding that I not foreclose the dialogue with the Germans?

the [my] home situation . . . that I was able to see that I was trying to reverse the situation through this presentation: Still in the role of "transference objects," you "Germans"/"parents (mother)" were now to experience the terrible imposition—so unbearably embarrassing to witness—of inadequate, uncontrolled self-exposure of the kind that "you" had imposed upon me in the past with "your" shameful, "mad" behavior.

I hope that sharing these insights with you—and thereby moving a step closer to being able to relate to you rather than to my fantasies—will facilitate a positive exchange between us during this presentation, notwithstanding the difficulties involved, in listening to as well as in presenting the material [p.21; in German].

In the course of writing my first self-analytic paper (Eifermann, 1987a), I had discovered that I had used my audience in the role of third party to whom I chose to "tell on" my early internalized object; now I discovered that in my complex relationship to my audience I was also placing the audience in the role of identifying with me in my relationship with my internalized objects. But at the same time I became partly aware that my audience might reject the role and consider me "crazy." Thus I apologized in advance for any infiltration of offensive unconscious tendencies.

Childhood Origins of the Threatening Dialogue—Working Through

So I realized that a preoccupation with "craziness" was in part behind my ambivalence about sharing my self-analysis with my audience. This realization was not entirely new to me. Earlier signs of this preoccupation and its effect on my self-analytic work were evident already in my two previously written papers (Eifermann, 1987d and 1989a), to which I shall now turn. It occurred to me that in those papers, as I was disclosing experiences with "craziness" while fo- cusing on other specific topics studied through self-analysis, I prob- ably wished to sense how my audience (and perhaps how I myself) would react to such disclosures. My fourth and fifth self-analytic papers exemplify this.

In my paper "Children's Games Observed, and Experienced" (Eifermann, 1987d), I contrasted my past investigation of games by means of external observations of children at play with, so to speak, the investigation of games "from within." Using an analysis of my reconstructed experiences while replaying a childhood game in my mind, I tried to illustrate the kind of general discoveries and insights about the child-at-play that can best be reached by means of this "within" search method.

It was a ball game that I played with/against the wall of our house, throwing the ball "hard" and "hot" at the wall and catching it on the rebound. It took me some days before I retrieved the complete game in my mind and associative writing, including the fact that it had contained "a secret element," a secret rule: I had to shout curses aloud between the time I threw the ball at the wall and its return to me. As the game became alive I found the curses, first elusive, now articulated—"May your name be wiped out" and "Go to hell" (in Hebrew). Replaying the game in my mind and reexperiencing the tensions and anxieties, as well as the pleasures involved, I became cognizant of frightening childhood memories. My associations were a blend of these memories, of the feelings of fear, anger, and frustration that these aroused and of ideas and feelings of control and coping— "The wall" of our house—which received the "hard" and "hot" blows of my ball, "was indestructible." At the same time I now reexperienced my curses as "shameful" and "silly," indeed "crazy." This feeling, that my whole game was crazy, continued to reemerge. I had a fear that "I shall be caught" in my game and then it came to me— "acting crazy would be what I would be caught at."

Despite the clear significance to me of such thoughts of "craziness" within the context of my ball game, they were essentially omitted from my paper on games. My main preoccupations in that paper were with (1) the functions of rules as I understood these functions through my reexperiencing and observing the playing child "from within," and (2) the place of creativity in such simple, repetitive games, as I recognized the enormous virtuosity involved in the performance of my game. To my mind, whether this virtuosity, the "master *performance!*," would be recognized for what it was depended on whether the onlookers of the game were in the know about its subtleties or were "uninitiated." For "just as the subtleties that add up to make a great artistic performance are lost on the uninitiated, much of the quality and special characteristics of children's performance in games is lost on the remote adult" (Eifermann, 1987d, p. 142). My associations to the craziness of my game thus did not directly belong to this paper and only later could be seen to have been implied—the "uninitiated" could not recognize the creativity and would see only the craziness. (The associations were eventually introduced only in the sixth, 1987e paper.) In describing my game to my audience at this point, I nevertheless revealed to them that I had a "crazy" game. By not taking this further in my public writing at the time, I seem to have taken a guarded step toward a dialogue on "craziness" with my audience. Here I was still unaware of this latent move. In the subsequent, fifth, paper, such a move was no longer latent—"craziness" was now actively incorporated.

Self-Analysis and Innovation—Parallel Dialogues with the Audience

In my fifth self-analytic paper entitled, "'It Suddenly Came to Me'— On the 'Occurrence' of Ideas and Their Sequel" (Eifermann, 1989a, p. 115), I meant to define retrospectively some of the conditions that facilitate and others that inhibit these "occurrences." But as I continued working on the topic of the process of discovery, I found that once again I was both attracted to, and afraid of proceeding with my revealing enterprise. And I was advised, by both inner and external better judgment, that I would do better to look in the many notes I had made for my papers for a more "neutral" example than that related to my further associations to my game. But as I searched through my associative notes, I observed the same thing again and again: all the new revelations and insights I had arrived at, as well as those which I had inadvertently avoided reaching, even though I came remarkably close, or those which I had made without noticing their significance, were always associated with sharing and exposing these new discoveries. There were always anxieties and wishes regarding making public my discoveries and through them myself. For while such exposure could lead to sharing, recognition, and admiration, it could also invite rejection and derision, even to the extent of being treated as "crazy."

It was the repeated observation of my wishes and fears regarding "exposure" and the fear of being, or being considered, "mad," that turned into a central subject in my paper.

As I was preparing the paper and repeatedly encountering my ambivalent feelings with regard to "exposure," the idea occurred to me (with a calming effect) that my feelings were not any different from those of most people suddenly "struck" by a new idea. In discussing some of my thoughts, I pointed out, for example, that the fear of losing one's mind or of being regarded by others as having lost one's mind, is expressed blatantly every time someone introduces a new and exciting idea with the phrase, "I may be crazy, but listen to this"; or, "You'll think I've gone mad, but . . ."—preambles often used when we share our latest, exciting ideas. I then observed that "by sharing them, we plainly express our hope for recognition and admiration as well as for having a partner to our excitement. But the underlying anxiety is also made quite explicit" (p. 118). In my further work for the paper I turned to Freud, recalling that he often expressed feelings of apprehension with regard to the "wildness" of his ideas in letters, as well as in his analyses of his own dreams. I quoted from his letter of December 12, 1897 to Fliess (Masson, 1985) in which Freud says how much he was looking forward to sharing with him "the most *meschugge* ["crazy" or "mad" in Yiddish] matters"; and from his dream, "Goethe's Attack on Herr M" in which Freud quotes his dream thoughts, "Naturally, it's he [Fliess] who is a madman, a fool" (*"ein Verrückter, ein Narr"* is translated inaccurately as "the crazy fool" in Freud, 1901, p. 664). According to his own interpretation, these thoughts reflect his fears concerning himself being "a madman." I also discussed his fears of "ridicule and derision" (p. 664) in connection with his revelations.

It was in the context of these discoveries about myself and others that the story of Archimedes occurred to me: Archimedes made his discovery regarding the weight of the water displaced by a body as he was stepping into a bath; he then ran out into the streets of Syracuse stark naked, shouting excitedly, "Eureka, eureka." My understanding of the story of this discovery and its sequel was for me further confirmation of my own inner experiences and their repeated reflections in my notes. In my paper (1989a) I took the case of Archimedes as prototypical for the moment of revelation and its immediate sequel. I wrote in this connection:

> The risk involved in excited sharing of one's original ideas is most poignantly present in Archimedes' story—for unless his uncontrolled excitement and the behaviour to which it led were "excusable" considering the importance of the discovery he made—he would have remained, to use a common and telling Hebrew expression, *bekhol ma'arumav* ('in all of his nakedness') [p. 117].
>
> Had Archimedes eventually had only his nakedness to show for all his excitement—and in running through the streets shouting 'I have found it' he revealed nothing else—he would have been in the sad position of many a madman, whose uncontrolled behavior brings him neither recognition nor fame, nor even sympathy [p. 118].
>
> [Furthermore:] The sequel of Archimedes' story of discovery is about physical exposure, the exhibitionism that is the most "primary" or "original," and originally the most exciting and the most vulnerable. As a success story it may raise our hopes; but it also signals that we had better make sure of a genuine, well-founded and convincing "cover-story" before we reveal our "originality" in public. Otherwise we may be regarded as "mad," inviting pain, shame, derision and rejection [p. 118].

I expressed a similar fear, alongside hopes, with regard to myself. Writing about an analysis I had made of a section of one of Freud's dreams, I said that

> I was planning to write [it] up . . . for the purpose of public presenta-
> tion to psychoanalysts . . . [hoping to] be admired for it, but at the
> same time reluctant to do so, "for analysts may 'see through' what I
> show them—as I feared they had done in my earlier presentation—and
> scorn me for it" (Eifermann, 1989a, p. 122).

I was referring to the 1987c paper I had presented in Germany, in which I had acted out my fantasies with regard to my audience and feared that they had recognized that I had performed "as would a little girl."

A Threatening Self-Analytic Dialogue and Acting Out

As further inner connecting links kept emerging, I became even more fully aware of the extent to which my analysis of the sudden occurrence of ideas, as well as a great deal of my earlier work served as such "cover stories." In my original conception of the paper I meant to present the thoughts and associations, put down in writing, that eventually led to my ideas regarding Archimedes. But as I worked on this material I once again became apprehensive. I decided instead to analyze the new idea that occurred in the course of writing the paper. After I tracked down the sequence that had led to it, I felt confident and yet wrote to myself in notes from which I later quoted in the paper, that "there is nevertheless an anxiety about mishaps or also about the possibility of a total *broch* (literally a break, a rupture, or a hernia, meaning a disaster in Yiddish, and in Hebrew slang)" (Eifermann, 1989a, p. 123). That, indeed, turned out to be no idle fear. As I explained in that paper, as I was planning how to integrate my new idea into its last draft, a sequence of thoughts and feelings occurred to me, unsuspecting of what it would lead to:

> I had a pleasurable, fleeting fantasy that I would show the paper to a
> couple of people—whose appreciation of me I valued but felt far from
> certain of—who would as a result give me their undivided, admiring
> support. Following this fantasy I decided to first take a long deserved
> rest, and switched off the computer. But in so doing, I did the
> "unbelievable": Inadvertently, I erased (or shall I say "cut out"?) a
> considerable part of the edited draft from the word-processor on my
> computer. All that remained of my work was a printout of the first
> draft, and some notes. This dramatic, and to me traumatic event took

place as I switched off my machine without following any of the
necessary, totally routine procedures [p. 123].

Once again acting out, this time of my conflicted need to "protect"
myself from my fantasied audience, was incorporated into the paper
I was writing. The threat that the audience held for me was the very
topic of what I had to say to the audience. I was writing to the public
about writing to the public, and thus what happened in the course of
writing was not only very relevant to my work but *was* my work, as
became increasingly clear to me in the course of writing to my
audience about my self-analytic work.

SELF-DISCOVERIES THROUGH CREATING AUDIENCES

Public Audiences—Real and Fantasied

In reviewing my papers, I focused on my public audiences, real and
fantasied. These audiences were repeatedly integrated into my texts
as their presences and their real and fantasied meanings for me
became explicit. There was a development in this awareness that can
be traced through the various texts. But from the start I recognized
that the meanings that the audience had had for me were integral to
the inner processes I had undergone and was reporting about. That
is, I recognized that my audience not only affected what I said and
what I refrained from saying, as well as how I said it, but also affected
the very inner processes themselves. The distinction between real
and fantasied audiences is not clear-cut, of course. Usually, at least
some fantasies regarding the real audience come to mind, however
fleetingly, while I am preparing a presentation as well as before,
during, and following it. When the presentation involves the personal material of self-analysis, sensitivity to the audience may be
sharpened, since concern about the audience's real responses is more
keenly felt. My repeated attempts to assess the reality of my conscious fantasy with regard to my audience—and the fact that this has
become an integral aspect of my self-analytic process—can be viewed
in the light of this increased sensitivity. These attempts to assess my
conscious fantasy drew me closer to my unconscious fantasies and
intentions with regard to my internal objects. They also allowed me to
identify the various roles I assigned to my real audience in relation to
these objects.

   In the first two papers of the "series," I regarded the audience
simply as audience; that is, I did not search for the inner represen-

tations for which it stood. Even when I recognized the role the audience unconsciously served for me, I kept on regarding it simply in terms of an "object" to whom I had assigned, in fantasy, a role it knew nothing about. In listening to my papers, they were to respond to and satisfy my need to "tell on," and they were to share in my excited, though not unembarrassed, oedipal triumph. It was only in the third (1987c) paper that I explicitly identified the role of my audience as transference object, and revealed the internal representations for which it stood, both as "the Germans" and, at a deeper layer, my early internalized objects. As I pointed out in my discussion of that paper, this move inward—as long as it remained an effort at self-analysis not intended for publication—was a way of undermining the significance for me of the real, external audience and my relationship with it.

Yet my decision to report on this piece of self-analysis in a paper and republish it in German translation, and the decision to present it in Austria upon invitation there, reflected my recognition that the real audience had important meaning and significance for me. These decisions were an attempt to share my effort to differentiate fantasy from reality with both my past real audience, and another, similar audience. Thus, in my sharing with my German-speaking audience my discovery of whom they had stood for, I was inviting a new kind of dialogue with them. Yet again, this initiative at the same time also served defensive purposes. I described earlier how I denied the significance of the *real* audience for me by focusing, in private self-analysis, on latent meanings. Conversely, the powerful *transference* feelings to the German (speaking) audience that still remained were denied as I made this piece of self-analysis public. Before these feelings could be uncovered, three papers further into the "series," I had to recognize and work through the emerging theme of my dialogue with my transferential objects—as well as "test" responses to this theme on audiences emotionally less loaded for me than the Germans (e.g., in Denmark, Sweden, and the United States). The theme was craziness and the necessity to accept it as belonging to oneself and thus be freer to be truly creative.

In the two papers that followed the "Germany" paper (1987d, 1989a; the fourth and fifth of the "series"), my engagement with my future audience receded into the background in the sense that its presence in my mind did not lead, directly and consciously to new insights that I then included in my text (as I had in the earlier papers and once again in the sixth). Yet the audience continued to be present. It was now present in a role that was a reversal, in a sense, of the earlier role. While in the three earlier papers (1987a, 1987b,

1987c) my preoccupation was with the roles I had assigned in unconscious fantasy to my audience, in the two later papers (1987d, 1989a) I was preoccupied with the role my audience would perceive me in: crazy, or creative. And I was fluctuating between fear of being regarded as acting, or thinking, "crazy" and hope that my creative attempts would evoke recognition, even admiration. In my paper on games (1987d), this fluctuation between hope and fear found expression through "the child within me," preoccupied with how its playing would be perceived: Would it be looked upon as "acting crazy," or would its performance be recognized for its "creativity" by the "onlookers"? Only "uninitiated" onlookers/audiences would perceive the "craziness" of my game while failing to recognize that it was "creative."

Thus, that paper contains an analogy between the child's relationship to the onlooker and that of the adult with the audience. The fears and hopes of the performer lie at the heart of the analogy. My "eureka" paper (1989a), which followed, focused on adult audiences and fears and hopes with regard to how creative enterprises may be perceived and responded to by such audiences. I first discussed Archimedes and Freud from this perspective. Then, turning to myself, I had a fantasy about a specific audience—two experts whom I would ask to read my paper—a fantasy that led to my acting out (causing the paper to vanish from my computer) in an attempt to prevent the reading of the paper. My fantasy was guided by feelings of self-satisfaction and the hope of recognition and appreciation; my acting out was similarly unconsciously guided by fear of rejection. Thus, while in my earlier paper (1987d) I suggested that it was only an "uninitiated" audience who would be unappreciative and disdainful, I recognized in the paper that followed (1989a) that my acting out was in response to a fear of how a very "initiated," in fact an expert "audience" would react to my creative attempt.

Neither in the game paper (in which my immediate audience remained altogether implicit) nor in the "eureka" paper did I identify additional, early internal objects that were represented by my audience. I know that uncertainty about how I would have been viewed by some of these objects—as well as how I perceived them—contributed to the intensity of both my hopes and fears in relation to my audience. But it was only after I had worked through and spelled out my anxieties about being considered "crazy" and my hopes of being recognized as creative that my audience, real and fantasied, again took central stage. Thus, in my sixth and last paper (1987e), I spoke directly to my German audience about my fears of "madness" (*she' gaon*), the striving for genius (*gaon*), and the need both personally and as a people to be in touch with the closeness of the two. As I integrated these insights concerning my fantasies about my audience into the paper, my earlier revelations were not invalidated but, rather, were given an added dimension.

Context and the Value of Self-Analytic Findings

Despite my repeated acknowledgment of defensive uses of self-analysis, I have also tried to demonstrate that such uses do not a priori render its findings entirely worthless. The revelation of blind spots and distortions in my self-analytic writing, as well as the discovery that it was unconsciously and defensively motivated, often led to new discoveries, without necessarily invalidating all my earlier observations. This realization allows me to see in a more positive light self-analytic work that even the analyst himself has rejected. Arlow (1990), for example, self-critically describes a piece of his self-analytic work as "a ludicrous, almost laughable form of denial" (p. 20). He is referring to a self-analysis carried out while objectively faced with "horrifying information" regarding his life-threatening illness. Arlow explains how his self-analysis based on this information led to a sense of pleasure, instead of the horror that should have emerged; the content of the analysis confirmed his theory on the formation of "a continuing entity, the self, existing in time" (p. 14). Although the details that Arlow offers indicate that his thought was indeed a form of denial, this fact does not negate the thought. Moreover, the content of the thought suggests how important the wish for the survival of one's ideas can be in a "near-death" situation. Respect for our ideas, the truth they contain at the moment of their discovery, and awareness of their origin also allows for the discovery of errors they may contain. This point has been brought out by Blass and Simon (1992), who convincingly demonstrate the importance of following the history of our ideas. In this context, Freud's abandonment of his seduction theory is considered to have resulted in part from his having come in contact with the influence of his personal "wildness" on the development of that theory (Blass, 1992).

Freud had reservations about and recognized the limitations of self-analysis, but he continued publishing self-analytic material as late as 1936. There he describes the aftermath of a piece of self-analysis of a parapraxis:

> I felt very pleased with this solution. But in self-analysis the danger of incompleteness is particularly great. One is too soon satisfied with a

part explanation, behind which resistance may easily be keeping back
something that is more important perhaps [p. 34].

Freud proceeds to describe how his daughter, with whom he
shared this self-analysis, pointed out an oversight that then allowed
him to arrive at a more "complete" analysis. While pointing to its
limitations, Freud does not dismiss his earlier interpretation as
senseless or entirely superseded by his daughter's addition. In this
last piece of Freud's on self-analysis, he first publicly reveals another
dimension of the self-analytic process, in reporting on his exchange
with his daughter: the role of the private audience. By sharing his
self-analysis with his daughter, Freud reached discoveries worth
making public.

Private Audiences—Real and Fantasied

Anzieu (1975) concludes his in-depth study of Freud's self-analysis
with the realization that: "There can be no proper self-analysis unless
it is communicated to someone else" (p. 569). He discusses Freud's
communications to Fliess. "When Fliess ceased to play the role of
Freud's 'only audience' " (p. 568), Freud communicated with Minna,
and with other private audiences (p. 554), including his daughter. I
suggest that a private audience is an essential part of self-analysis.
This is confirmed by my own experience that there must be a real
object, who can, and wishes to, meet my needs to communicate and
exchange.[5]
    There is another kind of private audience—the exclusively internal
audience. We frequently conduct dialogues in our minds with our
internalized objects. At times these dialogues are loving or soothing;
at other times, painful or upsetting. They differ in the degree to which

---

[5]In the course of my writing this paper, Rachel Blass has been a most valuable
"private audience." Her help in thinking through and formulating major issues
discussed in the paper was also essential. In the course of writing my self-analytic
"series," Erich Gumbel's presence as an extraordinarily discreet and sensitive "audience" helped me develop and apply self-analytic skills. Regine Haesler was a most
understanding, tolerant, and patient "audience" as I was struggling with my ideas and
my doubts. She was also extremely helpful in working over the German texts,
translated from the English by Ludwig Haesler. An editor has a special role as "private
audience"; he or she must be open to the spirit, style, and idiosyncrasies of the writer
and use his or her talent to allow these to be expressed more fully. Norma Schneider,
who has edited most of my papers, has taught me how important this role is. I have
had many private audiences, even counting only those of whom I am conscious. Some
of them were physically present; with others I have corresponded. To all of them I am
grateful.

the other is listened to. If the other is not heard, they may become monologues. Such inner exchanges are no less "alive" if the partner to the dialogue is deceased. In the course of the self-analyses I have described, I was constantly maintaining dialogues with my internalized objects, which, though not directly presented in my papers, are nevertheless more than implied. For example, I have had repeated, intensive inner dialogues with my internalized mother about her, and about us both. There were dialogues with my internalized father, brother, and each of my grandparents. Making self-analysis public has added a new and significant dimension to these dialogues. In making aspects of my inner world public, I exposed not only my own self, I exposed my inner world of objects as well, and in this I experienced myself as if exposing people deeply significant to me. There now emerged a new dialogue within myself with these internal objects, about what it was that I was doing with/to them and why. At the source of these exchanges with my internal objects was a deep need and a feeling of responsibility, particularly since I was writing about objects with whom a real, live exchange was no longer possible. How to be true to one's inner self, while at the same time coming to terms with what one decides to publicly reveal about internalized others, is thus an additional preoccupation of self-analysis, when self-analysis is made public. This preoccupation introduces a new perspective into one's inner dialogues and thus enriches them, opening up a new path to important insights.

REFERENCES

Anzieu, D. (1975), *Freud's Self-Analysis*. London: Hogarth Press, 1986.
Arlow, J. (1990), The analytic attitude in the service of denial. In: *Illness in the Analyst*, ed. H. J. Schwartz & A.-L. S. Silver. Madison, CT: IUP, pp. 9–45.
Blass, R. B. (1992), Did Dora have an oedipus complex? *The Psychoanalytic Study of the Child*, 47:159–187. New Haven, CT: Yale University Press.
_____ & Simon, B. (1992), Freud on his own mistake(s): The role of seduction in the etiology of neurosis. *Psychiat. & Humanities*, 12:160–183.
Eifermann, R. R. (1987a), Interactions between textual analysis and related self-analysis. In: *Discourse in Psychoanalysis and Literature*, ed. S. Rimmon-Kenan. London: Methuen, pp. 38–55. Also in: *Essential Papers on Literature and Psychoanalysis*, ed. E. Berman. New York: New York University Press, in press.
_____ (1987b), Fairy tales—A royal road to the child within the adult. *Scand. Psychoanal. Rev.*, 10:51–77. Also in: *Das Märchen—Ein Märchen? Psychoanalytische Betrachtungen zu Wesen, Deutung und Wirkung der Märchen*, ed. J. Stork. Stuttgart-Bad Cannstatt: Frommann-Holzboog, pp. 165–206.
_____ (1987c), "Germany" and "the Germans": Acting out fantasies and their discovery in self-analysis. *Internat. Rev. Psycho-Anal.*, 14:245–262. Also in: *Jahrbuch der Psychoanalyse*, 20:38–55.

_____ (1987d), Children's games, observed and experienced. *The Psychoanalytic Study of the Child*, 42:127–144. New Haven, CT: Yale University Press. Also in: *La Psychiatrie de l'Enfant*, 33:457–478, 1990.

_____ (1987e), Zustände von Überwältigung im Umgang mit "Verrücktheit" (oder Psychose). *DPV Informationen*, 2:19–28.

_____ (1989a), "It suddenly came to me"—On the "occurrence" of ideas and their sequel. *Internat. J. Psycho-Anal.*, 70:115–126.

_____ (1989b), Varieties of denial: The case of a fairy tale. In: *Denial: A Clarification of Concepts and Research*, ed. E. Edelstein, D. L. Nathanson & A. Stone. New York: Plenum, pp. 155–174.

Freud, S. (1901), On dreams. *Standard Edition*, 5:633–686. London: Hogarth Press, 1953.

_____ (1936), The subtleties of a faulty action. *Standard Edition*, 22:233–235. London: Hogarth Press, 1964.

Masson, J., trans. & ed. (1985), *The Complete Letters of Sigmund Freud to Wilhelm Fliess: 1887–1904*. Cambridge, MA: Harvard University Press.

10

Mutual Supervision, Countertransference, and Self-Analysis

Adrienne Harris
Therese Ragen

What is wrong with you?
What is wrong with me?
What if I told her what really is wrong?
There are answers.

What if something happens to you and what if I can't do it? I dreamed my secretary said you called and left a long message saying you no longer wanted to be a therapist. I concluded you were dying.

I dream there is a phone message from a patient who has moved away. There are all sorts of words written down that aren't complete thoughts. I get the gist of it. She's in dire straits and if her father contacts me I shouldn't tell him anything and she wants me to call her.

I dreamed I lifted my hair and underneath was another layer that was absolutely iron gray, totally gray.
If I didn't have her to worry about, I might be much more depressed.

My head gets a swirling feeling writing this all down.
I don't know. Do you think I'm getting these headaches because things are getting stirred up?
That would have been different and I guess I'm angry . . . and I think I'm angry at you too.

195

My mother doesn't want to know.
Why don't I remember it?
I had no one else to turn to but my mother. I felt ashamed. She made
me feel it was all in my head.
My mother seemed so excited about me coming home.
I feel so possessive of my mother.

I told him I won't stand for him speaking to me that way. It's abusive.
I'm going to tell him he's going to have to stop some of the ways he
talks to me. It's just too abusive.

It's strange not to ever remember being in my father's arms.
It is the father's hatred, the battle against hatred which I think cannot
be won.

My body knows ahead of my brain.
I feel dizzy.
I feel the medication has glued my head together and everything is
coming out in my body.
I am afraid you will get depressed and collapse.
And then my husband will have to bring me trays in bed.

These are excerpts from an interlocking set of dialogues that took
place over a 6-month span of time between the two of us, and
between each of us and our patients in two separate treatments.
These words constitute the conscious, articulated discourse, but, of
course, at the same time contain many levels of experience and
awareness for our patients and ourselves. Like most analysts, we are
struggling to advance our own self-analyses and to encompass and
make use of our unconscious countertransferences for our patients'
benefit. There are many ways analysts pursue these goals. This
chapter records our particular path.

We have organized this material in an attempt to evoke the
complexity and richness of the multiple transferences and countertransferences, the unconscious dialogues, the resonating themes, and
powerful commonalities which always occur in analytic work. In the
course of a mutual supervision, which we elaborate here, we spoke to
each other about our own and our patients' questions, worries, and
experiences. We grappled with the complexity and multiplicity of
representations—back and forth between patient and analyst, and
between analyst and supervisory colleague.

We shared an initial broad interest in learning more about the
process through which colleagues discover psychoanalytic knowledge. We wanted to take as our starting point the finished product

typically presented in a scientific paper and to try to identify the processes operating behind it. We thought this exploration might mean not only carefully observing the working interaction between us, but also developing a new method of investigation. We attempted to set up a process that would help us become more self-conscious about the resonances and reverberations between our analytic work and our experiences of ourselves. Perhaps we were doing no more than elucidating the intuitive working method of many analysts.

In retrospect, as we now write about this experience for publication in a book on self-analysis, it is clear how deeply we have needed to explore our own inner lives in concert with intersubjective experiences. Here, too, we suspect we are merely articulating what has long been a working assumption of analysts, namely, that analytic work inevitably touches on all the places of struggle and difficulty in one's own life. These matters have been addressed elsewhere in the literature as they appear in more extreme forms. There is writing on the impact of an analyst's illness or pregnancy or known losses on the work and on the patient. And there is the phenomenon much addressed, at least in personal conversation among analysts, of the patients who seemed equipped with some psychic radar and were able to touch and stimulate most acutely very dark and vulnerable points in the analyst. But perhaps there is a more general assumption underlying these dramatic clinical moments, that the psychic struggle and unconscious web between patient and analyst is always finely resonant and interactive. One contribution of this essay might be to suggest that self-analysis is, can be, or should be an abiding feature of analytic work and analytic supervision.

Drawing on Sándor Ferenczi's experiments with mutual analysis, as recorded in his *Clinical Diary* (1932), we came to call the process "mutual supervision." For about a year we had been separately and collaboratively investigating Ferenczi's work. Much of our professional reading and writing had been focused on new work on intersubjectivity and the role of mutuality in analytic work. Analysts who are important to us—Winnicott, André Green, McDougall, Bollas—write about the demands upon the analyst to deepen the work, to reach primitive levels in oneself, to expand the analytic instrument in response to powerful archaic phenomena in patients. These contemporary concerns resonate with the courageous work Ferenczi reported in his last writing.

Ferenczi's life as an analyst was marked by an adventurous, searching spirit. His experiments in technique were always in the service of a profound clinical commitment; to understand and relieve suffering by demanding of the analyst whatever process of work and introspection and self-examination was necessary. He seems to have been driven more by an empathic connection to the patient's depths of psychic anguish and confusion than by theory building. Although he is best known for the last work, the *Clinical Diary* (Ferenczi, 1932) his interest in the nuances of transference–countertransference experiences and analytic subjectivity was lifelong. Ferenczi believed there was always an unconscious dialogue between patient and analyst running parallel to the explicit dialogues.

These attributes, along with Ferenczi's openness to patients, left him receptive to the belief of one of his patients, RN, that despite his brief analysis with Freud and his ongoing self-analysis, his own unresolved conflicts presented such countertransference obstacles that her further progress in treatment with him depended on their resolution. She proposed that she, herself an analyst, do a simultaneous counteranalysis of Ferenczi, who would take up the position of analysand, working through with her his countertransference difficulties toward her. Thus began Ferenczi's experiments with mutual analysis, as disclosed in the *Diary*.

Reading the *Diary*, one is struck simultaneously by contradictory feelings and thoughts. How daring, how on the edge. And again how careful, how quietly thoughtful Ferenczi is about his own character, the knots and snarls in his own psyche that are touched by clinical process with his patient. He struggled deeply with the viability of mutual analysis. At times we find him writing of feelings of dread, vulnerability, terror, humiliation, and depression which he experienced in the restructuring and personal disclosure involved in this new analytic relationship. In other diary entries, he speaks of the intimacy, consolation, and comfort, tenderness and richness that emerged between him and his patients in their shared mutuality. He never settled within himself the question of exactly what the extent and nature of his openness and counteranalysis needed to be. And he never gave up the question.

Ferenczi's stance in relation to transference and countertransference is what is remarkable and inspiring to us, despite his failures at the project. There are several aspects to consider. Take the term "mutual analysis" and consider both aspects—the mutuality and the analysis.

Ferenczi (1932) believed that as a consequence of mutual analysis "our entire attitude towards the patient changes" (p. 129). His view of the analytic process was one of a collaborative endeavor requiring an emotional openness, immediacy, and accessibility between both individuals. Disclosure of the genuine reactions of the analyst to the patient are as vital to the work as the exploration and resolution of the transference and countertransference. The relationship with a real other who is emotionally alive and spontaneous and reactive is essential for growth in this paradigm. It is only in such a relationship that the patient develops a new sense of self and of other and experiences the powerful curative difference between pathogenic features of past formative relationships and the analytic relationship. The relationship itself is at the heart of the treatment.

But his research also focused on "analysis." It is, in retrospect, easy to see that Ferenczi consistently wished for more analysis, from Freud above all. Perhaps the fact that RN was an *analyst* is relevant. Recently György Hidas offered the speculation that Ferenczi's presentation to Freud of the "Confusion of Tongues" paper (Ferenczi, 1933), with its plea for empathy and understanding in the analyst, was an unconscious criticism of Freud and of the limits to their work. In the *Diary*, Ferenczi speaks of the requirement to push on, look deeper, remain relentlessly curious about conscious and unconscious forces. In a way his work is fundamentally faithful to the deepest insight in psychoanalysis—the limitlessness of the unconscious. To the end of his life, his professional commitment was to continue the project of self-analysis and to capture and utilize the power of the unconscious in analytic work.

When we began this project, we puzzled over the viability of mutual analysis. Looking at Ferenczi's paradigm, we observed three critical elements. First, both people were mutually disclosing, second, the work that was being done was analytic work, third, the analyst's countertransference was a focus of the work.

What we have done is create a new model that preserves these three critical elements at the same time as it eliminates perhaps the one untenable aspect of Ferenczi's model, that of burdening the patient with the countertransference work that the analyst needs to do him-or herself. Our model is one of mutual supervision or mutual countertransference analysis between colleagues. We decided not to preserve the usual distinctions between supervisory and analytic issues but attempted to move more fluidly across these boundaries.

We have struggled with the term "mutual supervision." It does not fully describe the flow between consulting with a colleague over a case, presenting personal material, and allowing the consultant to do, almost simultaneously, analytic work and supervisory work. It also does not do justice to the shared attempt to examine the integration of the personal and the professional. It does not capture the serious attempt to shift usual arrangements of hierarchy and power. In finally settling on the term "supervision," we want to capture the belief that mature professional work will also entail a dialogue in which the analyst—the one who knows—asks for insight into what he or she does not and will not know, and asks for this insight in the service of analytic work.

Many of the contemporary speculations on the power and potential of the analyst's subjective and unconscious involvement in the analytic dialogue, and the patient's access and insight into the analyst's unconscious process, focus on technical choices between analyst and patient. There are other possible ways to develop our understanding and use of countertransference. Our efforts have focused on deeper and different explorations in supervision. This work clearly draws on many ideas already developed and practiced in the supervisory and analytic processes. Our contribution is the suggestion that analysts can put into play a process which integrates and synthesizes mutual supervision and analysis in the service of expanding the analyst's instrument and understanding the unconscious participation by the analyst in the patient's material. In this project we have undertaken to advance our self-inquiry, to expand and deepen the analytic instrument, and, in particular, to find ways of enhancing the analyst's awareness of and capacity to represent the complex multidirectional processes of intersubjectivity.

In establishing a mode of work, we were determined to be conscious and explicit about the distinct phases of what we were doing, to act rather deliberately, and to establish a formal structure to our collaborative activities. Each of us chose a patient with whom there were complex countertransference issues. The presenting analyst focused the countertransference issues as clearly as she could see them and then moved into presenting patient material for supervision. She did not arrange notes or otherwise structure the presentation but employed instead an intuitive and perhaps unconsciously driven mode of discourse. She presented material more as a set of associations, so that the unconscious blind spots in the analyst might be more accessible. Moving from supervisory to analytic process was done with a specific demarcation. The analyst/supervisor, while commenting and supervising, was also listening for countertransference issues and stopped the presentation of the patient material when she felt she had heard sufficient indications of the countertransference material to pursue it. At that point, more explicit analytic work began and the patient's material moved to the background. Ending this phase, which constituted the greatest portion of the session, was by mutual agreement. At the end of the hour we then worked on the countertransference of the analyst/supervisor, who talked about what had been set off in her. Postsession work consisted of journal writing, noting dream work, and continuing work with the patient. To summarize, our process consisted of five steps:

1. The presenter broadly identified countertransference issue.
2. The presenter then presented the patient's material. The supervisor supervised while listening for countertransference undercurrents.
3. The supervisor felt she had heard sufficient countertransference material to switch to its exploration. She refocused the session to working on the presenter's countertransference.
4. By mutual agreement, the countertransference work was ended, and there was a brief period of processing the supervisor's countertransference from that session.
5. Each person continued working individually postsession, making journal entries, noting dream work, and continuing work with the patient.

This was the process as we designed it. The fact of the matter is that in any given session we did not always move through each stage, but remained in one or the other. It then became a point of meaningful reflection as to why we stayed in a particular phase. Actually, these stages are more loosely and usefully thought of as elements of a process that can occur over time rather than necessarily in any one session.

One of the surprises of our work was the power of the element of mutuality. It provided a unique experience in which we opened ourselves with a colleague to the exploration of personal issues that affect and are affected by our work, and in the same relationship offered our clinical competence to the other in her exploration and analysis. It created a deep and rich colleagueship, a sense of wholeness not found in other collegial activities. Outside of our own analyses, other professional forms of working with each other are significantly more limited. They occur in relationships that are either hierarchically structured or more restricted in their focus, whether emotional or intellectual. The multiplicity of personal and professional dimensions called upon in this process approaches a rare integration and wholeness of personal and professional identity. One is both knower and known, competent and confused, helper and helped, active and passive, mired in personal thickets and possessor of emotionally integrated and insightful perspectives.

For the person presenting, the commitment to explore and analyze problematic countertransference as fully as possible called for a depth, a candor, and a vulnerability unusual in our professional activities. The openness was expanded by framing the countertransference question and then allowing one's unconscious to organize the material in a freely associative way. Similarly, in the position of supervisor we were called on to allow our clinical competencies to come to life and share them to an unusually full degree with a colleague. This, too, was heightened by the technique of assigning to the supervisor the task of stopping the presentation to refocus on the countertransference question.

Each of these sides of the mutuality carried its own inherent and subjective risks. As the two of us discussed our anxieties about the project prior to our first session, our concerns lay on different sides of the coin of mutuality. Therese's main anxiety lay on the side of clinical competence. She was afraid she would fail to grasp the core issues at stake for Adrienne. On the other hand, Adrienne was worried that Therese's ability to empathize with her would stir disturbing affect in her that she had been defending against. This was our first articulation of the multiple transference and countertransference issues that would arise in our work together, partially shaped by joint history. Initially, Therese had been in Adrienne's class and a subsequent study group. As we evolved a more collegial professional relationship, we also became friends, spent time together socially, shared an intense interest in sports and athletics, and even prior to the evolution of the formal working process, had developed a dialogue about deeply personal matters in both our lives.

While the overt purpose of mutual analysis as conceptualized by Ferenczi was analysis of the countertransference, there was another crucial purpose it served. It is clear from reading the *Diary* that the personal and professional closeness engendered by mutuality was very important, if not as important as the countertransference analysis, to Ferenczi as well as to his patients. By abolishing the "distancing by inferiority" and the personal opaqueness of professional aloofness, Ferenczi made way for an emotionally close and alive relationship. This is clearly one of the values of mutual countertransference analysis. In a profession so involved with helping people forge connections and relationships with others, we are often relationally isolated and insulated by the solitary nature of our work. The preponderance of hierarchically structured relationships in our field adds greatly to this isolation. Mutual countertransference analysis opens up a new way of being with each other that is simply more related, perhaps a value in and of itself.

It may help to clarify further the nature of countertransference analysis by discussing its relationship to more traditional supervision as well as to one's own personal analysis. Customarily in supervision there is an ambiguity, and often a high degree of ambivalence, about analyzing countertransference. Each supervisory dyad arrives at its own comfort level in dealing with the deeply personal roots of countertransference. Over the course of working together, there develops at least an implicit point beyond which exploring the countertransference becomes too personal for one, the other, or both. At that point the issue is often referred to one's personal analysis.

That particular countertransference dilemma with that particular patient, however, seldom finds its way into one's personal analysis, and for good reason. One's analysis has a life of its own. While the root of the countertransference difficulty most likely will emerge in the personal analysis, it will do so in its own time and in the context of that relationship, not the relationship with the patient. Having a different arena in which to work on personal issues as they arise in immediate ways out of particular patient relationships preserves the integrity of one's own analytic relationship. At the same time, it ensures that countertransference problems will get the attention they need.

In short, mutual countertransference analysis provides a forum for a rich pursuit of countertransference issues. It gives them room to expand and be understood in the context of the relationship in which they are occurring in a way that no other relationship in the field does. It fulfills the analytic purpose of mutual analysis without impinging on one's own analysis or on one's patient's analysis.

In thinking about presenting our work, we were aware of the many different ways in which we experienced the work. We wanted to give you an idea of how the process worked within the frame we had established. Most important, we wished to communicate a sense of the power of unconscious phenomena as they swept across us, within and among persons bound together in a powerful, emotionally laden set of interlocking bonds. Lastly, it seemed important to attend to the ways in which we found ourselves living out some of the answers to our questions. In the midst of all this, we were keenly aware of our vulnerability and anxiety in mixing personal disclosures of the analyst with excavations of patients' material and offering this mixture to a professional audience. It led us to question the ease with which we write and speak of patients' material and the difficulty of exploring in a public way our own material, no doubt mirroring the issues of power and disclosure between analyst and patient.

In the course of the work many strands of narrative emerged. It was amazing to track the wash of feeling and unconscious process emanating from the collaborative work. Here we will just briefly follow one strand. The theme we track can be represented by the interrelated polarities of active–passive, responsible–negligent, determination–depression.

So far we have been speaking as a collective and collaborative "we." Now we change the format, speaking in our own particular voices, both about our work with our patients and our own experience. We make this shift to recreate aspects of the working dialogues, the variations in experience as well as the commonalities.

AH: I began presenting material of a young woman in her mid-20s, several years into treatment. I just spoke associatively, and what emerged was a picture of tremendous fragility. Even the presentation seemed to me somewhat chaotic and fragmentary, like the patient's experience. This is a young woman who is highly anxious, fragile and tremulous, paranoid, prone to panic and dissociative states, often excruciatingly despondent and tense.

My earliest experience of the patient was a deep worry over the level of her confusion and fear. Whole sections of the city seemed to be off-limits. Many routines of daily life were too spooky or dangerous. States of light and weather, particular streets, could trigger fear or upset. In a simple walk to work she could be focused intensely on one of the army of homeless street dwellers.

There were dramatic discrepancies in the patient. In the realm of work she appeared poised, articulate, charming, and stunningly skilled. Early in the treatment she vaulted, seemingly with ease, into a position in which she trained for high-level analytic work in the world of finance. Yet often in session she sat curled in the big chair very much the frightened child, often uncertain and inarticulate. And inconsolably sad.

At first what she could tell me about her childhood was fragmentary and frightening. Great empty spaces, appalling images, and memory fragments of dirt and contamination and muddle. It took a year to get a coherent life narrative, and what emerged was a childhood experienced in frightening loneliness. She was aware in herself of a desperate attempt to hang on and keep order, within muddle, family disruption, and depression, and within a frightening internal world. Her nightmares were chaotic and violent. Over and over again she would say in session, "I woke up after a night of dreams, and I thought, what happened?" It could take hours for her to feel settled and present in daily life and routines.

One continuing preoccupation in the treatment, shared and discussed with a consulting psychiatrist, was how to titrate medicine, treatment, and support. The patient was like some exquisite, delicately constructed creature who could be wiped out or strengthened by tiny shifts in psychic, environmental, or biological structure.

TR: Listening for the countertransference, I found that I followed material about the patient closely but heard it as the background out of which a picture of Adrienne emerged. As I listened to the material about the patient, her history, her current inner and outer life, the treatment, and her relationship with Adrienne, I was forcibly struck by the level of Adrienne's concern over the patient's fragility and potential for decompensation and the tremendous feeling of responsibility Adrienne had for the patient. While I envisioned a woman in great pain, at times precariously carrying that pain, I also formed a picture of someone with strengths and resources who was willing and able to use those. I felt that Adrienne could rely on her—that was how it came to me. She did not need to feel so responsible about holding this woman together. She could rely on her patient to carry her pain. I wondered about Adrienne's weighty feelings of responsibility.

The primary countertransference set off in me during this session had to do with the fact that the patient was on antidepressant medication monitored by a psychiatrist. Being quite skeptical about the use of psychotropic medication in general, I found myself having to rein in my urge to question its role in the treatment. My difficulty was compounded by the fact that the backup psychiatrist was on staff at the hospital where I had done my internship, enduring a most unpleasant year of the worst of psychiatry's attitudes toward psychology. It was a place where my opposition to medication seemed to increase in direct proportion to my perception of an inability among hospital staff to tolerate emotional suffering.

AH: When we processed this later, it led to my thinking and talking about depression in my life and family, my guilty responsibility for this. It also called up a long-standing and probably characterological worry—the fear of doing damage inadvertently, through some moment of negligence. Therese's very different take on the medication question made me wonder if the drugs, and more particularly the psychiatrist, were functioning for me as a holding environment so I could feel I was working effectively and helpfully with the patient. I realized that this probably recapitulated a family dynamic for me. I could see the transference to the psychiatrist and the comfort from talking to her, and by extension the holding environment that Therese was providing.

As we talked, I had the worrying thought that the patient was having to bear my depressive feelings as well as her own. Again the worry of doing damage. Then Therese commented on the patient's luck in now having the chance to go through her anguish with me. Yes, she is alone, so alone, but now she's with you. I realized I was caught by surprise at this comment. Sitting hour after hour with this despondent girl who is finally telling another person how alone she has been, I absorb what she says, but in thinking of my responsibilities to her, I can imagine only not being enough, and I underestimate my own presence as a source of consolation. I think of Winnicott's idea of the healing aspect of being alone in the presence of another.

TR: I presented material a year into treatment with a woman in her late 20s who experienced her mother as very depriving by virtue of her extreme remoteness, a patient who quite likely had been sexually abused as a child, although she has no conscious memories of this, and up to the time of our supervision had fleetingly had the idea cross her mind in a few sessions only to dismiss it quickly. In the countertransference I am struggling with the fact that this patient stirs maternal feelings in me, but then I feel a gate come down against them. Adrienne hears me interpreting and being empathic, but from what she describes as an adult place rather than meeting the patient in the child-place she is experiencing. We approach the block to the maternal in me from various perspectives. The one that most strikes me is Adrienne's thought that it will automatically put me in touch with my own experience of being a child. In repeating my patient's mother's remoteness, I remain aloof from painful aspects of my own childhood.

Two sessions after our supervision my patient found herself struck by a strong unbidden thought about having been sexually abused. This ushered in a stream of affective and cognitive associations that she continues to unravel, including evidence of sexual abuse her mother has substantiated. Might a shift in me, detected by my patient, have taken place in my supervision with Adrienne that made room for this material to come forth?

AH: In the aftermath of these working sessions, we began to notice that we were splitting the polarities of active–passive, responsible–negligent, determination–depression. We made a conscious decision to include experience that was outside our formal sessions in order to illustrate the reverberations of our work playing out unconsciously in our lives.

We go to the Degenerate Art show at the Art Institute of Chicago, a reconstruction of extraordinary modernist painting and sculpture originally displayed by the Nazis, who labeled them "degenerate."

TR: I was holding myself back with much effort, wanting to weep, and thinking that if I could run out and go ahead and weep, I might know why. I felt that there was something wrong with me for my emotion. I didn't know why I was so overcome by feeling. I recall Klee's statement that appeared at the entrance to the exhibit: "I am here now [in Switzerland]. There was no place for me in Germany," and the statement of another artist: "We collectively and deeply feel the pain, the shame, the indignation." I walked back to the beginning of the exhibit trying to understand my feeling. I saw two different men crying. That calmed me. It made me know my feeling was okay, normal, natural. And so I need not feel upset about it because I didn't know what was happening to me. I could own my feeling rather than be overwhelmed by it.

AH: I was numbed to much of the pain. I found myself in an oddly intellectual spin, thinking of the craziness of this attempt to destroy art and spirit. The Nazis had graffitied anti-Semitic and fascist slogans on the walls of the rooms where the paintings were hung in Munich in 1938. Here, in 1991, the paintings survive on gleaming walls, their beautiful muted palettes, oranges, dusky browns and greens, somber and beautiful. But Therese and I have split the experience. I don't immediately read the fine print in the catalog—the designation "Fate unknown" beside so many works, signifying the thousands of canvases lost, like so many other lost souls of that time.

Weeks later we talk. I realize that I have been making use of Therese's comment that I try to notice the patient's strength and sense of responsibility. Her words have been like a life raft in a sea of despondency in the treatment. I use the metaphor of water deliberately. In this time I have been reacting to the news of a friend from childhood whose son has drowned during a last week of summer holiday. I know the theme of lost sons resonates quite personally for me. I tell Therese my dream. I am looking in the mirror and I am admiring my new hair color, lights and vibrancy on the top layer. I lift a lock of hair, and, to my horror, it is all steel gray underneath. My association is to the hair of another friend who went gray-white upon the death by drowning of his son. Fear of sadness, of what is beneath the surface, under the water.

TR: A vivid visual image of Adrienne depressed comes to my mind. I have the thought and then share it—Oh, let's stop; let's not do this. What if Adrienne gets too depressed? What if she collapses?

AH: We then spend some time parsing out whether Therese's worry is her feeling or mine. It's actually unlike her to draw back from emotion and pain in others. I try to address whether her voiced worry is really mine. Is this induced countertransference? I say, apparently only humorously, well if I collapse then Bob (my husband) will have to bring trays. I have visions of agoraphobic Victorian ladies taking to their beds; hysterics on strike from their lives. I'll stay in bed, that wouldn't be so bad. I actually in retrospect think this was an important organizing moment for me. I was less afraid of burdening my patient and of her burdens.

TR: As we reflected in the aftermath of our experiences, a number of things came slowly into focus. I am struck by how each of us relentlessly pursues issues with the other when we feel her to be mired in the thicket of her own personal confusion, unable to experience her resources and potentials. I characterize it as a kind of fierce maternal protectiveness, a persistent urging that the other grasp her own capacities.

AH: The split in ourselves is divided between us in fascinatingly interchangeable ways. One person driving things onward and the other in the lassitude of hopelessness and denial. Somehow in our work we need to find ways of consistently listening for the disowned side. We have fantasies of what would occur if we let the disowned sides play themselves out.

TR: I have us in adjacent executive suites, each running the other's life. Adrienne adds that Bob would have to bring trays for all of us. Even in these fantasies we are splitting.

AH: What we have presented here is a slice of the interaction that occurred between us, with the hope that it captures the spirit of our work. We turn our attention now to one of the abiding questions we have had to take on: What was the impact of this work on the patients and treatment?

TR: Questions about mutuality have been in the forefront of my thinking throughout this project. The openness, the realness of Ferenczi drew a clamoring response from that part of me which is lively, spontaneous, and emotionally present in a very immediate way with others. It is a way of being that in my professional work was more often than not constrained, sometimes strangled, by my own opposing tendencies toward reserve and inhibition buttressed by a good deal of my training in psychoanalytic psychotherapy and psychoanalysis. However, my own analyst's very immediate and open way of relating to me, this particular patient's pulls for realness from me, the dissatisfying constricted experience of myself I had in my work, and the mutuality of the work between Adrienne and me, all converged to focus me on questions concerning the nature of the relationship in psychoanalysis—its genuineness, spontaneity, and mutuality.

As I lifted constraints on my reactivity, which had seemed required by a more highly interpretive model in which my function was more exclusively as a transference object than a real other, I found myself simultaneously feeling both increasingly liberated and uncertain in my work. In relatively uncharted waters, I was less informed by my own experience, reading, thinking, and supervision. Feelings of uncertainty plagued me, but as I observed the differences in what transpired between myself and patients when I more openly brought more of my real reactions—positive or negative, superficial or deep, affective, cognitive, or fantasized—into the treatment, I saw my patients work in deeper, richer ways. The alliance and connection between us strengthened. They, too, became more open to venturing into the unknown, to exploring previously closed off parts of themselves and our relationship.

The way that I have come to think about this theoretically is that the shift toward the realness of the analyst as a more vital element of the treatment enables the patient to discover her- or himself in ways that are different from what occurs when the analyst's role is more exclusively as a transference object. With the analyst as transference object the patient discovers through the analysis of the transference what the analyst is not. Through the repeated noticing of the patient's persistent experiencing of the analyst as a transference figure, rigid conceptions of others and self in relation to others, slowly erode. Psychic conviction gives way to curiosity and the dawning awareness of the distortions involved in the transference. Gradually the analyst is seen not to be who he or she appears to be.

The question then becomes, if this is not who the analyst is, who is she or he? Analyzing the transference leaves the patient to build a picture of the analyst by implication and inference. In contrast, when the analyst also at times presents herself or himself as a real other who is genuinely affected by and has authentic personal responses to the patient, the patient has a different kind of experience. She or he discovers and engages a new object and out of this builds new psychic structure. The difference is between actively presenting a new object with which the patient grapples in her or his psychic schema, in contrast to disassembling an old psychic schema through the analysis of the transference. These are not mutually exclusive processes. Rather, they are complementary processes between which patient and analyst can fluidly move back and forth. It is a matter of which is figure and which is ground at any moment. Interpreting oneself as an old object and presenting oneself as a new object together strengthen the forces at work in treatment.

An important aspect of being more emotionally open with patients is that for the most part one is simply articulating what is already known to the patient, and in doing so is more fully using the person of the analyst as a vehicle for the patient's growth. As Ferenczi (1932) stated, "in one or another layer of his mind the patient is well aware of our real thoughts and feelings" (p. 178). Our willingness to bring our real thoughts and feelings into the treatment as a resource for the patient enables the patient to work toward a new experience of self, of other, and of relationships.

An example from my work with this patient may help to illustrate. Questions arose as to her ongoing financial ability to continue treatment. The problem involved possible upcoming changes in her finances. It also involved issues with her parents, who were helping her finance the treatment, and the dynamics of her relationship with them played themselves out through the money. In addition, there clearly were transference issues.

As we talked through the many dimensions of the problem, nestled in among all the other considerations was the question put to me by the patient, "Do you like me?" Of course, that question itself had many dimensions to it. Included among them was her conflict over feeling dependent. If I liked her and she liked me, she would feel dependent, which both appealed to her and frightened her. The idea of our liking each other also quickly raised separation anxieties. She wanted to be attached, but ending would only hurt. Then there was the painful problem that if I liked her, she wanted me to like her the best of all my patients. She also feared that if I liked her, then some day I could stop liking her. Further, she experienced, partly defensively, her mother's parenting as so infused with a sense of duty that sometimes she felt the only reason her mother cared about her was because she was her daughter. Similarly, perhaps the only reason I liked her was because she was my patient. If she was unable to pay me any longer, she would see how much I really did like her. As she did with others, she tried long and hard not to care whether I liked her, but she did care.

All these were dimensions of the question, "Do you like me?" They needed analysis and working through. In the transference I was being experienced and related to with the anxieties, conflicts, defenses, and deprivations of the past.

Nevertheless, the question remained at the level of the real. Did I like her? In fact, I did. I wondered why she needed to defend herself from her knowledge that I did, and I asked her what she really thought the answer to her question was when she stepped back from it. As it turned out, she not only knew I liked her, but she had a very clear and accurate idea about what I liked in her. I told her that indeed I did like her and that I liked her for the very reasons she thought I did as well as for some others, which I went on to detail for her.

Being real to her in this way seemed to have a positive paradoxical effect. On one hand, letting her know that I personally liked her more clearly brought to the surface her anxieties about being liked so that we could work with them. On the other hand, it helped her feel secure and anchored in the real relationship, giving her more clarity about the transferential base of her anxieties. I was not only not the transference object she had constructed, but in actively letting her know how I felt about her, I was a new and different object. Thus, our relationship bore the possibility of transforming her internal representations of self, other, and relationship.

I am aware that my positive feeling represents only one level or strand in the subtle, multilayered fabric of the relationship between the two of us. But it is a truth, part of my subjective experience. The critical point is that this was a moment in the treatment at which it seemed that my responding at this level of personal feeling would facilitate the patient's growth and deepen our relationship. To use Bion's term, this was "the selected fact" that needed to be addressed in that session.

AH: In my thinking on how our collaborative process affected the work with the patient, I would focus first on the replication of an emotional rhythm between Therese and myself. On one hand, the patient experiences a sense of greater efficacy and the conviction that something had happened, that there was trauma. On the other hand, there were still frightening dips into great despair. Every time she became settled in her conviction that she was responding to something that had injured her, the ground seemed to settle under her. But these certainties were not themselves certain. The conviction was still transient. I could see that these feelings ebbed and flowed between us as well as within her.

I think another phenomenon occurring was that I began to have moments of strong identification with her, moments when I would notice something and think "this is how she sees the world."

After a working session, Therese and I go for a walk through Washington Square Park, and I catch sight of a man on the grass. I see him just in my peripheral vision. He is slight, odd looking, talking to himself. He is lying down; perhaps he has fallen. I see that his limbs and hands shake. He seems mad and ill. I think, he has AIDS; he is homeless and dying in the park. Afterwards, when I write about it, I recognize that this is the sort of urban detail my patient is always noting and worrying over, a representation of someone lost, dispossessed, possessed, alone.

Once when Therese and I were talking about my fears for my patient, I was able to articulate a deep and settled worry in me that the patient would not be able to bear knowing the intensity of her father's hatred. From my direct and indirect knowledge of this man I felt him to be icily enraged and contemptuous of both ex-wife and daughter whom he lumped together as fearful and inadequate women. Therese pushes me to think about this for myself. I describe several situations in my life of considerable difficulty and realized that there must be some question about my hatred. I have to ask myself, how is it accommodated? Where does it surface? This leads me to think about omnipotence, both personally and in the context of the patient Therese and I are talking about. When is an omnipotent wish a defense against loss and powerlessness? What if you have to accept that someone got away with murder? What if you have to live with it rather than take revenge through the destruction of your own life? This line of questioning is relevant in clinical work with many patients, and it draws me to think about people in my personal life whom I sense have been in deep internal battles over their hatred.

Several months after our working sessions, the patient had a dream, different in quality and texture from so many of her violent, fragmented nightmares. It was terrible and upsetting but coherent; the events felt known and clear, viscerally like a memory rather than fantasy or dream. There were elements of distortion and transformations, and she knew this. There was a central episode, a parent transgressing sexually. But what struck the patient and me most forcibly was another feature of the dream, the conviction in the dreamer/child that at last the secret was out. The parent was culpable, something had happened. She was not crazy or inadequate because she felt afraid and anxious. The deepest feeling in this dream was that of conviction, clarity, and sanity.

I realize that I have been looking at the impact of my working with Therese, as it affected the content of the patient's experiences and communications. What of process? Where did the process of our work on mutuality and authenticity have an impact on this patient? In fact, I realized that the issue of the realness of the analyst and the analytic relationship had actually exploded quite destructively in another treatment, where the issue of payment for the work of analysis came into impossible conflict with a patient's determination to ward off her dependency, her need to be in treatment, and her envy of any capacity in me to give or take care of her. She and I had explored her sense of the ways in which we were similar. We were both women, clearly similar in age. She had asked the referring person to find someone who had a family. The feeling tone in our sessions was often warm and easy, with each of us feeling collaborative and compatible as we worked. I had been struggling to find a way to work with this patient's anger, a part of her experience which was very buried and inaccessible, but carried by the patient as a dangerous bad part of the self. She had shown me some writing she had been doing revealing the cynical, bitter, almost sardonic observations with which she moved through the world. I suggested some writers — all women — who seemed to write and think in the same vein as the patient. Perhaps you can imagine the list: Angela Carter, Fay Weldon, Rachal Ingalls, Emily Prager, Mary Gaitskill. The patient felt recognized and relieved of her lonely feeling that she was trapped in isolation with these rageful thoughts and feelings. She read voraciously and delightedly, talked to me about the books and the sessions in this period of the work clearly drew on the shared assumption that she and I liked this kind of writing, felt amused and stimulated by it. It was a period of hopeful energy and activity for the patient.

Then there were several disruptions in the treatment. I went on vacation and made a referral for some couples work. The inescapable "fact" of my vacation and the experience with a new therapist led the patient to a dramatic repudiation of the "real" relationship. Another reality had come sharply into view. The conjunction of our experiences and interests and collaboration was at odds with the other "reality" the patient now focused on, the feeling that really therapy was just my job. These facts canceled any sense of the authenticity of our work.

The "reality" that I had many dimensions in my life and offered her only the experience within the treatment was painful and demeaning to her. I think something else was going on as well. One struggle in the patient's life was to find meaningful work. I know that she sensed but often denied, that my work, including my work with her, was important to me. It had meaning and value to me. Her envy was not of the particularities of my life but of its investment with meaning. This proved to be intolerable. Her answer was to attack the "reality" of the work. Therapy was not a "real" relationship. It was no different she surmised than being a checkout clerk at the grocery, a construction of our relationship which expressed her sense of powerlessness and mere object status, and her sense of contempt and rage in her construction of a degraded identity for me. In this treatment the dilemma over what was real, what was shared and authentic, proved tormenting for the patient.

The contradiction, the reality and spontaneity in the analytic work, and the reality of structured and purchased time, can, of course, if handled thoughtfully, lead to a productive integration. In this case it led instead to a more melancholy foreclosure. Where did we go awry?

Too much mutuality and sharing, too little transference analysis and work with the patient's experience—full/empty, dependency/equality, love/hate?

CONCLUSION

As we write this paper now seven months after the working sessions, we are both struck with the richness of the experience. How we come back again and again to the events of the sessions together, the experiences between sessions in our individual and collaborative lives, and in the work with our patients. We have new insights and new worries every time we reconnect to the material.

At the moment the theoretical point that seems most salient to us has to do with the experience in us and in our patients of rapidly oscillating positions in which we moved from one polarity to its opposite, often within the same hour. As we worked together and analyzed our work together, the phenomenon that seemed most palpable was the way we split aspects of our experience, but often (consciously and unconsciously) reversed fields or positions quite dramatically: passive/active, healer/healed, knowing/confused, determined/reluctant, persistent/vacant, container/contained. We think that this experience of having to move oneself across these polarities, or to see the other person change states so radically, is a factor in promoting integration.

In working with our countertransferences, we were working with core personal issues of considerable depth and intensity. In the midst of the process of being supervised, we often entered our own turbulent psychic spaces, and as we switched roles only a short time later we experienced ourselves in competent and strong ways as supervisor/analyst. This kind of quick and profound change of state had the effect of making movement within ourselves and between segments of ourselves more fluid. Internal boundaries became more permeable. This disrupted the usual rigidity of patterned self and object representations which typically occurs in relationships.

We hunted around for other examples in which this type of transforming mental oscillation occurs and found one in the work of the contemporary Kleinian, Ronald Britton (1989), who conceptualizes the mental and emotional impact of the Oedipus complex in the following way. In this stage the child comes to the realization that the same parent who is the object of desire in one version (the positive oedipal stage) is the hated rival in the other (the negative). In struggling emotionally and therefore cognitively to grasp this complex psychic fact, a new space in mental functioning opens up in which reflection, observation, taking multiple perspectives, and self-consciousness become possible. There is a healing of splits and a capacity to think reflectively about the complexities of dynamically fluctuating self and object representations and reflections.

Cognitive developmental psychologists, trying to elaborate Piaget's model of cognitive transformation via a model of disequilibration and reequilibration, are speaking of the same process. A rapid movement across different and initially contradictory experiences leads to resolution of contradiction at a more integrated and higher level of cognitive functioning.

It raises for us the possibility that mutuality, either in the collaborative and collegial experience we developed, or in the experience with patients, creates the conditions for this kind of mutative transformation.

Our last observation. Each of us experiences a rather intense split and oscillation of feeling in relation to the paper. In preparing the work first as a talk and then as a paper to be published, we have each felt, sometimes within the same day, sometimes more in alternation, either that it was stupid and banal or delightful and interesting. This work had been almost simultaneously loved and hated, inhabited and repudiated. We each think from time to time, "You can't say that." Or with pleasure, how good it feels to write and work more spontaneously. We have also talked about the internal dialogue that accompanies our analytic work. It is a parental voice, sometimes harsh, sometimes protective and maternal. Sometimes it operates defensively, "Ignore this, it's nothing, don't be so sensitive." Then alarm bells go off. One thinks, "Wait, stop, do something." There is often the nagging question, when are you doing too much, going too far. But when is neutrality neglect? These were Ferenczi's questions as well, we believe.

It is important for us to notice that we circled and recircled these questions in the light of the conservatism in our field, the draconian superego of technical rules, and the important demand and value we place on rigorous self-examination. The split between active and passive, moving on relentlessly, or lying low and waiting, appeared and reappeared in us, in our patients, and in the countertransference tugs.

We have worried over what to include and what to censor. It has certainly been illuminating in terms of power and hierarchy to write about oneself and about patients, another split which it is frightening and exciting to integrate.

We leave you with this last mix of voices:

I don't think my mother lets herself get excited. I've never seen her excited but she
was excited this morning.
It could open you to excited and exciting feelings of mothering.
I want a child so much.
I don't want anyone to get close to me . . . unless I had a child.
Then I'd let the child close but nobody else.
I started thinking the ultimate gift to give you would be to resolve this so it's not
something I just want to do for myself but for you too.
I reflected on how a child being healthy and happy is a gift to the parent. I thought
of you, wondering what it does to a parent to be refused that gift.

I had this urge to hurt her baby.
I started thinking about why I cared if you or my mother like me . . .
I'm not special. She probably likes everybody.
I feel so evil.
He speaks of his daughter as evil, as bad seed.

The stepmother stands by completely impassive.
My mother just sat there in the car and I was so scared.
When is neutrality neglect?
Our relentless pursuit of issues with each other feels like a fierce maternal protectiveness.
It's not voracious but goes into action.
I say nothing.

Can she bear this? . . . I feel she cannot stand it.
I want to know what motivates you—if you went into this profession because you
suffered so much pain yourself. Then I wouldn't have to question who are you
to sit there and try to help me.
The reason to do any of this is to liberate yourself.
I can have more confidence in her sense of responsibility.
What is hopeless and lost and what can be repaired. A question for the analysts
and the patients.
I found your sense of conviction liberating for me, liberating me to take myself more seriously.
I try to notice my patient's strength and sense of responsibility and this has been like
a life raft in a sea of despondency.
I feel relentless.

REFERENCES

Britton, R. (1989), The missing link: Parental sexuality in the Oedipus complex. In: *The Oedipus Complex Today*, ed. R. Britton, M. Feldman & E. O'Shaughnessy. London: Karnac Books.

Ferenczi, S. (1932), *The Clinical Diary of Sandor Ferenczi*, ed. J. Dupont (trans. M. Balint & N. Z. Jackson). Cambridge, MA: Harvard University Press, 1988.

_____ (1933), Confusion of tongues between adults and the child. In: *Final Contributions to the Problems and Methods of Psychoanalysis*, ed. M. Balint (trans. E. Mosbacher). London: Karnac Books, 1980, pp. 156–167.

11

Self and Other in Self-Analysis

Warren S. Poland

"The only true voyage of discovery, the only real rejuvenating experience, would be not to visit strange lands but to possess other eyes" (Proust, 1981, p. 260). So regularly do we see what we expect to see that we must struggle to try to see afresh, to see with other, with new eyes. Just as that is true for how we see outward, so is it more so for how we see when we look within. Too often our self-portraits are like the delightful images painted by court artists, portrayals of loveliness with an occasional beauty mark intended to mask the idealization. Contented, we then call the beauty mark "insight."

Clinical analysis offers a way to move beyond such self-serving reflections, to aim toward greater truth. In a formal analysis, self-serving reflection is corrected as the image is refracted through another's eyes. A patient comes to someone else, an analyst, and tries as ever to structure the present so as to refind the past. For his part, the analyst strives to avoid conventional and predictable reactions, instead working to hold to a position of candid and non-self-serving description of what unfolds. In such a way does the analyst lend his eyes to the service of the patient, the analyst's eyes becoming the needed "other eyes" until the patient is able to develop his own ways of looking within afresh.

I am indebted to Stanley Needell, M.D. and Janice Poland, LCSW for their substantial contributions to the development of this paper.

219

What other eyes are available for a person alone so that inner vision can yield to re-vision, so that re-vision can lead on to in-sight? Without the benefit of "other eyes," is such a thing as self-analysis truly possible? And, if as I believe it is, then how can it come about by one person alone?

Before turning to the sources of "new eyes" in self-analysis, I want to address background questions that relate to both clinical and self-analysis.

WHAT IS ANALYSIS?

First, what do we even mean by analysis? Whether two people are involved or one person is alone, just what *is* analysis and how does it differ from what is non-analytic? If we do not consider this, then every rationalization can be presented in the guise of analysis and called a beauty mark.

We cannot say that analytic work has been done unless at other times we can say that it has not been done. To consider a new idea the result of analysis, it must not have been known before and it must have become knowable only with difficulty, through work.

This is, of course, already well known to us in our clinical experience. We may struggle to define analysis behaviorally (for instance, in terms of a patient lying down on a daily basis and saying what comes to mind to a technically appropriate interpreter sitting behind him). We may define analysis conceptually (for instance, in terms of an analyst working on the basis of concepts of the unconscious, transference, and interpretation). But when we sit among colleagues to hear a case said to be ready for termination, no matter how technique is defined and no matter how good the analyst's technique may have been, we ask whether core issues have indeed been touched, whether "real analytic work" has been accomplished.

The problem is the same with self-analysis. The proof is in the outcome. Both clinical analysis and self-analysis must demonstrate genuine inner change and outer opening subsequent to emotional work for one to say that analysis has taken place. Self-absorption is not self-reflection, and self-reflection is not by itself self-analysis.

Using a semifictional model, when Proust's Marcel spoke of feeling happy, he described his state of feeling. When he wrote that his sometime lover Albertine had been responsive, he reflected on the immediate source of his pleasure. When he let his mind move on to his childhood longings for his mother's kiss, he extended and deepened his reflections. Then when, *laboring hard against considerable inner resistances* he managed to open the universe of memories and ghosts, struggling for candor about his own loving and lustful, envious and hateful urges, he extended his reflections to a breadth as well as depth which permitted him major new freedoms and choices in his personality, in the entire structure of his life. There is a continuum from conscious awareness of a feeling to reflection to deeper reflection to profound opening of buried memories with increasingly candid and even merciless self-exposure. Also, steps along the continuum from emotional awareness through levels of reflection to deep insight take increasing levels of work, that is, the expenditure of energy despite increasing discomfort.

For one to say analysis has gone on, hard work has had to be done. An understanding that was not emotionally available before must follow the inner labor of overcoming prior defense. If all seems easy, with the end carrying the tone of self-congratulations, we question what work has been done.

It has been said that an understanding is a place where the mind comes to rest. One, and especially someone intellectually bright and psychologically sophisticated like an analyst, can easily satisfy himself that a comfortable conclusion based on self-reflection is the result of a piece of self-analysis. Whether in clinical analysis or in self-analysis, insight and understanding are always partial; proclaimed self-analysis is always open to the question of how far it has gone beyond self-satisfying self-reflection. Respecting the continuum of psychological depth, our question now about analytic work is how much and in what ways an insight is authentic and how much and in what ways the same insight serves to protect against deeper exposure.

Recognition of the importance of degree when considering self-knowledge and self-mastery exposes a further problem that is similar yet different in clinical analysis and self-analysis. In each, if analysis is always a question of degree, then when is one finished?

In clinical analysis the question of termination is complex. There is always the temptation for a patient to quit while moderately ahead but still wishing to feel safe. Such defensive retreats require interpretation rather than enactment. Nonetheless, a time arrives in a clinical analysis when analysand and analyst agree that central issues have been mastered and it is time to stop.

What of self-analysis? At first glance there would seem to be no termination in self-analysis. Yet when we turn to those specimens of self-analysis we most often examine, the resolution of eccentric engagements by analysts at work, we see they are relatively well-defined instances with beginnings, middles, and ends. This is so for each example of an analyst's self-analysis while at work, even if each clinical analysis carries with it, as I believe, a continuing series of reciprocal patient and analyst self-inquiries.

In clinical analysis we are aware of work undone even when there is a successful termination. Aiming at the least for analysis of the core neurosis, we also try to aim higher, attempting to analyze as much of the character structure as we can. Even with success, we never presume to have analyzed all of the character.

How does this apply to self-analysis? Stepping back from the self-analysis of circumscribed episodes, such as countertransferential engagements, we are left with the vexing question of character analysis. We all are limited by and partially blind to our characters, a difficulty I had in mind when I wrote that the major problem in self-analysis is that of case selection (Poland, 1984). In self-analysis we are faced with the distinction between segmental analysis and character analysis. Can a self-analysis go so far as to yield character changes?

What is left untouched by the bits and pieces of self-analysis? When we limit ourselves to repeated fragments of self-analysis we may master crises but end like Eugene O'Neill's father, spending our lives over and over replaying the same old familiar role. Regrettably, the tennis coach was right when he said, "Practice makes permanent." Without the benefit of reflections from another person in regular attendance, self-analysis runs the risk of becoming a series of never-ending reruns, a sophisticated version of a neurotic symptom, perhaps like examination phobia dreams in which recurring dangers provoke self-assurances without proceeding to more difficult personal structural changes.

With the analyst at work as our major focus for studying self-analysis, we fall short of answering whether self-analysis can lead to significant character analysis. We await multiple longitudinal studies which could demonstrate clear alteration in character beyond repeated small steps. Until we have such data, in recognition of the power of the repetition compulsion we must be cautious about the defensive nature of self-analytic conclusions. As Gardner (1991) observed, the main business of self-inquiry may be trading yesterday's illusions for today's.

Caution in evaluating analytic gains does not imply nihilism. Both clinical analysis and self-analysis do take place and both do work. Let us now turn to the dilemma of "self" in self-analysis.

COMPARISONS BETWEEN SELF-ANALYSIS AND CLINICAL ANALYSIS

So far, vignettes offered by analysts at work have been the main building blocks of our understanding. Deutsch, Fliess, Gitelson, and

Racker in the early years, and Calder, McLaughlin, Jacobs, Gardner, Silber, and Sonnenberg more recently have been among the major contributors in this work. None has explored the subject of self-analysis more incisively than Eifermann. Rather than here offering yet another such vignette of my own, I think there may be more use in my stating briefly how an aspect of my character colors my views as I approach the question of self-analysis.

After a lifetime of curiosity about myself and others I have found one major thread running through every aspect of my life and my thought. It is the marvel of otherness. With more than mere curiosity, rather amazed with intense and permanent puzzlement, I am taken by what it is like to be somebody else, what it means to be someone other. Indeed, after following this theme to its professional application, I have come to believe that *the fundamental principle from which all other principles of clinical analytic technique derive is regard for otherness, in the analyst's marrow a deep respect for the uniqueness of the patient's self as an authentic other.* In parallel, I find that *in self-analysis, in looking at oneself as an other, dedication to truth with ruthless candor is the highest respect that one can pay oneself.*

We all know the multiple phases of a life in progress from earliest moments through aging. My own life has been both as representative of the universal and simultaneously as idiosyncratic as any of our lives must be. Whether I start with my earliest infantile memories or move to the later sexual and hateful unfolding of my oedipal struggles, or continue up until this very moment when I walk in the warm afternoon sun of maturity chilled by the dusky cool shadow of nonbeing always at my side—whatever the level and whatever the inner forces, I see that the struggle to recognize the essential separateness of people is always present. The uncanny realization of being alive, and alive as one person and not someone else, the mind-spinning awareness that I am another person's "other"—these senses of self and otherness color every moment of my life. For me, grasping reality always requires a stretch to try to realize what self and otherness mean, to try to contain with great difficulty the awareness that you and I share the same world but have different and equally valid realities.

We ask whether and how a self-analysis can exist, indeed, whether a self can exist, apart from a universe of others. We ask how there can be a *self*-analysis without the presence of others, and, as an unavoidable parallel, also how there could be a dyadic clinical analysis without having at its center one soul's self-analysis in the presence of but apart from the analyst/other.

Unfortunately, we use the same language to talk of our private worlds and our public interactive worlds, at times misleading ourselves into thinking the two are identical rather than overlapping and similar but also different. At times we even foolishly sound as if we can know someone else in the same way we know ourselves.

In contrast, Anna Freud (1981) suggested that insight and understanding be distinguished. She suggested reserving "insight" for the kind of awareness one can have of oneself and "understanding" for the very different level of awareness one can have of another. Expressing no quaint daintiness of semantics, she cut to the center of our analytic plight.

When we say that we analyze a patient, and when we say that we analyze ourselves, do we even use the same word in both instances or are we using a single word-symbol to stand for two importantly different meanings? "Analyzing," when applied to the search for inner truth in oneself, and "analyzing," when applied to the professional technician's efforts to help another in the other's own search, are not identical. In the sense of true knowing rather than knowing about, analyzing refers to the self-knowledge that arises within. In appreciation of the private nature of inner experience and self-knowledge, it has been put provocatively that the only person in an analysis an analyst can analyze is himself. Certainly it is legitimate to say that an analyst analyzes the patient, but one must keep aware of what a different technical use of the word "analyze" that implies. Anna Freud's distinction between insight into oneself and understanding of another reminds us to distinguish the world of inner emotional experience from the professional tasks involved in approaching another's inner world.

As understanding of another and insight into oneself differ, so also the processes leading to those distinct states differ. In a clinical analysis, the patient takes the analyst at first as a distinctly other person, but with growing investment in transference actualizations the analyst/other comes to seem as if a part of the patient himself, an actor of those emotions and expectations which the patient assigns from his inner drama. With the aid of the analyst's interpretations, the patient comes to re-cognize, to realize anew, that the analyst is, indeed, an other, not part of himself.

In a self-analysis, in contrast, one must be open to oneself but then must aim for candor to see that self as if it were an other. Just as in clinical analysis the processes of the dyadic interchange must themselves come to be the object of study, so also in a self-analysis must the subject of one's own analyzing submit to the scrutiny of self-investigative skepticism.

How can one develop the ability to see oneself with increasing candor? What "other eyes" can be adopted so one can extend vision to one's own blind spots? At present, we are learning much about the clinical two-person interchange from studying the analyst's self-analysis. Paradoxically, we may yet learn much about how "other eyes" are taken in in self-analysis from the study of interaction and internalization in dyadic clinical work.

It is in the search for knowledge of the inner workings of one person's mind that the ultimate similarity between self-analysis and clinical analysis is to be found. Yet, behind that similarity lies an essential difference. The paradox that discomforts our usually ordered way of thinking is that one's inner emotional experience is unique and internal even when one is sharing a moment with an other, and at the same time one lives within the network of human connection even when one appears to be alone. The seemingly self-evident difference of solitude of self-analysis and shared intimacy in two-person clinical work is not so simple as at first appears.

In clinical work, although the patient invests the relationship with private meanings, the patient's mind functions in the privacy of inner emotional experience. Although there may be a longing for merger, probably in both patient and analyst, and although there may be fantasies of merger, perhaps also in both, the two clinical partners remain separate people.

The fantasy of fusion is not the actuality. Clinical success brings with it the realization that intimacy exists within a framework of essential separateness, "intimate separation" as Stone (1961, p. 91) described. The two analytic partners come to share respect for the essential otherness, the unique individuality, the authenticity, each for the other. The mutual respect of two separate people connected in shared contact, but apart in selves, replaces fantasied symbiosis.

In self-analysis, the person alone is not quite so totally alone as at first might appear. Just as dyadic analysis is more inwardly private and solitary than its two-person interactive context may suggest, so also a self-analysis unfolds more within the fabric of human connections than seeming individuality suggests. One lives in the context of current external life engagements and internal reflections of earlier engagements. When offering a poignant fragment of his own self-analysis, Silber (1991) noted, "When I work upon my dreams I feel I am in the company of analysts." Nonetheless, the complication in self-analysis is the seeming absence of a single, clearly defined other as apparent coparticipant.

Consideration of self and otherness leaves us with the question of how much clinical analysis actually is a patient's self-analysis in a setting structured to make possible the contributions of the expert assistant in attendance. For self-analysis the question turns to one of how much is not done by one mind in solitude but subtly depends on and draws from external assistance.

THE PLACE OF OTHERS IN SELF-ANALYSIS

How do engagements with others contribute to the "new eyes" of objectivity which make original discoveries possible in self-analysis? As in clinical analysis, so is it in self-analysis. An other is needed for two main functions: first, to provide a supportive structure and, second, to provide the interpretations which can come from an other's views. I shall turn to both functions.

Supportive Others in Self-Analysis

In the following examples, illustrative fragments which might seem merely incidental or educational out of context, were crucial parts of active self-analyses in each instance cited. Were it feasible to spell them out more fully, each would fit our criteria of inner labor followed by inner and outer growth. I have selected narrow aspects of experiences only for the sake of offering illustrations.

Looking for the sources of "other eyes" we are led directly to our learning from others. While learning implicitly raises the question of teachers, education and self-analysis are not the same. An analyst provides the analytic situation in which an analysis can unfold and the interpretive tools that help open doors through which a patient can proceed. In like manner, what at times appears to be teaching may also provide an emotional holding environment as well as new ways of looking necessary to self-analysis.

Taking in the Different Eyes of a Teacher. Since all contributors to one's self-analysis can be considered teachers, I shall start with an experience involving an actual teacher, in this instance a teacher from relatively late in my life, the chief of the department of psychiatry where I had my formal training.

During the first week of my psychiatric residency I met with my new chief, who asked me how I would like to spend my time in training. Thinking in terms of formal requirements for board certification, I began, "Well, for my three years . . ." My chief looked confused and interrupted me. "What do you mean, three years?" It was my turn to be confused since I was sure that he knew full well, but I stated the requirements for certification. I have thought of the incident often and I am certain he appeared genuine in his surprise when he answered back, "Are you telling me that you're the kind of guy who would let a bunch of old men in another city tell you what you are going to do with your life?" I felt abashed as I was forced to recognize that yes, I *was* telling him exactly that. But I did not know what I was telling him until *he* told *me*.

That brief interchange was of pivotal importance to me in my coming to recognize what has been called my own agency, the sense that I am the one living my own life, the realization of my proprietorship of my own life and of my own responsibility for whatever choices I make. Is that a new insight? A clinical analysis would certainly take credit for such an internal shift. Is this not, then, part of a self-analysis? My coming to my new realization required my recognizing my earlier ways of seeing my place in the world and my appreciating how those earlier views had developed in order for me to move beyond them. As McLaughlin (1988, p. 374) wrote: "No fresh and mutative insight occurs in our work excepting as some previous and compelling insight, i.e., some former understanding of one's self by which one has lived, is worked over and discounted." My experience with a teacher offered the vision through new eyes that widened my own view of myself in the world as I proceeded with my self-analytic work.

Taking in the Eyes Behind the Eyes of a Teacher. At times others who contribute to our self-analyses are not only those we know we see but also that flood of many whom we do not know we see when they approach us through others. Having just quoted him, I shall turn to my involvement with McLaughlin to show the presence of others behind an apparent other in the facilitation of inner growth.

In an earlier published fragment of my self-analysis (Poland, 1977) I focused on how children identify with the unconscious conflicts within their parents, values and conflicts thus transmitted as traditions across generations. The grandfather I never knew suffered from inner conflicts developed in his relationship with his parents, conflicts which my father internalized and spent his life struggling to master, conflicts which I also labored to put to rest yet another generation later.

In my professional career, McLaughlin's intellectual engagement and emotional encouragement have clearly influenced my own thinking and questioning. Transforming competitiveness into support, he has helped me venture to explore. For the sake of my present point I cite out of context two sentences about his own life that McLaughlin (1988) had occasion to publish.

> I had lost my physician father in the great flu epidemic shortly after my birth. . . . At the same time I was fortunate in having frequent contact

with a paternal outdoorsman uncle, a journeyman carpenter and ingenious craftsman, who summered with us and taught me much until his abrupt and permanent departure to the west coast in my early adolescence [p. 378].

I have no doubt that his uncle's warm light is reflected in the prism of McLaughlin's own personality. It is probable that the "ingenious craftsman" was vital in forming the skills that were in the next generation realized in an ingenious psychological craftsman who was able to help me gain some bits of mastery of myself in my own effort to develop my craft. Our paths are lit, colored, and influenced from within our conscious reservoirs by the traces of ghosts we could never know we knew. The selves we hope to analyze and the skillful parts of our selves that do the analyzing have in them both assimilated and unassimilated others. Our selves *are* the others at the same time that they most keenly are ourselves, *not* the others.

Interpretive Others in Self-Analysis

Let us move from the nourishing and educational to those relationships which might be deemed more interpretively informative.

We are open to taking in most readily from those in whom emotionally we are most invested. Those closest to us not only have greatest access to seeing us most fully but also greatest opportunity to speak to us when our defenses are down. Spouses, children, parents, patients, friends, and enemies—all have ways of looking at us and opportunities to tell us more of what they see of us than at any moment we may wish to hear. Similarly, in those moments when we relax our control and open ourselves, as when engaged with reading, theater, and music, we allow ourselves to be vulnerable to learning more about our worlds and ourselves than we might have expected.

Analytic patients are central contributors to an analyst's continuing self-analysis. This is not only because repeated engagements with regressive states of emotion provide the opportunities and demands for repeated self-analysis. In addition, patients have their own perceptive capacities and repeatedly inform an analyst of aspects of himself he often would prefer not to know. Analysands are, thus, primary contributors to their analysts' own analyses. However, since this area has been the most common focus of previous study, I shall here merely acknowledge it and move to other sources of other eyes.

Others as Contributors—Children and Segmental Focus A primary (I sometimes think *the* primary) category of facilitators of self-analysis is that of one's children. If patients contribute to the self-analysis of analysts by their impact from the firing line of daily work, then one's children are even more potent, knowing their parents from having grown up behind the lines. Also, a person's identification with and investment in his children is greater than that with and in his patients.

One demand for self-analysis comes each time one faces one's own child's confronting the pressures of moving to a new life phase. Indeed, growing older as one's child grows older, and reworking developmental crises as one's child confronts that child's first edition of those crises, may well provide the major opportunity for carrying self-analysis beyond the narrow into broad reaches of character structure.

I have described elsewhere (Poland, 1977) my self-analytic use of a pilgrimage in response to the pressures of my son's rite of passage from childhood to adolescence. When writing then, my interest was in the place of action in self-analysis. Only later, in retrospect, did I come to appreciate how much the pressures of my son's moving from boyhood to manhood shook me, upset my prior insights, and demanded further self-analytic work. In the process of reworking earlier self-analysis I had to learn again the importance of degree rather than absolutes when considering insight. Cherishing insight, one comes to realize that what one cherishes is always tentative; one comes to have increasing respect for the tentativeness of temporary convictions.

Children often serve as our most useful, if at times most painful, interpreters. For an example, I turn to an early moment in my son's growth, to one of the initial steps in his move from infancy to independence.

When my son was about 3 he and I engaged in a defining power struggle. Full of a growing sense of himself, he challenged the usual rules beyond tolerable limits and repeatedly did so to such a point that I sent him to his room. Still defiant, he left his room. I carried him back. Again he left, and again I carried him back. The back and forth continued several times until I was sitting on the floor at his doorway holding him in while he pushed to come out. Exasperated, I told him that if he left his room one more time, I would spank him. He left.

Forcefully, I picked him up and announced, "All right, that's it! I'm going to pull down your pants and spank you." And just as clearly he answered, "If you have to spank me, then spank me. But you don't have to pull my pants down."

It would be difficult and a bit embarassing to try to estimate how many times in my life I have been in the position of apologizing to my children. I *did* spank my son, though after his words I spanked lightly, half-apologetically, and never spanked him again. I certainly did not pull his pants down. Instead, I found myself confused (a choice state for self-analysis), wondering about old conventions, wondering about myself both as current father and as former son. The incident set off considerable private discomfort and anguished extension of my insight into previously hidden aspects of myself and my relationship with my own body, and with my father as I had been a boy, as I had grown, and as I had experienced myself in the world.

Others as Contributors—Children and Characterologic Focus. The question has been raised whether self-analysis can extend beyond specific areas of symptoms to character issues. I turn to a second instance of a child's contributions. My daughter has equally contributed to the painful extension of my self-awareness. I choose one time for the sake of brevity. It was a time when she was central in forcing me to see— and fragilely master—narcissistic pressures.

It was a time when my narcissism was running rampant, a time I was newly in private practice and impressed with myself as a "promising young doctor." Then 5, my daughter must have been fed up with what undoubtedly had been my pompous lectures. One time that she must have found one time too many, she heard me out and then answered me simply but forcefully, "You don't know everything just because you're a doctor."

Again, on the surface that might seem to be an ordinary if apt comment not related to the question of self-analysis. But in the context of the vulnerability of intimacy, it was as powerful as any interpretation of resistance I had ever heard in my formal analysis for its effect in forcing me to take a pained new look at myself. My readiness for self-analysis must also have been present, but that, too, is always a matter of degree.

Nothing that I have learned of myself of true value would I ever at the time have chosen to learn. In self-analysis we take our breakthroughs where we find them and we find them when we are most vulnerable in our attachments.

Each of my children has helped me learn more about myself and my unconscious dynamics than I can specify. I have learned greatly from each even if it often has taken me a long time to forgive them for having enlightened me.

Much is made in the analytic literature of the role of the parents, especially the father, in introducing principles of reality to the growing child. More notice is due to the extent to which the growing child introduces principles of reality to the still growing parent. This offers a new level of meaning to the poet's observation that the child is father of the man.

Others as Contributors—Non-Family Members. Friends and enemies, those we love and those we hate, even strangers to whom we open ourselves—all help us look into ourselves in ways we otherwise could not. Greenson (personal communication) said that he believed that analysts' needs included having good spouses and good analytic friends, friends who could listen to one's concerns with friendship enriched by analytic wisdom.

An instance of a classical analytic interpretation offered by a stranger was described by the writer Michael Arlen (1975) in his book about his inner struggles over his Armenian heritage. Struggling against an Armenian identity against which his father, too, had struggled, Arlen undertook a voyage of discovery to Armenia. Once there, however, he found himself still pulling back from all links to Armenian tradition. He felt contemptuous of those earlier Armenians who "accepted subservience"; he seemed to agonize as he continuously rejected the very identity he was traveling to explore. Finally, it was a tour guide who offered him the crucial interpretation he at last was able to hear. "I know what you want. You want to tear down your father."

The full report details the substantial emotional turmoil, the reworking of hitherto forgotten memories, the shift in dreams, the change in his character structure and way of life. The guide had indeed been a guide on both of Arlen's journeys, the inner as well as the outer. As a helpful escort on the outer journey, the guide offered the immediate personal connection that facilitated the unfolding self-analysis. In that context the guide could put into interpretive words what had to be said for Arlen to open his eyes to self-knowledge. In Arlen's published description, it was a stranger who offered the crucial statement needed for Arlen to hear from an other in order to open his eyes to new views.

Others as Contributors—New Sensations Contributing to Reworking. Others once removed, their effects evident in their creative products, can also serve. New experiences can also elicit sensations which trigger memories, the new sensations thereby introducing the possibility of new understandings.

Two categories of experiences particularly contribute to self-analysis: experience of changes as part of aging and aesthetic experiences.

As we age we have renewed opportunities to view with new eyes the inner landscape as previously seen. Recently, at a time of uncommon exhaustion and without immediately visible prospects for a vacation, I had a day of disheartening fatigue. I love my work, but at the end of that difficult day I turned to my wife and said I would love never to work again.

In bed that night, that is, at a time of relaxed reflection, my mind turned to my father during those early years of my life when I had considered him my enemy. Not able to defeat him in the multiple ways I then wished, I had often consoled myself with a private attitude of disdain for him.

Now older than my then young father, I found myself thinking back to my childhood during the nineteen thirties. The world, I later learned, was in a terrible depression, but the circumstances of life were all I had ever known and I took them to be the essence of normality. My father had three jobs. One was his regular daytime work; a second was on weeknights, far across town; for the third, he worked behind a counter in yet another remote section of the city. At the time I had convinced myself I was glad the old man was always out of the house, but privately I felt hurt, rejected, and furious. I was certain that he preferred being at work to being at home. As far as I could see he was having the time of his life.

In the years between that childhood and that tired moment of my own when I was reflecting on that childhood, I had had two conventionally successful analyses. But it was not until I was 15 years older than my father had ever lived to be that I came to realize that my father must have felt then something akin to what I felt now, that I came to recognize how I had distorted my view of my father, how much I sadly had blamed him for what undoubtedly had been his effort to protect me from having to see his fatigue and unhappiness. And, at that moment, very late in my life, I came to appreciate parts of my father I had previously labored to repudiate. At that moment, I came to be able to extend my own self-analysis to levels and areas to which I had not before had access. A small step in my own natural development had enabled me to re-view how I saw myself and others in my life who mattered to me.

Others as Contributors—An Immediate Sensation's Contribution to Reworking. Before moving to the last major category, that of aesthetic experiences, I share a hint of self-analysis *in statu nascendi*. At work now, while writing, I have been constantly distracted as each point has revived yet further questions and further observations in my mind. For just one instance, I am struck how often I have turned to examine ambivalent struggles with my father and with his later stand-ins. Seeing that, I then notice how uncommon it has been for me to choose to write of matters touching on my mother. I realize how a self-analytic broadening in this regard likely was influential in shaping my last paper, one in which I turned my attention from Freud, whose self-analysis of his involvement with his mother was limited, to Proust, whose relationship to his mother was central to his self-analysis (Poland, 1992).

I shall not speak more of myself other than to notice how work, the process of writing about matters I already had considered that I knew, forces to my attention notice of areas I had not as openly considered, questions of possible resistance which demand further self-scrutiny. General reflection broadens the vista for further self-reflection.

Others as Contributors—Aesthetic Experiences. The final category of contributing others, that of aesthetic experience, is so broad and vital as to merit a full study in its own right. What gives art its power? Sensitive involvement with reading, drama, music, and art can open inner emotional areas which had been closed. Willing suspension of disbelief is a literary description akin to what we clinically think of as partial regression Walls between inside and outside weaken; reality testing is relaxed. In such a state one is particularly receptive to engagement with the creative works of others.

I once worked with an obsessional young man who was consumed by the intensity of his hatred and buried adoration for his industrialist father. A transference neurosis had crystallized, and we labored hard to try to expose how his passions colored his views of himself and his world. Our progress was slow.

One day everything seemed to change, to loosen, and to open. The previous night, like many such previous nights, he had watched television. That evening, however, *Death of a Salesman* was shown. The young man had never seen it before and its impact was explosive. The father whom he had described as detestable was suddenly reconsidered, even seen with sympathy. Tears brought forth hidden longing to be loved by his father. Hate and love, previously compartmentalized from each other, were now felt together. No doubt, prior analytic work had contributed to his receptivity when he saw the play. However, it is equally doubtless that continuing analytic work might have maintained its snail's pace had it not been for the overwhelming power of his experience of great art. Great art can move greatly.

We frequently learn from ourselves and from our patients of times that some book or drama or work of music or other art had vast personal importance. Although I have known of analysts who, based on that experience, have suggested particular books or movies to their patients, I have never known instances when such prescriptions were of notable value.

Play is relevant as a personal art form. Play, adult play as well as child's play, offers the opportunity not only for discharge but also for bringing hidden conflicts to where they can be seen with new insight. In the context of relationships with others, unconscious fantasies can be brought forth which then can be seen and analyzed, one's eyes strengthened and enriched by others' eyes.

SUMMARY

The analytic endeavor, whether in a dyadic clinical setting or in a self-analysis, requires effort to extend insight into areas previously kept in the dark. Earlier limited vision into oneself is extended with the assistance of an other, someone available to help one see what one could not see for oneself.

Every clinical analysis unfolds within the framework of the pair of resonating and interactive self-analyses, the patient's manifest one and the analyst's more silent one. Similarly, every individual self-analysis is nurtured by the communicative and interactive interplay between the individual and the human world of which he is a part.

True self-analysis is always a struggle against inner defensive forces, never the simple delight of self-admiration. Its outcome, the freedom that comes from insight and self-mastery, is always partial, always vulnerable to continued scrutiny.

The seemingly lonely task of self-analysis opens within the matrix of connection to others in the world, others known and not known to be known, others as close at hand as one's spouse and children and friends and enemies, and as far removed as the presences hidden in the inner lives of other people and their works.

The appeal of simple dualisms can mislead us. The two major errors into which we fall when considering self-analysis are first, those of making a subject–object split (that is, thinking that self and other exist apart from a relationship) and, second, failing to make a subject–object split (that is, as if the other is part of the self and the self part of the other).

Each view, that one is separate, *apart* from others, and that one is *a part of* others, is, of course, correct. Though separateness and connectedness seem contradictory, they are both true and both true at the same time. To be a person is always to be alone and simultaneously always to be in relationship to others. The loneliness of self-analysis unfolds in the fabric of otherness.

REFERENCES

Arlen, M. (1975), *Passage to Ararat*. New York: Farrar, Straus & Giroux.
Freud, A. (1981), Insight: Its presence and absence as a factor in normal development. *The Psychoanalytic Study of the Child*, 36:241–249. New Haven, CT: Yale University Press.
Gardner, M. R. (1991), And who will analyze the analysts? Presented at panel on "Self Observation, Self Analysis, and Reanalysis" at annual meeting of American Psychoanalytic Association, New York City.
McLaughlin, J. T. (1988), The analyst's insights. *Psychoanal. Quart.*, 57:370–389.

Poland, W. S. (1977), Pilgrimage: Action and tradition in self-analysis. *J. Amer. Psychoanal. Assn.*, 25:399–416.

_____ (1984), On the analyst's neutrality. *J. Amer. Psychoanal. Assn.*, 32:283–299.

_____ (1992), Transference: "An original creation." *Psychoanal. Quart.*, 61.

Proust, M. (1981), *Remembrance of Things Past*, Vol. 3 (trans. C. K. Scott Moncrieff). New York: Random House.

Silber, A. (1991), Analysis, reanalysis, and self analysis. Presented at panel on "Self Observation, Self Analysis, and Reanalysis" at annual meeting of American Psychoanalytic Association, New York City.

Stone, L. (1961), *The Psychoanalytic Situation*. New York: IUP.

V

SELF-ANALYSIS, WRITING, AND CREATIVITY

Just as doing analytic work can be a spur to our self-analysis, so can writing about our work. Sonnenberg explores the ways in which his clinical and theoretical writings (and his continuing reflections on them) both facilitate and impede the self-analytic process. The written document becomes a repository of our thoughts and feelings. It holds them for us and can serve as a tool for further self-investigation or as a source of repression and resistance. Sonnenberg touches on both aspects:

> Writing, and thinking about what I write, provide me with unusual opportunities for autonomous and creative introspection in the service of organizing clinical material, thinking about how I listen to analysands, examining my blind spots, recognizing my resistance to self-analysis, and deepening my understanding of myself. . . . At the same time, writing can be used as a resistance to self-analysis and as an impediment to growth.

Sonnenberg presents the write-up of his first completed analytic case. He goes on to describe his complex relationship over many years to the case report and its evocation of powerful transferences toward patient, supervisor, and institute. He would "forget" about the report, put it aside for long periods of time, until some event challenged his resistance, such as a phone call from his former patient

237

or an interview with an analyst researching termination issues. As he became more able to tolerate the discomfort, he became more aware of the earlier collusive avoidance involving himself, his patient, and his supervisor around the nature and depth of aggression (and defenses against its emergence into full awareness) in the treatment. Of particular interest is the way he accomplished, through his ongoing relationship with the written material, a piece of self-analysis, only to see those gains eroded and fall victim to rerepression and subsequently to be recovered through the self-analytic process.

Sonnenberg's experiences help us think about self-analysis, terminable and interminable. Some self-analytic insights involving encapsulated segments of our psychic life, such as those described by Poland, chapter 11) may remain in place. Other self-analytic insights (involving core characterological issues) are continuously shifting and require ongoing self-analytic efforts.

Like Gardner, Gedo, and others, Sonnenberg at times finds himself surprised when the self-analytic process seems to be activated outside his awareness and to start by itself (autoanalysis). Unlike those authors, he also engages in a self-conscious, deliberate, and systematic self-analytic process at the end of each work day:

> The self-analytic process begins with my awareness of my free associations and my associations to dreams, symptoms, slips, interactions with family, friends, and colleagues, observations of patients and what I thought about them or said to them, or anything else I might consider. I allow myself to experience passively these associations, and eventually I engage in relatively passive yet self-conscious introspection, attending to what ideas might come to mind about my freer associations. I next think over these ideas, considering more carefully and with more directed effort what I know about myself, what conflicts I am currently struggling with, what hypotheses I have about the way my mind has been working. Eventually, I develop interpretations, and think more about these.

Significantly, the process described by Sonnenberg progresses (or moves back and forth) along a continuum from passive–receptive to active–interpretive. Also, the boundaries between different stages are quite permeable.

Sonnenberg believes that, gradually over the years, "it has become easier to engage in helpful self-inquiry." Like many other contributors to this volume, he feels that his self-analytic capacity did not preexist his personal clinical analysis, but was an outgrowth of that experience.

Through the example of Samuel Beckett and his analysis with Wilfred Bion, Anzieu explores the connections between clinical analysis and self-analysis, the conditions necessary for a fertile self-analysis, and the relationship between self-analysis and creativity. Despite the uniqueness of Beckett's genius, his example, according to Anzieu, illustrates common characteristics of an intense, sustained self-analysis: "It follows a psychoanalysis; it is carried out in writing (in this case, In a second language); it occurs in interaction with a correspondent; it takes place in the fictional presence of a psychoanalyst and of the rule of free associations; it occurs on the occasion of a midlife crisis."

Anzieu calls our attention to the way in which Beckett advances his self-analysis while experimenting with new modes of artistic expression. Beckett incorporates the psychoanalytic situation into the form and content of his early novels:

> The Beckettian narrator is alone when he speaks, but he imagines himself as a patient in a psychoanalytic situation. He speaks to a fictional psychoanalyst according to rules of fiction homologous to those of psychoanalysis. The psychoanalytic frame is the organizing code of the narrative. This frame allowed the novelist to make the narrator speak more freely than he himself could speak to Bion, at the time of the real psychoanalytic sessions, about the "night" part (blackness and mud) of his psyche.

For Anzieu, self-analysis is essentially a narrative activity, albeit one fraught with problems: ". . . the risk of fascination with the content of a narrative about an unconscious fantasy; effects of style in the service of defense mechanisms of the ego; and the resistance to becoming conscious." In the dyadic analytic situation, the analyst functions in part to remember and preserve the patient's psychic productions. In self-analysis, the written narrative serves similar functions. "Conservation returns to the very leaf of paper, the inscribed surface functioning as the psyche's envelope."

The written narrative is necessary but insufficient. Anzieu also stresses the role of the other in self-analysis. A self-analysis that remains a solitary activity runs the risk of becoming "a narcissistic solace and/or an obsessional rumination." "A self-analysis cannot be operative without a witness called upon to be the symbolic guarantor and to protect the self-analysand against the traps of his countertransference toward his own psychic work."

Lussier elucidates Anzieu's thesis that Freud's self-analysis was simultaneously a therapeutic and a creative effort. It significantly alleviated his train phobia, his anxiety about dying of a heart attack, and his severe bouts of depression. It also enabled him to discover the meaning of dreams, the rules governing their production, and the role played by unconscious fantasies in symptom formation.

We may be generally aware of the interconnections among Freud's self-analysis, his discovery of a new method of investigating unconscious derivatives, and his development of theoretical constructs to explain his findings. But Lussier specifically describes Anzieu's careful reconstruction of Freud's self-analysis through his dreams and their multiple linkages to his ongoing creative work.

As Lussier states, Freud's self-analysis was more than a soliloquy. Not only did he draw on his dreams and associations to further his self-analytic efforts, but he also relied on his work with his patients and on his cultural milieu including myth, folklore, and art.

Self-analysis, like clinical analysis, is always incomplete. Despite the magnitude of Freud's self-analytic accomplishments, they were nonetheless severely limited. Lussier examines those limitations, while maintaining an appreciative attitude toward Freud's interior journey.

12

To Write or Not to Write
A Note on Self-Analysis and the
Resistance to Self-Analysis

Stephen M. Sonnenberg

In this essay I am influenced by several important trends in the thinking of psychoanalysts in the United States. These trends include the heightened interest in the analyst's use of self-analysis throughout his or her life; the recent interest in the process of writing about psychoanalysis, and its role in analytic education throughout the analyst's career; and the nature of various specific forms of resistance which affect analysts as they work. The central issue I seek to explore concerns an aspect of self-analysis, and can be stated in the form of two related questions: (1) What is the potential positive impact of writing about psychoanalysis on an analyst's self-analysis? (2) What role might the product of analytic writing play as a resistance to self-analysis? There are many important related questions which are beyond the scope of this essay, though I hope others will consider what I say here when answering them in the future. Two obvious ones are: (1) What might be the role of resistance to self-analysis in the work life of the analyst who wishes to write, but cannot? (2) In what ways might resistance to self-analysis influence the writing analyst as he writes?

This study, then, builds on the interest among analytic educators in writing and its place in the education and development of the psychoanalyst. Reflecting that, Stein recently contributed two essays on psychoanalytic writing, in which he makes several observations and suggestions (1988a,b). Among these are: (1) clinical reports are

241

remarkably difficult to prepare, for reasons of accuracy and the need for confidentiality; (2) the analytic writer faces conflict because the desire to gain distance from clinical material is both a motive for writing and an interference; (3) spirited creativity is often lost by the time the potential writer accumulates sufficient experience to make a substantial contribution; (4) excellent writing requires a degree of painful self-revelation and self-assessment of the writer's errors; (5) senior colleagues can and should do much more to encourage and help junior colleagues to write; (6) fears of criticism from colleagues and of the impact on patients inhibits the clinical writer; and (7) the desire to write an interesting paper might influence the clinician as he performs his analytic work. Most of these points have particular relevance for my study, and I shall return to those at the close of the paper.

As I perceive it, there is today a movement among some analysts who advocate the use of their self-analytic reflections as aids in their work with analysands (McLaughlin, 1975, 1981, 1988; Kern, 1978; Calder, 1980; Gardner, 1983; Beiser, 1984; Silverman, 1985; Jacobs, 1991), and this, too, influences what I have to say here, just as it has influenced my work in recent years (Sonnenberg, 1990, 1991).

Finally, efforts to define and study specific processes of resistance among analysts at work is the third area of analytic inquiry on which this study rests. One such resistance was considered by Gray (1982), when he recently called attention to the resistance to uncovering the resistances. This, of course, is an old concept, but one which nevertheless had been neglected, to the point where Gray believes there exists a "developmental lag" in technique. Schwaber has also recently identified a special form of resistance (1983, 1986), the one the analyst experiences with respect to the way he is experienced by the analysand. She believes this resistance represents a substantial interference for the analyst in his effort to attune himself to the patient's point of view. Rangell (1982) also has identified a special resistance afflicting the analyst, which he describes as a difficulty in remaining aware of the derivatives of oedipal impulses. He believes this occurs in psychoanalysts as a consequence of deficiencies in their training analyses, superimposed on pathological group processes within psychoanalytic institutes and societies. He, himself, did not call this a resistance, preferring to discuss negative transference to psychoanalytic theory, but clearly he has studied a special form of resistance in the working analyst.

In my thinking about resistance I find myself moving in two directions. As I have indicated in the past (Sonnenberg, 1990, 1991), I am very aware of my continuing battles with it, and I realize that these are necessary because of my ongoing conflicts. So I often focus more on my conflicts, and less on the specific form of my resistance. Yet I also feel that it is useful to consider my resistances from the perspective of form, because as plastic as are my defenses, there are still patterns which define broad categories, which I can usefully identify. So in this paper, with the work of Gray, Schwaber, and Rangell in mind, I am bringing into focus what I consider to be a specific form of resistance, the resistance to self-analysis.

Finally, a word about my method. As in the past (Sonnenberg, 1990, 1991) I shall rely on my own self-reflections for clinical material, and I shall tell my story in the first person. Again, I am indebted to Stein (1988a, pp. 122–123) for suggesting that it is desirable to write in that way, and possible to do so without being exhibitionistic. I shall try to follow his lead.

SELF-ANALYSIS AND WRITING ABOUT PSYCHOANALYSIS

There is, at present, no clear understanding nor widely accepted definition of what constitutes the analyst's self-analysis, for as Firestein has put it (1978, pp. 253–254), it is an area "not sharply defined." He notes that since analysis has been described as a dyadic process, we have as yet no certain picture as to how it can be conducted by a single person, on himself.

I have attempted to describe a range of self-analytic activities and functions (Sonnenberg, 1990, 1991), and I will elaborate here. For me, self-analysis is a self-conscious and self-disciplined process, which begins with my awareness of my free associations, and my associations to dreams, symptoms, slips, interactions with family, friends, and colleagues, observations of patients, and what I thought about them or said to them, or anything else I might consider. I allow myself to passively experience these associations, and eventually I engage in relatively passive yet self-conscious introspection, attending to what ideas might come to mind about my freer associations. I next think over these ideas, considering more carefully and with more directed effort what I know about myself, what conflicts I am currently struggling with, what hypotheses I have about the way my mind has been working. Eventually, I develop interpretations, and think more about these. I engage in this kind of self-inquiry at various times during the day. Sometimes, by my active choice, this occurs while I am with patients, because I am puzzled as I try to understand what is going on. At times this process just seems to start by itself, either with a patient or during a wide range of activities, such as when I take a walk. But always, in a self-disciplined fashion, I self-analyze at the end of my work day.

I believe the mental activities I have just described have much in common with what Arlow related when he described the roles of empathy, intuition, and introspection in the analyst's efforts to develop interpretations (1979). I would add that in calling this a process I wish to convey the idea that my self-analysis is made up of a series of connected experiences, through which I develop self-awareness about what is going on in my mind, and my life. Sometimes the individual experience is productive of insight, sometimes of confusion, and usually of both.

Much of my self-awareness involves understanding consciously what was previously unconscious, and much of it involves the exploration of more or less intense transferences. I believe I repeatedly resolve conflicts of the moment, but I find that they return. Optimistically, I think as time has passed I've learned more about myself, and that it has gotten easier to engage in helpful self-inquiry. Finally, I want to stress that without the experience of my personal analysis I believe this mental activity would not be possible. Indeed, I believe that my self-analysis is a continuation and extension of my personal analysis.

I have also found that there exist in my experience of both clinical and theoretical analytic writing potential aids to my self-analysis. This was first mentioned by G. Ticho, almost a quarter-century ago (1967, p. 314), and others have recently commented on that idea, or illustrated it in personal accounts.

Calder describes how clinical writing, in the form of a record of one's self-reflections, might support self-analysis (1980, p. 6). He writes:

> My method [of self-analysis] consists of three stages: I collect certain primary data about myself and *write them down*, then I associate to those data and *write that down*; finally I attempt to understand the primary data on the basis of the associations. *I record both the primary data and the associations to permit a freedom to associate without having to make sense of either type of material and to permit comparisons at different times over the weeks, months, or years.* [italics added].

Another observation about self-analysis and writing came at the close of Silverman's paper about the transference and countertransference he observed in the conduct of an analysis (1985, p. 198). There he expressed the sentiment that analytic writing can aid the analyst in self-inquiry.

In the example I shall now give my experience spans what Calder and Silverman describe. It involves an effort in clinical writing, which at the time served as a stimulus to self-reflection, and indeed has continued to do so for many years since. That self-reflection included attention to matters of personal conflict, to clinical and theoretical issues in psychoanalysis, and to the experience of self-inquiry itself. This essay is one product of that experience of writing and subsequent thinking, and I can add that the process of self-inquiry related to the recording of that original clinical description is in no sense at an end.

PSYCHOANALYTIC WRITING AND RESISTANCE TO SELF-ANALYSIS

Any written record represents a potential counterbalance to one of the most dramatic effects of repression, total amnesia, and by being available for reconsideration might also serve as a positive stimulus to self-inquiry. But the resistance to self-analysis is formidable. Freud recognized its existence (Gay, 1988, p. 99), and that recognition is supported by the comment of Calder (1980, p. 6) as to the infrequency of self-analysis of dreams among colleagues. Further, Calder (1980, p. 17) offers observations as to the forms this resistance takes: (1) comparisons with Freud may have an inhibiting influence; (2) the implication of grandiosity may serve as a check; (3) reluctance to replace one's analyst because of fear of competition with or separation from him may serve as a resistance; (4) disappointment with one's personal analysis may lead one to refuse to self-analyze; and (5) all the other common resistances to insight or change may be operative. So now, as I attempt to describe the ways in which a piece of my analytic writing has been used by me to further my self-understanding, I shall also emphasize the resistances to self-analysis which my writing product concurrently produced. My story, a specific clinical example of a self-analyzing analyst at work, should supplement Calder's description of the resistance to self-analysis.

An Example

It happens that for a long time I have found that the written report of my first completed analytic case has been especially useful to me as I have learned about myself, and about my resistances to learning about myself. What follows now is a disguised summary of that case report, which was originally prepared for academic purposes. In preparing the summary I have both paraphrased and quoted from the original write-up; only space and the need for disguise prevent inclusion of the entire record. I have taken pains to ensure that what is included here accurately conveys both the content and style of the original. Yet each time I revise this essay, and review the case material, because I know different things about myself, and learn more about myself in the process of rethinking the material, I consider minor changes I might (and sometimes do) make. So in studying the process of self-analysis using this vehicle, it is clear that we are looking at a cross section of an ongoing, evolving, dynamic process. That is both the strength and weakness of this particular method of investigation: it allows us to appreciate the process of self-analysis starting with a "piece of my mind" frozen in time, yet the appreciation and description of that "piece of my mind" is ever changing. It is, then, only partly true that a written record represents an unchanging starting point for studying the evolution of an analyst's self-analysis.

The analysand was a 32-year-old unmarried woman, a social worker, who came with the complaint "I can't get along with my father." This woman, whom we shall call Susan, was bright, serious, and pleasant appearing. Yet from our first contact she was anxious about our relationship: she anticipated that I would argue with her when she proposed a very low fee, that I would say she wanted to pay too little. She imagined that she would present a written budget, that I would challenge her, and that she would then dissolve in tears. At our second meeting we set the fee at $2 per session, which was consistent with her proposal, and she began on the couch. She tearfully stated "My father, I can't relate to him . . . I surrender, cry, lose control, he always argues, tells me what I should do . . . lately, he's had a hard time . . . he may lose his job and it's clear he has no job security . . . he's a broken down man. . . ."

The history which unfolded during the first several months indicated that Susan was the first of three children, born in a comfortable small town in the Northwest. Her father was a civil servant, with a background in accounting, whom Susan remembered as hardworking, pragmatic, distant, and taciturn. Mother was a housewife, warmer than father, but still quite reserved. Neither parent was considered particularly empathic, but mother's role in the family was to let the children know how she and father felt.

When Susan was 2 her sister Sarah was born, and Susan was aware of resentment toward Sarah all her life. While Susan never married, Sarah had, and this won her the approval of father and mother, especially when she produced a grandchild. When Susan was 4 Joe was born, with a congenitally malformed leg, and a borderline normal IQ. Mother became depressed at the time of Joe's birth, and Susan was aware of feelings of guilt about her lifelong dislike of Joe, as well.

Throughout high school and college Susan was often asked out, but she found sex repulsive, and quickly rejected each boyfriend. The pattern she described of her social life in recent years was somewhat different. She would usually become involved with a man from a minority background, he would prove unreliable by not keeping his promises or commitments, and eventually find himself on the receiving end of Susan's rehabilitative efforts.

But as her twenties gave way to her thirties, and as Susan recognized a basic interpersonal emptiness in her life, she sought psychotherapy. Her therapist, after a year, referred her for control analysis.

During the first year of analysis Susan discussed her fear that she would be rejected by me. The analysis of this fear focused on her belief that her father was overly critical, and that she would invariably be found wanting by him. She went on to note that in response to her father she felt hurt and very angry, and that each time she recognized her anger she concluded he would, too, and reject her in response. She said that her feelings about me paralleled this pattern: I, a critical man, would critically reject her, she would become angry in response, she would recognize her anger, and then anticipate that I would further reject her for it.

Next Susan became silent in her analysis, and again a transference construction was possible. She wanted to be a perfect patient for me, just as she wanted to be a perfect daughter for her father. She felt she would appear stupid if she freely associated, so she found she could not talk. With father, she believed she tried to be a perfect daughter, to earn his love and approval. But he never appreciated her.

There was, next, a shift as a result of this analysis of Susan's silence: she recognized in a seemingly global way that the past was living on in the present; that she was preoccupied with her love for her father; that her competitive feelings with regard to her mother were strong and related to her desire for her father's love; that her resentment toward Sarah and Joe was similar in origin; and that her avoidance of sex was related to her guilt over her wish to be close to men as representatives of her father.

At this point she had been in analysis for 15 months, and we both took vacations. When we resumed our analytic work she angrily asserted that she wished to stop. The analysis of this also seemed productive. She recognized that she had come to believe that I had given her an impossible task: she could not give up her wish for her father's love, and therefore, analysis was not helpful. She recognized that her vacation trip home had stirred her memories of happy moments in her childhood, which included close moments with father, and that this led her to be particularly angry with me now. There were no conscious thoughts about how father and I had recently treated her — I had taken a vacation and father had been away on business when she visited her family home — and how she felt about us in this connection. But in response to what she did recognize about her current state of mind, she decided to continue the analysis.

Yet the analysis was once again characterized by Susan's silence. Again, analytic understanding seemed useful: this silence was a derivative of potty behavior, was central to a pattern of sadomasochistic behavior she directed toward father. She noted that: "I was always unhappy . . . I never felt happy because I would never allow my father to know I was happy, or satisfied by him . . . and really, I never was happy because of him. . . ." Susan recognized that this sadomasochism had pervaded her character development, and once again, there was some lifting of her silence.

We were now well into the second year of Susan's analysis, and for its remainder, and through the third year, as well, we worked on understanding her relationships with men. She came to see that she chose men whom she would experience as abusive, in order to expiate guilt feelings about angry wishes toward her mother and her siblings. This was particularly troubling to her, and she recognized that Joe's birth defects led her to feel a particular sense of responsibility and guilt. The result of these analytic efforts were a waning of feelings of guilt, and certain steps in the direction of closer relationships with women. I felt the analytic alliance was better than ever, and evidence included fewer periods of silence.

Yet at this point the analysis became stalemated. We were confronted with the reality that Susan was not willing to change her pattern of relationships with men, which she described as designed to recreate a past in which she was disappointed. She also rejected change because her current pattern allowed her to expiate her remaining guilt for her fantasized evil impulses and behavior toward mother and Sarah and Joe. And, she added, she would never stop wanting her father's love.

Finally, about 5 months before Susan's analysis came to a close, and with recognition that her masochism, while still present, was better understood and controlled, we decided on a termination date. From my side this was a reluctant decision, but I felt that perhaps this woman had gone as far as she could, at this time, and I did hope that she would benefit from an orderly termination process. Susan, I should specify, had unequivocally demanded termination.

During the termination phase much productive work was accomplished. In fact, the quality of this work was so surprising that it altered my view, as well as those of Susan and my supervisor, as to the success of this analysis. Susan stated that I was selfish and uncaring about her, that I did not care about understanding her. I was able to hear this clearly and work with it, so that analysis could reveal that she had felt this about mother, and that the feeling had primarily preoedipal roots, though Susan focused on the later experience of Joe's birth, after which mother had become depressed and withdrawn from her. Susan concluded that this experience, resting on its preoedipal foundation, cemented her inability to give up her oedipal strivings for father: Mother was "gone" so father became that much more important; also, with mother withdrawn and depressed, father "seemed" that much more available. Susan felt she now, for the first time, understood why she so often felt people neither cared about her nor understood her.

At this point, about 3 months before the end of analysis, Susan had a dream in which she renounced a humiliating triangular relationship with an older couple. Susan's analysis of the dream indicated that she believed she could now give up the demand for her father's love. She then began to talk about what she would take from the analysis: a new sense of self-esteem, a diminution of guilt, an understanding of herself, and an ability to gain understanding through introspection. Dreams were interpreted in a fashion consistent with this view. She dated a new man, and while he was another minority group member with a tendency to abuse her, he also was highly educated, and she felt he had the potential to be an appropriate partner. She was able, certainly, to assess his strengths and weaknesses, and to enjoy sex with him more than with others, before.

At her last analytic session Susan reported a dream which she interpreted as indicating that she felt she could take with her what she wished of the past, and leave behind what she deemed unwanted: in its manifest content she was living in an old residence, and working in a new job. Finally, Susan indicated that she would call me for help if, in the future, she felt she needed it.

WRITING AS SELF-ANALYTIC ORGANIZER AND THE ONSET OF RESISTANCE

The piece of analytic writing summarized above was prepared during the final months of my candidacy, and immediately after my graduation from an analytic institute. This coincided with the final months of Susan's analysis: her termination date was the week after my graduation. To put this effort into perspective, then, I must say a word about how I felt about what I was just then going through, insofar as those feelings are relevant to the beginnings of that part of my self-analysis which was aided by this effort at writing.

Wallerstein (1972, p. 598) has suggested that there is a cult atmosphere in analytic institutes, and Kernberg (1986, p. 799) has stated that analytic education is "conducted in an atmosphere of indoctrination." Arlow (1972) recognizes that the candidate may develop a mature identification with an important intellectual tradition, or, as a result of a training experience which is actually an initiation rite, an identification with the aggressor, which is far less useful.

I mention these observations because I believe they touch on what was a part of the educational experience of many, if not most, analytic candidates of my generation. As a group, in addition to integrating into the fabric of our life experiences what were feelings of disappointment as we came to grips with the limitations of psychoanalysis as therapy, we faced the challenge of coming to grips with a process of psychoanalytic education which was far less supportive of thoughtful diversity and therapeutic creativity within a classical context than is the case today. As I completed my formal analytic education, then, during the 6-month period in which I completed my first analytic case and wrote it up for academic purposes, I was thinking a great deal about my training experience, integrating disappointments and satisfactions, and thinking about the evolution of my ideas about theory and therapy, and the ways those ideas had been both stifled and encouraged by my training.

So, as I wrote up the completed case report the process of reviewing my summary records and process notes, organizing my ideas, and writing them down became a stimulus and an opportunity for reflection on the ways my own conflicts had interplayed with my environment, and on the ways my own unconscious processes had contributed to shaping my learning experience. Through analysis of concurrent fantasies I had about the man who supervised my work on this case, I began to realize more clearly that some essential considerations had been outside my awareness during most of the analysis.

Specifically, after the termination date had been set and I began the writing project, I became uneasy with what I had come to see as my adaptive decision about this analysis. For I began to realize that my decision to concentrate almost exclusively on the analysis of Susan's oedipal conflicts reflected deference to what I believed was my supervisor's preference, as the representative of my institute. However, as I thought more about this, and allowed myself to both freely associate and reflect on my experience with Susan and my supervisor, I realized that included in my memories of the experience were clues that I had caricatured my teacher and what I was being taught. Indeed, I recalled specific exchanges in which I had been encouraged by my supervisor to consider more thoroughly certain hints of the ways preoedipal factors had shaped Susan's oedipal experience. I also came to recognize that I had created a caricature of my supervisor, a barely conscious image of a rigidly inflexible person. In this caricature I recognized elements of a way of thinking which allowed me to "know the rules" I needed to follow, in order to avoid what I thought would be for me a dreaded oedipal confrontation. I also recognized the ways in which all this was determined by the interplay of the reality I was experiencing and the transferences which I brought with me and superimposed on that reality.

As indicated in the case summary, all this was very helpful in the last months of my work with Susan: it enhanced my work with her by allowing me to hear what I believe I had been missing. This experience also illustrated for me in a memorable and discrete way the importance of self-analysis in the course of my work with each and every patient. Yet there was an equally important lesson here, and this was one I did not so easily learn. For just as I had experienced the usefulness of self-analysis of a range of factors which might impinge on my work, I was at almost the same instant learning that resistance could erode my capacity to conduct that process of self-inquiry. Of course, by its very nature, of that I was unconscious.

In fact, upon completion of my work with Susan, and submission of my write-up for an academic purpose, but still with many questions about that analysis very much on my mind, I put my written records away, and did not look at them for four years. From time to time I would think about Susan, and consider rereading what I had written, in order to better think about what I had learned, and still needed to learn, from my work with her. Sometimes there were very specific stimuli for such thinking, one being about one year after the analysis ended, when Susan called me. She had a new boyfriend, he was again a member of a minority group, and he was again a problem for her. Yet she felt he had potential, and wondered about the availability for him of low fee analysis. I referred her to the clinics of the analytic institutes in Washington, DC. I asked her how things were going, and she said they were "about the same": better than before, but not what she would ideally like.

Not surprisingly, while Susan's report that things remained better was encouraging to me, at the same time I found her call disconcerting. This was so because many among my remaining unanswered questions about her focused on how I might have done a better job. Certainly, I had never been entirely satisfied that I had done as well with her as I might have. Yet my questions continued to fester outside of my full awareness, and I did not experience the benefit that would have been mine if I had engaged in a thoughtful review of what I had written. Indeed, in retrospect the existence of the written record actually allowed me to more easily put off review of the case. For, I would reason, "since it's there in my files I can always look at it at some other time."

Then, several years later, I was interviewed by a psychoanalytic researcher. This interview focused on a discussion of analytic termination, and I described to the interviewer the process by which I became aware of a difficulty in Susan's analysis. Yet after the interview I was moved by a sense of curiosity to take my case write-up and other written material out of my files, and conduct a careful review. This was possible, I believe, because advances in my self-analysis allowed me to overcome my resistance to engaging in such an experience. What I discovered, as I read and thought and remembered, was that in my talk with the researcher I had demonstrated rerepression, as I conveyed again that transference-laden caricature of my supervisor. I found this interesting, and useful to me both personally and professionally, because it was a reminder of the importance of my self-analysis, but once again I put my write-up away for several years. My memories of my work with Susan still nagged at me, but I now know I used the stored written material as a rationalization for not thinking more about that nagging feeling.

I want to emphasize here that I am well aware that in this essay I am not focusing on all aspects of self-analysis, which is a subject of enormous complexity. I believe that by isolating the relationship among my self-analysis, my writing as self-analytic stimulus, and my use of what I had written as a resistance to self-analysis, certain points will be made. Certainly, while what I have described was going on I was learning about self-analysis and the resistance to self-analysis by engaging in both in other ways, for self-analysis and the resistance to it are multisourced and multimotivated processes. Yet at this point in this essay my focus serves an illustrative goal: to show that by using what I had written in a very particular way, over a period of several years I believe I held myself back from a thoughtful reconsideration of Susan's case. I believe this qualifies as an example of a specific form of resistance to self-analysis.

FURTHER SELF-ANALYSIS USING THE WRITTEN REPORT

I will not attempt to detail here all the self-analytic and other experiences which have resulted in my current practice of self-analysis, and my current appreciation of my resistances to it. But I do want to indicate that today I am far better able to use what I have written to stimulate my memory and my self-analysis than I was during the first years after I finished working with Susan.

I shall give one more example of self-analysis aided by the report of Susan's case. This example is taken from the recent past, occurred in the course of working on this essay, and is chosen because it illustrates the rich ongoing possibilities for learning through such activity. What I shall address is Susan's opening fantasy: that I would reject her fee proposal, and that she would fall apart. Susan began her analysis with what were associations to this fantasy, concerning her father's critical nature. As her analysis unfolded she explained that father's criticism frustrated her, made her angry, and that in turn made her feel even more vulnerable to the criticism of men.

I had always felt that further understanding of that fantasy was possible, and as I reviewed the case material self-analytically my thoughts turned to that fantasy, and I brought into conscious focus a persistent, though dim picture (often I experienced this as a set of ideas) I had of Susan's father. I had this picture from the very beginning to the very end of my work with Susan, but usually I was either unaware of it or didn't pay attention to it. In this picture I see a kindly gentleman, a sort of "Father knows best" character, who is benignly speaking with Susan. He sits in a dimly lit and inviting room.

But now, in vividly recalling and associating to that fantasied picture of mine, I know that room is a condensation of my supervisor's office, my office at the time, and the living room of my family of origin's summer home. My associations and my responsive interpretations, now less encumbered by previous needs to caricature and very much in summary form, include my current understanding that my supervisor was hamstrung by his kindly view that aggression was the result of frustration, and should be so analyzed. I now know, too, that I was then hamstrung by my transferred oedipal discomfort in my relationship with my supervisor, and that throughout most of the course of that analysis I had handled that transference by submission, rather than discussion and debate, or some other response. Looking back I also realize that I vaguely knew then, as surely as I clearly know now, that Susan's aggression was not simply to be understood as a response to frustration, that to understand it properly the defensive aspect of her explanation of it—that it was simply a response to father's nature—needed to be addressed.

I also realize now that I had "almost" understood all this back then, and do now, because of a contribution from my personal analysis, in which that family living room had been the scene in memories through which I explored my negative oedipal impulses, and my aggressive, competitive strivings toward my father. In personal analysis, in that remembered room I had learned that a muted and compromised form of oedipal aggression had taken the shape of my blaming my father for some of my own shortcomings. I now am able to comprehend how that dynamic similarity was during, and for years after, Susan's analysis an interference in my ability to understand her, just as understanding it is now, finally, an aid. I also know now how transference of this attitude influenced my view of my supervisor during and after the time we worked together: during the years of supervision it prevented me from learning from and with him as easily as I might have, and afterwards it contributed to the persistence of my caricature of him. Indeed, I now understand just how profoundly unable I was back then to comprehend and discuss with my supervisor our disagreement over the nature of Susan's aggression, and how those inhibitions, based on my oedipal transference, in turn led to my inability to explore that aspect of my analysand's personality.

But there is more, for as I recognized all this my self-analytic thinking deepened. I continued to think about Susan, and I realized that I felt both my supervisor and I were hamstrung; another mental picture of mine came into focus, which I knew I needed to address. I saw my old Jewish supervisor, and myself, his younger Jewish student, strung up in a smokehouse, like meat, by our Christian analysand. I saw us trapped, as we were adulterated . . . in a gas chamber. I saw us slaughtered. But, I asked, what does this fantasy of mine mean? Then, I remembered the second part of Susan's opening statement from the couch: ". . . lately, my father's had a hard time . . . he has no job security, and now I see him as a fragile, broken down old man. . . ."

It is then that I was flooded by associations to an essential aspect of my relationship with Susan, which was never once brought into focus. Susan, a sophisticated social worker, referred through my training institute's clinic and control analysis screening committee, never once acknowledged that she understood anything about, or thought about, or had fantasies about my job security. I, for my part, never became consciously aware of that issue: it is as if I and my supervisor had to pretend I was not a candidate, trying out for a job as an analyst.

In response to those thoughts I now look back on Susan's analysis and I recognize that while we often explored what seemed to be the transference neurosis, we were all too quick to relate it back to surface thoughts of the moment about father and mother. The consequence of this was that we never explored the existence of fantasies Susan might have had of me as a fragile man, whose job security was vulnerable to the way she treated me. Therefore, we never were able to consider and understand what may have been Susan's most powerful aggressive feelings toward me, the depth of her wish to harm me, to ruin me, to destroy me expressed in her silence and her refusal to be analyzed. We never were able to consider, together, the possibility that she did not always experience her destructive aggression toward me simply as her more or less appropriate reaction, secondary to frustration. We never were able to consider, together, how she might come to know that this was not the whole story. We never explored the possibly defensive nature of her agreement at the end to be "cured," for in this formulation her acceptance of "cure" allowed her to defend against understanding the nature of her aggressive fantasies, over the entire course of her analysis.

So now I recognize sources of my nagging feelings about Susan's analysis which lasted these many years: during her analysis I had not articulated to myself my belief that Susan had constructed a defensive way of thinking which for me was then impenetrable. Indeed, I am now able for the first time to consider fully that a more accurate formulation might have been that in Susan aggression was not simply an angry response to frustration, or even a powerful murderous fantasy far out of proportion to her frustration, but a way of thinking which led her to construct a life in which she sought out victims, driven by a wish to hurt others which transcended current experience, and which seemed to reflect a basic desire at the center of her personality. Further, I am finally able to fully consider that our not exploring this possibility resulted in the limitations Susan described one year after her analysis ended. While back then all this I could not explore, could not know, I am now able to recognize similar difficulties in understanding analysands, when they occur, and use self-reflection to gain valuable analytic information from those experienced difficulties, as they occur.

I wish to add that I realize many colleagues may not agree with my formulation about Susan, especially because it suggests what many doubt: the fundamental nature of the destructive component of an individual's aggressiveness, the component which to some even suggests the existence of a death instinct (Bird, 1972, p. 288; Loewald, 1972, p. 235). But whatever my theoretical position on the nature of human destructiveness might be or become, it could not be developed and investigated in Susan's analysis, because of limitations which are less restrictive now because of the specific self-reflective effort I have just described.

DISCUSSION

In this essay I have attempted to illustrate how I have used the process of writing about psychoanalysis, and a resultant piece of analytic writing, as an aid in my self-analysis. I have described the method I use when I self-analyze, I have called self-analysis a process, and I have revealed some details of what I have learned about myself. I believe I have shown that writing, and thinking about what I write, provide me with unusual opportunities for autonomous and creative introspection, in the service of organizing clinical material, thinking about how I listen to analysands, examining my blind spots, recognizing my resistance to self-analysis, and deepening my general understanding of myself. But even as I described how I have engaged in a process of personal and professional growth, I also illustrated the way a piece of writing has been used by me as a resistance to self-analysis, and an impediment to growth. I have by design, for reasons of personal choice, left out certain details of what I have learned about myself, which some might consider relevant. For example, one might wonder what else I have learned about myself which now allows me to articulate new ideas about the nature of Susan's aggressiveness.

I shall now return to Stein's suggestions about analytic writing, and discuss implications for analytic education and the analyst's development over the course of his or her career. To emphasize the complexity of the issues Stein has brought into focus I shall begin by noting that while he mentions that senior colleagues can and should do much more to encourage junior colleagues to write, he also recognizes that writing analysts are inhibited by the fear of criticism from colleagues. So the potential writer may feel he or she is in a bind, needing and fearing exposure to the thoughts of colleagues. Stein also states, and I have illustrated this, that writing can be used to gain undesirable distance from clinical material; I have described this as a specific resistance to further self-understanding and professional development on the analyst's part. Therefore, there may even be conflict experienced by some analytic educators about encouraging analytic writing in some of their students.

Yet I would argue against not encouraging writing in the beginning analyst, for anything can be used for purposes of resistance, and educational measures can be employed to counteract this tendency. Thus, if experienced analytic educators wisely and kindly involve themselves in fostering efforts by younger colleagues to write independently, the development of autonomy and creativity in younger analysts will be supported, and thoughtful teachers will be positioned to point out resistances resulting from writing, when these occur.

I can now address Stein's lament that older analysts don't contribute to the literature as they might, because they lose spirited creativity even as they acquire clinical wisdom. He seems to be saying that today's analytic writer is often too young or too old. In my view this underscores the importance of encouraging independent thinking and writing early in the analyst's education, for younger colleagues, once encouraged to think creatively and to write, may find themselves engaged in a process which may prolong their passion and enthusiasm for their work, no matter how elementary their early efforts may be. I have certainly found that to be the case.

There is no question that excellent writing requires a degree of painful self-revelation and self-assessment of one's errors, as I have shown by example, and that accuracy is particularly problematic, because as the analyst learns more about himself the picture he has of a clinical situation, even a "static" one which took place years ago, changes. But again, if senior colleagues who understand such difficulties share in the task of writing, and encourage the self-inquiry necessary in writing about psychoanalysis, younger analysts will learn that through writing they can not only contribute to the field, but also learn more about themselves.

Throughout this discussion of Stein's ideas it has been my intention to emphasize what is for me an important point: I believe there is nothing intrinsic in analytic writing that results in resistance, but there is something basic in the experience of writing which can enhance the capacity for introspection of many analyst writers. Certainly, for me writing is now primarily an aid in my self-analysis, and I believe Stein would agree with my view about the relationship of writing creatively and the potential for enhancement of introspective activity.

Finally, there is the question of just how much the desire to write an interesting paper might influence the clinician as he or she works. I understand Stein's concern, but I believe there is a more likely outcome when an analyst writes: he or she will be encouraged to see what is there. Because I believe every analysand is actually different from all others, and interesting in his or her own way, and that each analysis is therefore like no other, every analysis which becomes the subject of an analyst's writing will afford the writer the opportunity to convey something unique, if only he or she can recognize it. I cannot say with absolute certainty that this view is not a rationalization on my part, since I am a writing analyst. But as of this moment, as I complete this essay, my self-analytic reflections, my recollections of my experiences as an analytic clinician who is ever searching for unique ways to understand and communicate with analysands, and my perspective on my experiences as a writing analyst who is ever searching for new ideas, tell me that this conclusion does not represent a self-deception.

REFERENCES

Arlow, J. A. (1972), Some dilemmas in psychoanalytic education. *J. Amer. Psychoanal. Assn.*, 20:556–566.
_____ (1979), The genesis of interpretation. *J. Amer. Psychoanal. Assn.*, 27 (Supplement): 193–206.
Beiser, H. R. (1984), An example of self-analysis. *J. Amer. Psychoanal. Assn.*, 32:3–12.
Bird, B. (1972), Notes on transference: Universal phenomenon and hardest part of analysis. *J. Amer. Psychoanal. Assn.*, 20:267–301.
Calder, K. T. (1980), An analyst's self-analysis. *J. Amer. Psychoanal. Assn.*, 28:5–20.
Firestein, S. K. (1978), *Termination in Psychoanalysis*. New York: IUP.
Gardner, M. R. (1983), *Self Inquiry*. Hillsdale, NJ: The Analytic Press, 1989.
Gay, P. (1988), *Freud: A Life for Our Time*. New York: Norton.
Gray, P. (1982), "Developmental lag" in the evolution of technique for psychoanalysis of neurotic conflict. *J. Amer. Psychoanal. Assn.*, 30:621–655.
Jacobs, T. J. (1991), *The Use of the Self*. Madison, CT: IUP.
Kern, J. W. (1978), Countertransference and spontaneous screens: An analyst studies his own visual images. *J. Amer. Psychoanal. Assn.*, 26:21–47.
Kernberg, O. F. (1986), Institutional problems of psychoanalytic education. *J. Amer. Psychoanal. Assn.*, 34:799–834.
Loewald, H. W. (1972), Freud's conception of the negative therapeutic reaction, with comments on instinct theory. *J. Amer Psychoanal. Assn.*, 20:235–245.
McLaughlin, J. T. (1975), The sleepy analyst: Some observations on states of consciousness in the analyst at work. *J. Amer. Psychoanal. Assn.*, 23:363–382.
_____ (1981), Transference, psychic reality, and countertransference. *Psychoanal. Quart.*, 50:639–664.
_____ (1988), The analyst's insights. *Psychoanal. Quart.*, 57:370–389.
Rangell, L. (1982), Transference to theory: The relationship of psychoanalytic education to the analyst's relationship to psychoanalysis. *The Annual of Psychoanalysis*, 10:29–56. New York: IUP.
Schwaber, E. (1983), Psychoanalytic listening and psychic reality. *Internat. Rev. Psycho-Anal.*, 10:379–392.
_____ (1986), Reconstruction and perceptual experience: Further thoughts on psychoanalytic listening. *J. Amer. Psychoanal. Assn.*, 34:911–932.

Silverman, M. A. (1985), Countertransference and the myth of the perfectly analyzed analyst. *Psychoanal. Quart.*, 54:175–199.

Sonnenberg, S. M. (1990), Introducing psychiatric residents to psychoanalysis: A visiting analyst's perspective. *J. Amer. Psychoanal. Assn.*, 38:451–469.

_____ (1991), The analyst's self-analysis and its impact on clinical work: A comment on the sources and importance of personal insights. *J. Amer. Psychoanal. Assn.*, 39:687–704.

Stein, M. H. (1988a), Writing about psychoanalysis: I. Analysts who write and those who do not. *J. Amer. Psychoanal. Assn.*, 36:105–124.

_____ (1988b), Writing about psychoanalysis: II. Analysts who write, patients who read. *J. Amer. Psychoanal. Assn.*, 36:393–408.

Ticho, G. R. (1967), On self-analysis. *Internat. J. Psycho-Anal.*, 48:308–318.

Wallerstein, R. S. (1972), The futures of psychoanalytic education. *J. Amer. Psychoanal. Assn.*, 20:591–606.

13

Beckett
Self-Analysis and Creativity

Didier Anzieu
(translated by Pierre Johannet)

BECKETT AND THE FIVE STAGES OF A CREATIVE
SELF-ANALYSIS

Encounter with Mental Illness

Samuel Beckett (1906–1989) decided very early to become a writer in order to put an end to his adolescent crisis and to enter adulthood. He had felt misunderstood by his family and by others in the Irish Protestant environment in which he had grown up and pursued his studies. He was motivated by the hope that he would find in and through literature (as a reader, commentator, and author) those things he had missed. He hoped to hear people say what he had waited for in vain. He hoped to give voice to what he had never been able to say or known how to communicate.

To the great displeasure of his parents, particularly his mother, Beckett entered the exacting vocation of writer which led him away from any regular and remunerative professional activity. He was sustained in this vocation by his remarkable discovery in Paris from 1928 to 1930, when he was an English Assistant at the Ecole Normale Superieure at the Rue d'Ulm, and taught classical philosophy, modern novel, and poetry. In this cultural environment, open to artistic innovation, he met Irish writers who like himself were voluntary exiles and who could not fail to provide him with ideal identifications.

Out of this situation a first paradox arose. He wanted to live by his pen, but since he was almost unknown and wrote only minor works, he produced very little income. There came a second, more daunting paradox. Beckett wanted to devote his life to writing, but he had nothing to say. Wasn't this though the sign of a true vocation? Didn't Proust, to whom Beckett devoted one of his very early essays, begin this way? Writers who know in advance what they have to say touch us much less than those who venture out blindly into regions unknown to themselves and who lead us, as well as themselves, to guess at some unspeakable reality.

Beckett took two decades to solve these paradoxes. For years what he wrote was intelligent, amusing, but not moving. However, by imitating Joyce, whose son-in-law he almost became, by seeking inspiration from philosophers such as Descartes (and his Belgian disciple Geulinck) Leibniz, and Schopenhauer; from film comics who delighted him, such as Chaplin, Laurel and Hardy, the Marx Brothers; and from contemporary Russian, English, American, and French poets, he was training himself. When the time came to express something, he would be ready to write it.

While moving toward more radical misery, he learned to get rid, as of successive skins, of what Pascal once called diversion, and to shed, just as the mystics did, senses, imagination, and intelligence. (His characters invented fewer and fewer desires, stories, or arguments for themselves.) He reached a nothingness that at last he could attempt to talk about in a writing style similar to spoken language, since any great work is innovative in both content and in form.

For Beckett, nothingness, which for him is at the origin and the center at the same time, represents the emptying of everything the individual has lacked in his history, in order to come into being, to feel contained in a self, to emerge from the distress brought about by the dereliction and inadequate response of the first loved object.

There are novelists who save time in this phase of apprenticeship of letting go, who organize a scenario around their conscious fantasies. These are the writers of diversionary works. Beckett started that way, but later broke away from that method and revealed another method at once more existential and more essential. He became a novelist of man's misery, not of social misery, but of man's condition in its contingency, finitude, dependency, anxiety, and mortality, and also a novelist of the only human greatness, neither vain nor conceited, which consists of the thought of this misery. Such writers can become creators only after they have touched the bottom of that misery.

This first stage of creative work took place from 1930 to 1933, when

Beckett was between 24 and 27 years old, in periods of increasing seriousness, accompanied by more and more pronounced psychological regression. He failed as an assistant in French literature in his attempt to teach women students at Trinity College in Dublin (the university of the Protestant elite), where he himself had been a student. He went to his courses dressed like a hobo, wouldn't look at his audience, and would run off as soon as the class was over because of his horror of human contacts. He spent his time in pubs and with prostitutes, got into fights, and frequently came home drunk. He became ill with humiliating physical symptoms such as carbuncles on the neck and anus, or disturbing ones such as insomnia or signs of cardiac and respiratory illnesses. He eventually resigned his position, and stayed in bed in his room for days at a time with the shutters closed, his face turned to the wall, in darkness, refusing to speak or to eat. His family tried to conceal his condition, but when they were faced with the repetition and the worsening of the crises, their worry intensified. Medical care proved insufficient. At times his brother Frank, older by four years, had to share the bed with him, and thus reassured, he could finally fall asleep.

Beckett touched bottom when, seized by a feeling of suffocation, he thought he was about to die. His parents, who had been opposed to a plan for him to go to Germany to visit a cousin with whom he was vaguely in love and whose family they regarded as dissolute, finally gave in. He got better quickly, a sign that his depression should be attributed to a defect in narcissism rather than to a psychotic structure. But these events left their mark on him. He did not understand what happened to him; he knew only that he dove into the night and that this night occupied the deepest layer of his spirit. In every sense of the word he found himself in the dark.

In June 1933 Beckett was confronted with the brutal, premature death of his father who had run a flourishing surveying business, had been a dynamic athlete, and too much a bon-vivant. His father's death led to the increased domination of his prudish, unaffectionate, abusive mother who oscillated between moral rigidity and emotional storm. Attempting to pull himself out, Beckett began writing creatively and entered into psychoanalysis. He was aided in this double endeavor by the decisive influence of an old Trinity College colleague who at that time was a physician in the midst of his psychiatric training.

Dr. A. Geoffrey Thompson guessed that Beckett's ailments were part of a psychosomatic process. In the course of conversations, walks, and chess games, he enabled Beckett to begin to see the existence of a link between his physical symptoms and his psycho-

logical functioning which had become altered by mechanisms revealing a kind of madness. Beckett recognized himself in the stories
Dr. Thompson told him about his patients. He even managed to visit
secretly the psychiatric service in England where Dr. Thompson held
an appointment. He made contact with a few of the mental patients
who led him to the stupefying discovery that he was on the same
wavelength as some of them. He discovered there at last the mirror
reflection of what he felt himself to be, unlike his experience in the
mirror of his mother.

Beckett's first novel, *Murphy*, written in English, was conceived
before, started during, and finished after his psychoanalysis. *Murphy*
is the tale, written in the third person, of the pathetic adventures and
confused moods of a main character who runs away from love,
friendship, and the outside world by accepting a position as a
temporary nurse substitute in a psychiatric hospital. The author tries
to objectify his psychic disorder by describing how his hero, or rather
his antihero, manages madness—the madness in his patients and in
himself. Beckett also attempts to exorcise this madness and to
evaluate its risks by describing how, as Murphy becomes mad, he
becomes neglectful and begins to make mistakes ending up in an
accidental, quasi-suicidal death and a funeral even more pathetic than
his life.

MURPHY (1938)

Murphy prefers rocking himself naked in a rocking chair to love
relationships. His pleasure is to feel his spirit, detached from his body
and from the world of the senses, become free. He shuts himself up
in his "little bubble of noncommunication," a sort of Leibnizian
monad without doors or windows, perfectly closed, in which he can
escape time, changes, and vicissitudes. Thought shaken loose from
reality, fluctuation of the boundaries between the psychic ego and the
body ego, alienation and lack of integration—these are the kinds of
feelings which Beckett described in his correspondence with his best
friend Thomas McGreevy and which invaded him when his mother
came to see him (Bair, 1978).

Is this self-description by Murphy a naïve expression of psychoanalytic theory, or is it infiltrated by the latter? Sentences such as the
following lean in the direction of the second hypothesis: "Split in
two, a whole part of himself never left the mental closet imagined as
a sphere filled with light, half-light and darkness" (Beckett, 1938,
chap.6). Could Beckett have written "split" without knowing the term

splitting which would become so important for Bion? Could he have distinguished "light," "half-light," and "darkness" had he not been thinking of conscious, preconscious, and unconscious?

Beckett describes meticulously in *Murphy* the functions particular to each one of these three zones. In the zone "light," there are "forms in parallel" and also what we would call defense mechanisms, mainly reversal into the opposite: "Here the kick, given by the physical Murphy, was given by the mental Murphy . . . Here an entire physical fiasco would be transformed into a wild success" (Beckett, 1938, chap.6).

In the "half-light" zone, there are "forms without parallel": pleasure is no longer physical, it is aesthetic (the pleasure of daydreams, of visions brought by bliss). This imaginary world is not "afflicted by its homologue in reality" (Beckett, 1938, chap.6).

The "darkness" zone is made neither of elements nor of states, but of a "flowing of forms becoming continually incorporated one into the other . . . with neither love nor hate, nor with any conceivable principle of change. Here he was not free but rather like an atom in the darkness of an absolute freedom" (Beckett, 1938, chap.6).

This is a world akin to the passive, inert, will-less condition of the newborn, to his dependence upon the unpredictable moods of those around him, to his search for and loss of reference points, to the sense of discontinuity in his being, to his oscillation between "generation and collapse," to being a "projectile without origin or destination" (Beckett, 1938, chap. 6). Isn't Beckett describing here what Bion will conceptualize later as the screen of beta elements?

The mind, according to a subsequent remark made by one of the minor characters in *Murphy* is a "closed system" such that "for each symptom that is alleviated another becomes aggravated", and so it follows that he can state the principle, eminently economic, pessimistic, and parodic of Freud: "The quantum of wantum cannot vary" (Beckett, 1938, chap.6).

PSYCHOANALYSIS WITH BION

In 1934 and 1935, Beckett was in psychoanalysis three or four times a week with W. R. Bion at the Tavistock Clinic, where Thompson had introduced them. This was a miraculous psychoanalysis that brought about a spectacular disappearance of his symptoms. This was also a deceptive and eventually hated psychoanalysis because it could not prevent the return of the symptoms and because Beckett transferred onto Bion the negative therapeutic reaction he had in regard to maternal care and to existence in general. This was a psychoanalysis which only approximated a real psychoanalysis. The Tavistock Clinic was founded in 1920 by a neurologist for the purpose of practicing diverse psychotherapies according to an egalitarian representation of the various trends of the time—Freudian, Jungian, Adlerian—an eclecticism which did not end until after the Second World War.

Bion, who had been working there only a few months, was a beginner; he had not yet started his personal analysis and he knew nothing about Melanie Klein's ideas which he would espouse ten years later and which she herself had not yet organized into a system. Bion gave Beckett instructions: keep yourself at a distance from your mother, she is the one who makes you ill (which was not false but proved somewhat terse and clumsy). Beckett rebelled because he was beginning to tell himself he must do so, while at the same time he was overwhelmed by feelings of culpability at the thought of such a sacrilege. Bion, by making the decision for him, prevented his patient from arriving there on his own and repeated the attitude of Beckett's mother who never stopped making decisions for others based on her own rigid moral code. Beckett wrote to McGreevy that he has had some sharp bickering words ("une prise de bec") with his psychoanalyst, an expression all the more significant since the Becketts were originally a French protestant family who emigrated after the 1685 revocation of the edict of Nantes, and whose name Becquet derives from Bec, meaning the tip of the tongue, gift of gab, gossip. In making a definitive return to the country of his ancestors in 1937 and then to their language (Beckett wrote his works in French starting in 1946), didn't Beckett achieve the original meaning of his patronym: to write as when one speaks with a sharp tongue?

During childhood, Bion himself supposedly went through an autistic phase upon which he would later elaborate (also starting in 1946) in his works on the language and thought of schizophrenics. He seems to have developed a deep intuitive sense (but at the same time confused and clumsily handled) with regard to his patient. A great admirer of Jung at the time, he allowed Beckett (in a countertransferential acting out) to attend one of Jung's conferences restricted to physicians at the Tavistock Clinic. In the end Bion was helpful to Beckett by encouraging him in his vocation, and by letting him hear an enlightening description of the initial moment of creation as a phase of regression, a rush of emotion and depersonalization. Beckett decided then to end his treatment, setting the date of termination for Christmas 1935. He then returned to Dublin and to his mother, with the illusory hope that he would not be deceived. After the war started and after Beckett finally managed to flee his unbearable mother, he went to live with his French girlfriend, first in Paris, then in Roussillon-en-Vaucluse where he participated in the Resistance. He then had to confront a return in full force of his pathology, far from Bion and psychoanalysis. He wrote a new novel, *Watt* (1953a), in English. He projected on the character of Watt his own internal disturbances, his loss of reference points, the failures of communication, the mental and physical decay, the solitude, the rejection, the emptiness, the search for someone to talk to. This person first appears in the form of a master, Mr. Knott. However, as his name indicates and, as would a psychoanalyst, he does "not" answer the questions that are asked of him. Later on, it is a fellow patient at the psychiatric hospital where Watt will end his life in misery, with whom he manages to speak (and even then only backwards), only in close body-to-body contact, and whose first name is, not by chance, the same as the author's Sam. In this fashion Beckett takes a step forward in relation to *Murphy*. To the splitting between the author and the character is added the split between the author and the narrator. It is my thought that the novel *Watt* describes, in its first half, through the allegory of the two years of domestic service with Mr. Knott, Beckett's failed psychoanalysis with Bion. Then in the second half the novel reproduces the conversations between Watt and Sam, that is to say a dialogue become internalized, and the observation, as in Bion's later theory, of the person's psychotic part by the nonpsychotic part. Beckett engaged himself, by means of a novelistic creation, in a self-analysis whose therapeutic effect, even in the absence of any definitive resolution, is sufficient to preserve his sanity. At the end of the war, in a short novel written for the first time directly in French, *Mercier and Camier* (1975), Beckett reinforces this internal evolution by drawing a caricature of psychoanalysis (the failed voyage of two comrades, one of whom, Camier, is a private detective), and by showing the necessity of their separation so that Mercier (who doubles for Beckett) feels free to dive into his own "night" and to make "flowers," that is, his works, grow.

THE VISION OF THE WORK TO COME

Bringing back to light the pieces of that interior night (the first moment) into which the sudden rush of feelings and the regression had pulled the future creator, made up the second moment of the creative take-off. If nothing was gained from the first moment, it would have risked being forgotten, annulled, split off, disavowed and scattered, or it might have been experienced as a hallucination, as the beginning of a delirium, as the entry into madness. This second moment was reported afterwards by Beckett in a play, *Krapp's Last Tape* (1958a). It takes place in the spring of 1946, during a stormy night, on one of the jetties in Dublin Harbor. Beckett, at the height of his midlife crisis, came to spend his fortieth birthday near his mother who was getting progressively sicker and whose physical decay was to serve as a model for the impotent, handicapped, degenerate, disintegrating, and dying characters which Beckett would invent in his novels and his plays. His mother's progressive weakening liberated Beckett from the constraints with which she had imprisoned his spirit. Until August 25, 1950, the day she died, Beckett would know his greatest creative years. He wrote three novels, *Molloy* (1951), *Malone Dies* (1958b), *The Unnamable* (1953b), and the play to which he would owe his fame, *Waiting for Godot* (1952).

Beckett inverted the pathogenic equation that tied him to his mother. As long as she remained alive and active, he was reduced to a state of psychic death. Now that she was dying, he recovered both strength and freedom. But once she was actually dead he would know a long period of internal drought and infertility, until the crisis associated with the entry into old age provoked a renewal of creativity in which he would abandon the novel and give primacy to theatrical creation, to the composition of shorter, more sober, more synthetic texts, as well as to a partial return to the English language.

Thus in Dublin in 1946 in a familiar landscape, in the midst of unleashed elements, he had a vision of the work to come. He would move from the narrative in the third person to the internal monologue, or more precisely to the soliloquy. The classical novelistic frame with its places, its times, and its distinct actions would break up and reduce itself to a single voice speaking in echo to others. What this narrator, who speaks in soliloquy, would have to say—Beckett at last discovered it—was to speak about himself, not about his thoughts nor his emotions, nor his conscious or preconscious fantasies, that is to say his zones of light and half-light, but to allow his zone of "night" to speak: " . . . at last clear before my eyes that the obscurity which I fought all this time is in reality my most . . . indissoluble partnership, to my last breath, of the history and of the night with the light of understanding . . ." (Bair, 1978, chap. 15). From this point on there is no more flamboyancy in form or in background. Landscapes and characters are played out in three tones—white, gray, and black.

This obscure darkness would become the content of Beckett's work. His brief psychoanalysis revealed its existence to him without allowing him to understand it, while his novelistic and later theatrical creations would make him increasingly more familiar with it. An "I" was trying to come into speech by affirming itself and by differentiating itself from the voices around him which used to utter and were still uttering words which remained foreign to him, phrases the meaning of which escaped him, perhaps because having imposed this particular meaning did violence to him, or perhaps because, not being sure that he existed, he was not sure that this meaning was addressed to him.

Bringing his own obscurity into speech became a specific form for the writer during the second period of creation. Still, in order to move from the leading idea of the work to its realization, an organizing code had to be found. The discovery of this code and the putting it to work constitutes the third period of creation. This code, while probably remaining unconscious, gained in precision and sharpness as Beckett made progress in the composition of his novelistic trilogy, between 1946 and 1950. My hypothesis is that this code was derived from the psychoanalytic situation. A narrator speaks to someone who is there and who is not there, who at times listens and often doesn't understand him, who tells him he must speak without saying precisely about what, or how, or why. To be more exact, we are dealing with the literary reconstitution of a series of psychoanalytic sessions. An unknown person comes through, at regular intervals, to take the text of these sessions which the narrator is under obligation to write down. The narrator writes as if he were speaking. The voice counts more than the message. The narrator speaks as if he were in analysis but more freely than in the presence of a real analyst. He can speak to himself as if he were addressing a fictional analyst, while remaining protected in his monad. With Bion, in English, in London, Beckett had been able only to sketch out the process of free associations. Now in Paris and in French, he could really let himself go.

The archaic core of Beckett's psychological problems is not touched, not at all concerned with the relation of the lips to the breast, but rather with that of the mouth to the ear. As a child, he was well fed and attended to by a mother who had once been a nurse, but he hadn't been "spoken" in a sufficient manner. In the mirror constituted by the face and the body of his mother, Beckett as the very small child read only her moral code, and not a reflection of his sensations, emotions, actions, questions which would have allowed him to contain them, to elaborate them, to symbolize them. The writing of a soliloquy allowed him to break away from the negative effects of his mother's teachings/caretaking and from the psychoanalysis with Bion, while at the same time it enabled him to decipher their traces and to reappropriate the unused mental functions. The place in the body, from which the narrator in the *Unnamable* speaks, is significant:

It is the interface, the membrane which separates, while holding them together, the outside and the inside, the protective screen against the violence of intrusions, the tympanum which vibrates with external waves, which filters and registers sonic signs, which gives to the self its first envelope, and which establishes a foundation for the capacity to communicate.

> I must feel something, yes, I feel something, they say I feel something, I don't know what it is, I don't know what I feel, tell me what I feel, I will tell you who I am, they will tell me who I am, I won't understand, but the thing will be said, they will have said who I am, and me I will have heard it, without an ear I'll have heard it, and I will have said it, without a mouth I will have said it, I'll have heard it outside me, then in the same breath inside me, maybe that is what I feel, that there is an outside and an inside and me in the middle, maybe that is what I am, the thing that divides the world in two, on one side the outside, on the other the inside, it can be as thin as a blade, I am neither on one side nor on the other, I'm in the middle, I'm the partition, I have two surfaces and no thickness, perhaps that's what I feel, myself vibrating, I'm the tympanum, on one side the skull, on the other the world, I don't belong to either [p.196].

The narrator, inserted in this place in the body, functions on the principle of the "upside down spiral," as all or nothing. If he withdraws into himself he clasps only his nothingness and risks transgressing the limit between animate and inanimate, between existence and nonexistence. If he tries to realize himself, it will happen in an expansive movement with no boundaries, toward a limitlessness which aspirates him and in which he risks becoming dispersed and losing himself.

Added to his self-confidence stemming from his 1946 "vision" and his increasing mastery of the organizing code for his novelistic work, was the tranquillity, the stimulation, the confidence induced by the discreet presence of his French woman friend, by their conversations sparkling with humor, by her resonance with whatever he was trying to say. All of this facilitated the fourth period of the creative process which, strictly speaking, is the work of composition.

The actual composition posed very few problems for Beckett who for 20 years trained himself to write. He was inspired. He slept during the day, wrote at night, in a state of trance, going to the limit of his strength, endangering his physical health, which worried all his friends. He gave up his long wandering walks and his drunken bouts. He finished a novel and the next one followed. He was, however, concerned that his French might be incorrect and might make him

sound ridiculous. Every afternoon, assisted by one of his old colleagues (the widow of Péron)[1] at the Ecole Normale Supérieure, he
went over every page written during the night before to check his
French usage. To Charles Juliet, who was astounded that Beckett's
manuscripts contained so few erasures, he would answer that he
wrote only after sentences were composed in his head—no doubt an
effect of his bilingualism.

Each novel, first written by hand, he typed himself, as much to
save money as to make an ultimate review of the text. Later on, he
would translate his writings into English. Writing in French made it
easier for him, at least in the beginning, to express himself in slang,
in the scatological, spontaneously spoken language that he must have
learned from his colleagues at the Ecole Normale Supérieure.

The work of composing came regularly and rapidly, not without
tiredness or pain. There we can recognize the effect of the superego,
until then only dissolved in alcohol. By working, Beckett appeased
this superego and made himself loved by it. Thus did his writing exert
a regulating function on his psychic equilibrium.

Next remained the fifth phase of the creative work: to declare the
work finished and publishable. Beckett encountered no particular
difficulties in bringing to term a novel or stage play once the writing
was done. The characters, and even more the narrators, are all victims
of a fundamental inability to achieve. Beckett, however, knew very
well when the work which put them on stage was completed. In
addition, the older he grew, the shorter his works became. To the first
writings he decided to publish after the trilogy, he gave the title *Texts
for Nothing* (1955).

For Beckett the biggest problem was not the writing itself, but the
decision to publish. Without Suzanne, his French companion later to
become his wife, it was not certain that he would have gotten to the
point of confronting an editor, a stage director, or the public. She was
the one who served as the go-between with Jerome Lindon at
Editions de Minuit for the publication of the novel trilogy, and with
Roger Blin for the staging of *Waiting for Godot*.

There was the shame of giving away his most intimate thoughts,
the danger of losing the best of his substance by showing it to the
outside, the exposure of himself without defenses to a destructive
moral judgment as embodied by his mother and his original puritan-
ical Irish environment. We should note, in addition, the postpartum

---

[1]Alfred Péron was assistant of French at Trinity College, Dublin, when Beckett was
assistant of English at Ecole Normale Supérieure, Paris. They became friends. Péron
and his wife helped Beckett to translate *Murphy* into French.

depression, the anxiety of emptiness after giving birth to each work, an unbearable anxiety which provokes a temporary return of his old symptoms of roaming at night through streets and bars. But thanks to success, to financial ease, and to the esteem of his peers, Beckett was able from then on to restore his basic narcissistic security, and to pursue throughout his work, which became increasingly austere, the inventory and the synthesis of the narcissistic wounds from which a human being suffers when he lacks the ability and the knowledge needed to communicate with his fellow men.

SELF-ANALYSIS AND PSYCHOANALYSIS

The example of Samuel Beckett gives us the opportunity to approach a series of problems concerning the relation between self-analysis and psychoanalysis and the conditions necessary for an effective self-analysis. A first differentiation seems essential, in spite of its para-doxical aspect. In order for self-analysis to be fertile, it must not remain a solitary activity. Otherwise it quickly becomes a narcissistic solace and/or an obsessional rumination.

I once knew a devotee of Maine de Biran[2] who each day would blacken the pages of a notebook where he reviewed his sexual temptations and amorous wishes. For their failures, he gave reas-suring psychoanalytic explanations—which were not incorrect ex-cept, of course, that it was only in his head that all this took place. His psychoanalytic knowledge allowed him to save face, and the activity of his daily writing was his main pleasure in life, a masturbatory equivalent and a deflowering repeated each day on the virgin page. He had brought me to read and eventually publish, to his glory (and mine), a suitcase full of notebooks which I had great difficulty in getting him to take back after I had only skimmed them.

Freud's self-analysis had a double effect on him, one therapeutic, the other creative. It appeased his anxiety about a possible heart attack, his train phobia, and his fits of depression. It allowed him to discover the meaning of dreams and the role played by unconscious fantasies in the formation of symptoms. But Freud analyzed his own dreams in interaction with the analysis of his patients: His dreams and theirs were mutually enlightening. He dreamed about them at the same time as he dreamed about himself. In that way Freud's patients functioned for him as imaginary doubles, and he himself

---

[2]Maine de Biran (1766-1824) was a French philosopher. More than 20 volumes of his *Journal Intime* were published.

functioned for them as an imaginary double, in accordance with a play of mirror reflections between transference and countertransference. Equally, the rule was the same for them as for him: free associations of thoughts alternating with active interpretive thinking.

The Beckettian narrator is alone when he speaks, but he imagines himself as a patient in a psychoanalytic situation. He speaks to a fictional psychoanalyst according to rules of fiction homologous to those of psychoanalysis. The psychoanalytic frame is the organizing code of the narrative. This frame allowed the novelist to make the narrator speak more freely than he himself could speak to Bion, at the time of the real psychoanalytic sessions, about the "night" part (blackness and mud) of his psyche.

Ten to 15 years after the real and unfinished psychoanalysis stopped. Beckett was inventing the New Novel and the technique of soliloquy. At the same time Bion was inventing concepts which were renewing psychoanalytic theory: the container/contained, attacks on linking, about which Beckett was no doubt the first to provide him with a still somewhat confused grasp. Both of them continued in this way, through the activity of associating and through the activity of understanding what was at best only roughed out during the two-year course of the actual psychoanalysis. Beckett was cured of his alcoholism, fugues, arrogance, and psychosomatic disturbances. Bion went back for a psychoanalysis with Melanie Klein. Beckett and Bion were for each other an imaginary twin. A self-analysis that is curative and creative requires at least two persons, one of whom is imaginary.

An imaginary presence, however, is not sufficient. Freud in his letters kept Fliess up to date with his self-analysis. Beckett was doing the same thing with McGreevy, and it was the latter who, worried about the crazy letters he was receiving, had invited his young correspondent, smack in the middle of his struggle ("prise de bec") with Bion to do some reflecting about himself and to report his reflections back to him. These efforts attested to psychological introspection rather than to an authentic self-analysis, but they contributed to the preparation for the reversal in the spring of 1946 in Dublin when Beckett had the vision of his work to come: reversal of content and reversal of form.

A self-analysis cannot be operative without a witness called upon to be the symbolic guarantor and to protect the self-analysand against the traps of his countertransference toward his own psychic work.

Now we come to a second difference and a second paradox. Psychoanalytic treatment is oral; the patient is advised against taking notes. Self-analysis requires writing. Freud had noted it—however, he didn't indicate why—and he wrote down his associations to each portion of the sentence of the dream, the narrative of which he had jotted down as soon as he awoke. *The Interpretation of Dreams* (1900) could not have been written without the help of these documents. A self-analysis is therefore a narrative activity, which raises several problems: the risk of fascination with the content of a narrative about an unconscious fantasy; effects of style in the service of defense mechanisms of the ego; and the resistance to becoming conscious. Why then the necessity to write? In the psychoanalytic situation, the analysand produces the material, the psychoanalyst registers it. He serves in part as the auxiliary memory of the patient who then does not have to make a special effort to stock the material in the archives. In self-analysis, the function of remembering and conserving is not assured by the supplementary skin-ego which the attentive listening of the psychoanalyst represents. Conservation returns to the very leaf of paper, the inscribed surface functioning as the psyche's envelope.

In order to get a clearer picture, I experienced for myself different types of self-analytic sessions. If I am alone during the day and I stretch out on my own couch and attend to my associations, nothing much comes; what does come is only in a whisper. I have trouble verbalizing it, and the effort to articulate weakens the effort to follow the thread of my thoughts. If I imagine a listener seated behind me in an armchair, I try to make myself heard by him. I raise my voice but the stream of associations scatters unless I fix on a theme addressed to my own investigations: the relationships to the paternal imago, a current psychological conflict, an anxiety crisis. I learn nothing new about myself; only old awarenesses are revived. On the other hand, at night, half asleep, unable to fall back asleep or to awaken, the screen of my consciousness becomes flooded by a stream of hypnagogic images, deformed and grotesque, which I try to allow to calm themselves or to be replaced artificially with pleasant images; for example, by the anticipation of hoped-for pleasures. This form of resistance to an underlying state of anxiety can work; it reestablishes repression and I go back to sleep. If not, I get tired of it, and I tell myself that I must get to the bottom of the problem and proceed to a fragment of self-analysis. To do this, I must defuse myself from the desire to sleep and split my ego into an observing part. This idea alone, thanks to the change in perspective which it introduces, causes a word suddenly to appear or a scene which tells me something about the nature of my current anxiety. At one stroke this anxiety is swept away—the sign of a well-founded intuition—and I quickly go back to sleep. When I wake up, not only do I write for myself or for someone in my circle, a summary of what came to me as the link between my anxiety and this word or that scene, but also I note what I must do—

or avoid doing—during the next day or week to be in harmony both with my desire and with my superego. This type of nighttime self-analysis is, for me at least, the only one which can be fertile on the two planes of my personal therapy and my conceptual creativity.

I will now simply review other problems concerning the possibility and the efficacy of self-analytic work. Beckett's self-analysis and the psychoanalyst's self-analysis depend upon two conditions: they follow a personal psychoanalysis, and their aim is toward both therapy and creativity. Self-analysis prior to a psychoanalysis is quite different; it is a resistance and a preparation for psychoanalysis. On the other hand, self-analytic moments can be productive during impasses in psychoanalytic treatment. Freud's case, as exceptional as it is, verifies these conditions. He invented at the same time both self-analysis and psychoanalysis.

The psychoanalytic work of associations and interpretations is interminable; that is why self-analysis and psychoanalysis follow each other, alternate with each other, and become entangled in each other. That is also why an unfinished part of the treatment is necessary for the psychological work of creativity, as a heroic-masochistic attempt to get beyond this incompletion. Beckett and Freud illustrate this. Discontent can be a motor for progress. An unresolved negative transference is the ferment of a creative self-analysis.

Elliott Jaques described three creative crises, tied to the entry into adulthood, maturity, and old age (1965). Freud's self-analysis and Beckett's both correspond to their crises of entry into maturity. Can self-analysis be creative only if it coincides with a midlife crisis?

What psychological material can best allow the success of a self-analysis? Freud carried his own self-analysis through to a successful conclusion by having it bear mostly on his dreams. Dreams are almost absent in the works of Beckett. The materials for his self-analysis are memories of childhood and adolescence, and imaginary representations of his body and of his psychic apparatus. What is the influence of the material on the self-analytic process. A self-analysis of his dreams allowed Freud to become aware of his neurosis. A self-analysis of his narcissistic wounds helped Beckett to understand his borderline psychopathology.

There are many who become creators only after a serious psychological crisis forces them to modify their life-style and the style of their work, and, if they already are writers, to change their source of inspiration and their writing style. In what measure can this creative crisis be considered a self-analysis?

Freud and Beckett were polyglots. Their childhood languages were

Yiddish and Czech for the first, English for the second. Their self-analyses took place in a second language which they had mastered perfectly: German for Freud, French for Beckett. Wouldn't a second language be more favorable for self-analysis because it is less affectively charged and is more oriented toward knowledge than is the maternal tongue?

A successful creative work brings with it certain primary psychological gains: it serves as a psychic envelope and as a support for narcissistic illusions; it brings denial into the complex of castration; it permits escape from the reality principle, and concentrates the pleasure principle into thinking, mastering, and producing artistic material; it creates an intermediary zone, a protective, nonconflictual margin of experiencing; it absorbs an overload from the drives, be it from eros or from thanatos, and reestablishes the constancy principle.

There are also certain secondary gains: money, honors, fame, admiration and love. There are indirect gains: a decathecting of old conflicts, even an access to gratitude and to serenity.

But frequently the cure doesn't last. The ending of the work brings on a postpartum depression, an anxiety of the void, a suicidal risk, and a precipitation toward the setting up of a new work.

In conclusion it seems to me that a creative crisis is not necessarily self-analytic. We can speak of self-analysis only when there is a narrator who is the principal character in the work being created; and only when rules homologous to those of the psychoanalytic situation are set up. On both these points the example of Beckett is typical for self-analysis.

REFERENCES

Bair, D. (1978), *Samuel Beckett*. New York: Harcourt Brace.
Beckett, S. (1938), *Murphy*. London: Routledge.
_____ (1951), *Molloy*. New York: Grove Press.
_____ (1952), *Waiting for Godot*. New York: Grove Press.
_____ (1953a), *Watt*. Paris: Olympia Press.
_____ (1953b), *The Unnamable*. New York: Grove Press.
_____ (1957), *Stories and Texts for Nothing*. New York: Grove Press.
_____ (1958a), *Krapp's Last Tape*. Evergreen Review, II, V.
_____ (1958b), *Malone Dies*. New York: Grove Press.
_____ (1975), *Mercier and Camier*. New York: Grove Press.
Freud, S. (1900), *Interpretation of Dreams. Standard Edition*, 4 & 5. London: Hogarth Press, 1953.
Jaques, E. (1965), Death and the mid-life crisis. *Internat. J. Psycho-Anal.*, 46:502–519.

14

Freud's Self-Analysis

Martine Lussier

(translated by Ciaran Ross)

SELF-ANALYSIS AND CREATIVE DISCOVERY

On July 24, 1895, for the first time Freud self-analyzed one of his dreams—Irma's injection—and discovered the meaning of dreams as the fulfillment of an imaginary wish. He was then 39 years old. Didier Anzieu (1975) has shown how most of the elements of the midlife crisis, as described by Elliott Jaques (1965), are condensed in the Irma dream. Freud's self-analysis of it contained the germ of a new science, psychoanalysis, the name given by Freud some months later, at the beginning of 1896. Among all the dreams related by Freud, psychoanalysts have written the most about "Irma," as if many felt the need to rediscover psychoanalysis once again by taking this fundamental document as a base.

Between 1896 and 1900, Freud systematically analyzed his dreams, screen memories, lapses, slips, and parapraxes. He narrated them in articles and books that appeared between 1898 and 1904. But he was divided between two tendencies: publishing all the material out of a concern to tell the truth and to convince the reader, and censoring

This essay summarizes and synthesizes salient findings of Didier Anzieu's in-depth investigations of Freud's self-analysis. Originally published in 1975 by Presses Universitaires de France in two volumes titled *L'auto-analyse de Freud et la decouverte de la psychanalyse*, the second edition was made available to the Anglophone reader as *Freud's Self-Analysis* (Anzieu, 1975). In 1988 Anzieu published a third edition that took into account the bibliographical references including the publication of the complete Freud–Fliess correspondence (Masson, 1985).

those documents when they turned out to be too personal, indiscreet, and shameful. In an attempt to resolve this conflict, he used anonymity and fragmentation. Freud attributed to his patients and to those near to him dreams and memories that were in fact his own; he also cut up their interpretations into pieces and dispersed them throughout his text.

In *Freud's Self-Analysis*, Anzieu has reconstituted Freud's unconscious productions by reassembling disparate passages to indicate what Freud had said explicitly and what he had implied about his self-analysis. Anzieu has managed to date nearly all Freud's self-analytic documents. By chronologically classifying them and linking them to contemporary social events, and to Freud's biography and correspondence (especially the Fliess letters), Anzieu was able to reconstruct the dynamics of Freud's self-analytic process.

Freud's self-analysis led to the creation of psychoanalysis in its three dimensions: a method of investigating the unconscious, a therapeutic tool, and a body of theoretical knowledge. Our study of his self-analysis allows us to discern the stages involved in the creation of his work. Triggered by a personal crisis, his self-analysis required an epistemological breakthrough before he was able to fully develop his novel ideas. Remaining as close as possible to the spirit of Anzieu's text, I shall present Freud's self-analysis from three perspectives: as a source of personal benefit, as a discourse on methods, and as a source of conceptual discoveries.

BEGINNING SELF-ANALYSIS

"Freud's intellect is soaring; I struggle along behind him like a hen behind a hawk" (letter from Breuer to Fliess, 5 July 1895, in Freud, 1887–1902).

At the moment of beginning his self-analysis, Freud was nearly 40 years old. Everything he had learned during his university training was of very little use to him for curing the increasing number of neurotic patients in his practice. His social and professional positions were somewhat mediocre; his scientific works were published mostly in reviews or collective works and were mostly neurological in character. He benefited from a decent reputation, which afforded him hardly more than a modest way of life—all the more so, since a sixth child was on the way (the contraceptive precautions used having been insufficient); he thus made up his mind to give up all active sexual relations.

He was greatly preoccupied with various phobias and signs of somatic illness, including heart problems, which fueled his ideas about imminent death. Moreover, the death of his father, Jakob, in October 1896 initiated a long and complicated process of mourning. He was subject to depressive episodes that could be intense and long lasting. Lastly, he suffered from various phobias.

Seen in the light of these conditions, his intensive self-analytic work from 1896 to 1901 might at first glance appear as a defensive elaboration of his depression. Freud's social and professional life, however, was greatly transformed, and his scientific creativity freed, by his self-analysis.

On the professional front, Freud turned away from, little by little, physiological theories, and came to recognize the specificity of psychical processes. This path was to isolate him increasingly from the scientific community (although he did decide to take the necessary steps to be nominated Professor Extraordinarius). But at the same time he was able to obtain more satisfying results with his patients, develop his clientele, and improve his financial well-being. He finally created his own scientific circle by setting up weekly Wednesday meetings that were the beginnings of the Psychoanalytic Society of Vienna.

On the personal front, he did not give up smoking, but his somatic problems bothered him less, and his phobias eased off. He was able to mourn his father; his self-analysis seemed to have reestablished a narcissistically based security, which the "little golden Sigi" probably derived from his mother.

At the (temporary) end of this long period of self-analysis. Freud showed himself to be more serene; he no longer depreciated himself as he had been doing in his letters to Martha and Fliess; he expressed more confidence in the future—death no longer obsessed him—and a greater sense of personal liberty. Set free, his creativity could be boldly employed.

In looking at its end result, we should not underestimate the difficulties Freud encountered in his self-analysis—the extreme discomfort involved in recognizing or exposing his evil wishes, unworthy thoughts, dubious behaviors—in short all that led him to feel like "the only villain among the crowd of noble characters" (Freud, 1900, p. 485). But his ardor for self-analysis was never definitively dampened either by his painful discoveries or by his periods of silent resistance. In the midst of his struggles, he was even able to speak of "the intellectual beauty of this work" (letter to Fliess, 3 October 1897, in Masson, 1985).

SOURCES, METHOD, AND SETTING

True self-analysis is impossible [letter to Fliess, 14 November 1897, in Masson, 1985].

Self-analysis is a never ending process that must be continued indefinitely [letter to Putnam, 5 November 1911, in Hale, 1971].

With these contradictory statements, Freud is probably suggesting that in order for self-analysis to be fruitful, it must guard itself against obsessional rumination or indulgent narcissism. It may conceal its defensive functions, or it may lead to uncontrolled regression, preventing meaningful elaboration. In Freud's case, these dangers were not extended, and his self-analysis remained under the control of the ego (even an auxiliary ego). In his self-analysis, it was necessary for the maternal imago to be defused (i.e., a split made between the ego and the ego ideal), enabling Freud, through himself, to discover the general functioning of the psyche. Let us examine what were for Freud the setting, the sources, and the tools of this work.

It is important to emphasize that Freud's self-analytic work cannot be reduced to primary narcissistic regression, else no creative work could have emerged. His self-analysis was *spoken* to Fliess and doubtless, at times, to his sister-in-law, Minna. Each served as an auxiliary ego (Fliess in particular). Fliess was the friend capable of awakening fantasy, to use Khan's (1970) phrase; it was he who played a reflexive role in the self-analytic process and permitted Freud to see clearly. Fliess was "the gift of the Other, a critic and reader" (letter to Fliess, 18 May 1898, in Masson 1985). There was consequently a "transference" onto Fliess in which Freud was able to deposit his own fantasies and test them against reality or against the sometimes delirious imagination of his friend.

Anzieu emphasizes that Freud's self-analysis was carried out in a language (German) other than that of his early childhood (Yiddish, Czech). Anzieu puts forward the idea that Freud's use of German favored the effort of working through: it was, for Freud, a later language of conceptualization and representation and thus different from the earlier language of primary affects. Anzieu, in his contribution to the present volume, offers additional confirmation of this hypothesis by taking as an example Beckett, whose self-analytically styled novels were written in French, although English was his mother tongue. Thus Anzieu illustrates the gap between experiencing affects in one language and the possibility of representing them in another. In my view, we could generalize these observations without resorting to bilingualism. The gap is created not by the mastery of two languages, but by the practice of different levels of language, ranging from the familiar and homelike to the more distant and abstract.

Just as his self-analysis was more than a soliloquy, Freud's source of inspiration was more than himself alone, and included his patients and his cultural milieu. First, he drew on his past and his dreams but was sometimes held in check by Fliess, who, doubtless discreet, influenced Freud not to make public a particularly revealing dream, a decision Freud was later to regret. Although Freud was not entirely successful in exercising the disciplined self-control necessary in confronting and revealing aspects of his self-analysis, he attempted to do so without flinching. He later wrote to the pastor Pfister:

> Discretion is incompatible with a satisfactory description of an analysis; to provide the latter one would have to be unscrupulous, give away, betray, behave like an artist who buys paints with his wife's house-keeping money or uses the furniture as firewood to warm the studio for his model. Without a trace of that kind of unscrupulousness the job cannot be done [letter to Dr. Pfister, 5 June 1910, in Meng and Freud, 1963].

Second, he fueled his self-analysis with the work carried out with his patients, and "from the relationships with patients . . ." which provided him with another perspective: "I can only analyze myself with the help of knowledge obtained objectively (like an outsider)" (letter to Fliess, 14 November 1897, in Masson, 1985). Although the concept of countertransference had not been at all elaborated, it was precisely that element in his analytic work that helped fuel the self-analytic procedure.

Third, Freud postulated that there was collective as well as individual knowledge of the unconscious. Through myth, legend, tales, folklore, superstition, and works of art, societies provide their members with systems of representing the processes and products of the unconscious. Freud found in these sources confirmation of the results of his self-analysis.

According to Anzieu, these three sources, taken together, enabled Freud to discover psychoanalysis. Any valid interpretation of unconscious process and content must, in return, bear upon these sources. Such is the case, for example, for the Oedipus complex. Arising from Freud's dreams of the "one-eyed doctor" and the "sheep's head," the Oedipus complex, which is formulated in Sophocles' tragedy, also appeared in full light in the psychic productions of two of his patients: an obsessional man with parricidal desires, and a female patient to whom Freud administered injections (reminiscent of the case of Irma) and about whom Freud (1901) guiltily confessed, "I did violence to or committed a blunder on the 'old woman' " (p. 178). These three interwoven sources underlay the discovery process. When considered separately, they provide converging evidence of the validity of the interpretation of unconscious phenomena.

Throughout this period of intensive self-analysis and afterward, Freud relied on the intuition provided by his dreams and associations, both of which were in rich supply. His self-analysis permitted him to build up, in the form of images, an endless and ever available stock of new ideas. From 1897 onward, he also drew on parapraxes, slips, lapses, symptoms, screen memories, and jokes. Freud considered the figurative aspects of dreams to be a visual puzzle depicting the dreamer's desire. His brilliance lay in finding the code that rendered the dream images, as well as other signs, intelligible. He located and conceptualized (gave a language to) the transformations generated by the psychical work of the preconscious, and he was able to proceed directly from a figurative mode of thinking to a verbal operational mode. He explained the dream-work, its vocabulary, syntax, and grammar—condensation, displacement, representability, and secondary revision. He was able to "see" not only the way things were represented, but also the code by which they were organized. In addition, without giving them names, he described two other prototypical forms of psychical work: mourning and creativity.

LIMITATIONS OF FREUD'S SELF-ANALYSIS

The intensity of his self-analytic work led to the building of psychoanalytic theory.[1] There was a contingent relationship between the two. (Anzieu interprets each of Freud's dreams from five perspectives: the day's residues, the return of childhood memories, the transference to Fliess, the images of the body, and the gradual creation of psychoanalytic concepts.) By 1900 some fundamental concepts were specific and lucid; others remained to be discovered. But the structure was solid enough to constitute, in Kahn's term, a "paradigm."

However exceptional this work of self-analysis may have been, it left us in the dark concerning quite a number of points. The conditions in which Freud made his discoveries partly explain why, in 1900, there were still blind spots, uncertain areas, insufficiencies. The mechanism of his own "transference" to Fliess could not be

---

[1]For a list of the psychoanalytic concepts developed by Freud in the course of his self-analysis, refer to Table 6, p. 564, in Anzieu (1975).

clearly identified and thus analyzed by Freud. On the other hand, he had clearly located transference with his patients but at the time considered it a major obstacle to the smooth running of the treatment. (He wrote the Dora case study in 1901 but did not publish it until 1905.) He had not yet succeeded in turning this obstacle into a tool.

Given the context of a midlife crisis, the systematic self-analysis, triggered by the death of his father, was, as we have noted, also a defensive weapon against depression. Through his self-analysis he was able to understand, elaborate, and lessen his depressive anxieties. But the deeper fears of splitting and annihilation were not taken into account by his self-analysis.

Freud's understanding of the Oedipus complex, particularly regarding himself, allowed him to shed some light on the place of the father in the psychoneuroses. He remained vague, however, on the role of the mother in her relationship with the baby, the formidable importance of the imago of the phallic mother, and the identification with the all-powerful idealized breast.

His self-analysis and his psychopathological investigations of his patients occurred in parallel. In 1895-1896, Freud focused on hysteria; in 1897-1898, he was more attentive to obsessional neurosis; and in the following three years, he "hovered around" persecutory fantasies. But the analytic setting, which was gradually established by Freud, was particularly well suited to the treatment of neurotic patients, and psychoses were not thoroughly taken into account.

Without yet explicitly naming them, Freud sensed the existence of the self-preservative and the sexual instincts but was in the dark regarding the death instinct. He was therefore defenseless when faced with negative transference and negative therapeutic reaction.

Such restrictions and limitations, which we have come to accept, cannot diminish the exceptional adventure, the uniqueness of what was, in Mannoni's (1967) words, an "original analysis." Freud's self-analysis served therapeutic and creative functions. But these were secondary to the fundamental scientific necessity for Freud to establish—through himself—the truth of the existence of unconscious psychical processes, experienced by himself and his patients.

REFERENCES

Anzieu, D. (1975), *Freud's Self-Analysis*. London: Hogarth Press, 1986.
Freud, S. (1887–1902), *The Origins of Psychoanalysis*, trans. E. Mosbacher & J. Strachey. New York: Basic Books, 1954.
_____ (1900), The interpretation of dreams. *Standard Edition*, 4 & 5. London: Hogarth Press, 1953.

——— (1901), The psychopathology of everyday life. *Standard Edition*, 6. London: Hogarth Press, 1960.

Hale, N., ed. (1971), *James Jackson Putnam and Psychoanalysis*. Cambridge, MA: Harvard University Press.

Jaques, E. (1965), Death and the mid-life crisis. *Internat. J. Psycho-Anal.*, 46:502–514.

Khan, M. R. (1970), The catalytic role of crucial friendship in the epistemology of self-experience. *Dynamische Psychiatrie*, 3:168–178.

Mannoni, O. (1967), L'analyse originelle. *Temps modernes*, 22(253):2136–2151.

Masson, J. M. ed. & trans. (1985), *The Complete Letters of Sigmund Freud to Wilhelm Fliess, 1887–1904*. Cambridge, MA: Belknap Press/Harvard University.

Meng, H. & Freud, E., ed. (1963), *Psychoanalysis and Faith* (trans. E. Mosbacher). London: Hogarth Press.

Index